Bernard Henry Holland

Letters of Mary Sibylla Holland

Bernard Henry Holland

Letters of Mary Sibylla Holland

ISBN/EAN: 9783743324701

Manufactured in Europe, USA, Canada, Australia, Japa

Cover: Foto ©ninafisch / pixelio.de

Manufactured and distributed by brebook publishing software (www.brebook.com)

Bernard Henry Holland

Letters of Mary Sibylla Holland

LETTERS OF
MARY SIBYLLA HOLLAND

LETTERS

OF

MARY SIBYLLA HOLLAND

SELECTED AND EDITED BY HER SON

BERNARD HOLLAND

LONDON
EDWARD ARNOLD
37 BEDFORD STREET, STRAND
1898

As night the life-inclining stars best shows,
So lives obscure the starriest souls disclose.
                                        CHAPMAN.

PREFACE

THIS selection from letters has been made in order to embody in a permanent form a memorial of a nature of rare distinction. No books have a charm more great, or of more permanent value, than collections of letters written, with no thought but to please, convey affection, help or console, by persons gifted with sympathy, reason, and the seeing faculty, if—and this is essential—the writer has also the power of style, the inmost soul of expression.

Mr. Walter Pater has spoken of "the impress of a personal quality, a profound expressiveness, what the French call 'intimité,' by which is meant some subtler sense of originality, the seal on a man's work of what is most inward and peculiar in his moods and manner of apprehension; it is what we call expression carried to its highest intensity of degree. That characteristic is rare in poetry, rarer still in art, rarest of all in the abstract art of sculpture; yet, essentially perhaps, it is the quality which alone makes work in the imaginative order really worth having at all."

Possibly this characteristic is less rare in letters; yet rare it is in them also, when carried to a high degree. It is this which gives their exquisite value to the letters of the poet Cowper, and yet more to those of Edward Fitzgerald, quiet and uneventful as were these two lives passed, one on the banks of the Ouse, and the other in the homely Suffolk countryside. It exists, also, in the letters of Dorothy Osborne, and its presence will, I think, be recognised in those contained in this volume.

I will not attempt to describe my mother. The letters speak for themselves and show how beautifully blended in her were the qualities of heart and mind, how seeing was her eye, how quick, tender, and abundant were her sympathies. Children may err in estimation of their mother, and in their case to err is most pardonable, but it is impossible to mistake the impression which the writer of the letters made upon many persons of widely varied position and character, age and class, both those who had known her for years, and some also, now and then in unexpected quarters, who had never seen her but for a few days. One thing, however, her own letters cannot give, the impression made by the visible self, eyes, voice, and manner. Beauty, in the ordinary sense, my mother did not possess, but her look was very distinctive and striking. In her an ardent spirit was united with a high degree of intellectual and reasoning power, and a heart full of love and pity. The inner combination of spirit, reason, and love was manifested in her strong forehead and her dark eyes, now lit with the fire of rapid thought and feeling, and now again abstract in deep contemplation. Her voice was soft, moving, and clear. With it, in the minds of her children, the best English poetry—Chaucer, Spenser, Milton, Wordsworth, Keats, Tennyson, and Matthew Arnold—must remain for ever inseparably associated.

The letters contained in this volume may, perhaps, on the whole, give the impression of a spirit rather melancholy than cheerful. Yet this impression would not be altogether just. No doubt a certain element of melancholy must enter deeply into the nature of those who, like the writer of these letters, have a lively sense of the transient and precarious existence in this world of all happiness and beauty, and an imagination living as vividly in the past as in the present. Yet my mother derived happiness from many sources. A lovely day, or a beautiful book, the company of children, or the presence of a friend, could yield her a higher pleasure than such things do to many who feel sorrow less keenly. Certainly, when she was there, our home was always cheerful with laughter and lively imaginative talk. Her mind represented the humorous and amusing as well as the serious and tragic side of things. No one could tell a story better, or with more delicate rendering not only of the manner but of the essence of character of its heroes.

If space and the principles on which this book is compiled had allowed, I should have liked to include a study of my mother's peculiar genius in the education of children. Her own children owe to her an endless debt of gratitude for her devotion to them of all the best years of her life. Her influence constantly biassed their minds towards all that was most beautiful in nature, noble and chivalrous in art, literature, history, and essential in religion and morality. If, far off, they follow at all in these ways, it is due to her teaching and example. They can only say—

>Sed longe sequere, et vestigia semper adora.

On her father's side my mother was a Lyall, a name common along both sides of the north-eastern part of the English and Scottish borders. Her ancestors had long lived as yeomen near Berwick until commerce had brought them south.[1] Alfred Lyall, her father, was born in 1795, the youngest son of a large family.

He went to Eton and Trinity College, Cambridge, and afterwards lived for some years at Findon, in Sussex, with intervals of travel. In 1829, at the age of thirty-four, he took orders and worked, at first, as Curate at Findon.

My grandfather is described in the *Dictionary of National Biography* as a "philosopher and traveller." In 1827 he published an observant book called *Rambles in Madeira and Portugal.* In 1830 appeared

---

[1] George Lyall, my mother's eldest uncle, became Governor of the East India Company, and was also for some years a Tory member for the City of London.

a small work by him entitled *Principles of Necessary and Contingent Truth*, and in 1856, his chief work, *Agonistes, or Philosophical Strictures*. His genius was, perhaps, rather of the critical than the constructive kind. A silent and meditative man—my own childish recollection is of him pacing round the garden walk of Harbledown Rectory after breakfast on far-away summer mornings, abstract in thought, his gray and weighty head bowed a little forwards.

In 1832 my grandfather married Mary, a daughter of James Tschudi Broadwood of Lyne in Sussex. The Broadwoods originally came, like the Lyalls, from the Northern Borders, but they had also Swiss blood derived from the Tschudis, and Highland blood from the Stewart clan. My mother's maternal grandfather, James Broadwood, married Margaret Stewart, of the Stewarts, once of Glenbuckie, in Western Perthshire. The violent and mysterious death of this Margaret's great uncle, Daniel Stewart, chief of Glenbuckie, when on his way to join Prince Charles Edward, is narrated in Chambers' *History of the Forty-five*.

My grandmother, Mary Broadwood, was young, about twenty, when she married. She was of a quick, lively, practical disposition, with a high ideal of life and conduct, swift to think and see, and also to feel, and capable therefore at times of deep depressions. She had, perhaps, rather the realistic or artistic temperament, her husband the abstract or philosophic, two dispositions which may combine well in marriage, and produce something remarkable in the children.

My grandfather in the year 1839 became Vicar of Godmersham, a small and very quiet Kentish parish about eight miles from Canterbury, in the most beautiful part of the Stour valley. The church and vicarage lie beneath the rise of a splendid deer-park, crowned with beech-woods, where the river, skirting the churchyard and vicarage garden, ripples swiftly over its gravelly bed, through a steep opening in the chalk downs. In the year 1848 he moved to the rectory of Harbledown, a much larger and more important parish, situated upon the London Road, just outside and above the city of Canterbury, where his brother, Dr. William Lyall, was then Dean of the Cathedral. I remember my mother saying that Harbledown—in spite of the adjacent and large tangled forest of Blean—seemed most tame to the young Lyalls after the wild and free life of Godmersham, and that they felt surprised to hear their father admire the view from Harbledown hill, with the low-lying, red-roofed old city in the foreground, dominated by the great mass of the Cathedral, the Stour valley widening down to the Thanet marshes, and, beyond them, the long white line of the North Foreland chalk cliff, visible some sixteen miles away.

My grandfather's family was a large one, eleven in all, of whom five sons and four daughters attained to maturity. Two of the sons rose to the highest distinction in the Indian Civil Service. One of them, now Sir Alfred Lyall, ended a brilliant Indian career as Lieutenant-Governor of the North-West Provinces, while his brother, Sir James Lyall, became Lieutenant-Governor of the Punjab.¹ My mother, the eldest of the daughters, was born on the 14th March 1836. She spent her girlhood at Godmersham and at Harbledown, and was married, at the age of nineteen, in October 1855. My father was at that time Vicar of St. Dunstan's, a parish in the western suburb of Canterbury, immediately adjoining the parish of Harbledown. Here at St. Dunstan's, in a little house on the edge of the town, looking out over wheat-fields and hop-gardens, they lived till the end of 1861, and here their first three children were born.²

These selections from letters begin in the year 1861 when my mother was twenty-five years old. She died at the age of 55. By far the greater part of these letters were written during the last ten years of her life, but I have been able to include a few earlier ones, at irregular intervals. It is hoped that, with footnotes and some observations later on, the letters will make her way of life sufficiently intelligible to those who may read them without having known her at all.

---

¹ For some months in the early part of 1887 the Lieutenant-Governorship of the elder and younger brother coincided. It is worth observation, as a sign both of the greatness and character of the Empire, that these two vast adjacent Provinces, containing all the high places of the old Mogul Court—Agra, Delhi, Lahore—and having a total population of some sixty million people, should for a time have been subject to the supreme administration, under the Viceroy, of two brothers issued from an obscure Kentish rectory.

² In all they had six children, four sons and two daughters, born in the following order, Bernard, Agnes, Alfred, Lucy, Francis, Michael. Two of my mother's children, Alfred and Lucy, died before her.

My mother hardly ever prefixed the date of the year to her letters, and as often as not omitted the date of the month and day. In the case of most of the letters the dates given have been collected from post-marks on envelopes, or otherwise, and there are probably a few errors in them.

CONTENTS

		PAGE
1. Letters, 1861 to 1865		1
2. Letters, 1869 to 1876		13
3. Letters, 1877 to 1882		43
4. Note as to the Life of the Writer of the Letters after the year 1882		72
5. Letters, 1883 to 1885		84
6. Letters of 1886		112
7. Letters of 1887		136
8. Letters of 1888		159
9. Letters of 1889		195
10. Letters of 1890		237
11. Letters of 1891		278
12. Conclusion		298
Lines by a Friend		301

LETTERS OF
MARY SIBYLLA HOLLAND

ERRATUM

P. 290, lines 18 and 19.—*For* mourons and moura *read* mourrons and mourra.

LETTERS OF
MARY SIBYLLA HOLLAND

I

LETTERS 1861 TO 1865

To her Sister

St. Dunstan's (Canterbury), *4th January* 1861.

. . . I have not been up to Harbledown since you went away,[1] and was almost glad I could not go there this evening. I so dread the silence of the house. It has just begun to rain heavily. I hear the drops on the leads outside. How often you and I have heard that sound and said, "How shall I get up the hill." Oh! my Cathy, to the end of our lives that hill will be peopled with dearly loved images, some familiar foot and face going up or coming down. How I sympathise with James's dream of tramping unrecognised up that dusty hill and turning with a beating heart into the drive.[2] While I write it seems as if the old life were over for me too, so vividly do I realise what it will be, what I shall feel one day.

Good-night, my darling child! You can never be more or less dear to me than you are now. I love and embrace you with my whole soul.

---

[1] This sister had just been married and had left Harbledown Rectory to live at Cavendish in Suffolk.

[2] The dream of her brother James, then a young Indian civilian. The hill is from St. Dunstan's up to Harbledown.

To the Same

ST. DUNSTAN'S, *6th January*.

... Annie L. goes to-morrow, and with her disappears the last of the gay company who have been more or less with us since your wedding. With her an episode closes. While faces and voices are yet fresh in my memory I con over and over again this little chapter in our lives, so insignificant to others but so interesting to ourselves; especially do I pause in my story when I come to the place where you and I look out of the window at Winchester, and see the old close changed into enchanted ground, like a garden in a fairy tale. Do you remember how the little tree bent and shook, and sprang up freed from the weight of snow? But if I begin "do you remember," I shall never stop, and besides, do I not know that you remember it all well enough? Annie L. and I went to the Cathedral yesterday afternoon and heard "As pants the hart" not very well sung, but still most lovely and exquisitely devotional. And now good-night, darling, sleep well in the windy old house in which for a while your tent is pitched.

To the Same

ST. DUNSTAN'S, *23rd January*.

... So we shall live near the old nest for a while, and I cannot be sorry.[1] I have a dread of breaking this calm in which we have lived for five years and more, although I sometimes feel, with the old heathens, that *some* sacrifice will soon be necessary, or the Gods will

[1] There was a rumour of my father's appointment to London work, slightly premature.

be envious of our bliss and send a thunderbolt into our quiet dwelling. If living in a small and ill-built house would appease their wrath, how willingly would we occupy St. Dunstan's Terrace for ever. But who can look into the future? Do you remember Egmont's speech to the effect that we can indeed stand in the chariot and hold the reins, but that it is beyond our power to guide the fast wheels or restrain the fiery horses? After all there is but one future into which we should desire to look, and it is only Jacob's dream that we should desire to realise, the near presence of God and His angels.

To the Same

St. Dunstan's, *Saturday, 26th January.*

I wonder what you are doing this lovely bright spring-like day. If you were here perhaps we should be taking a walk together. As it is, having despatched all the children, I shall sit out the afternoon in this sunny little room with the window wide open. It is hard to believe that we are still in January; the air is soft and balmy, and the sun very warm and light. The corn is springing fast in the field under the window, and, from the field beyond, the rattling of the plough as it turns and the cry of the little scare-crow boy sound very pleasantly. I do hope that we have got over the very severe weather, though of course a continuance of this mildness is out of the question. We have all our east wind to come.

To the Same

St. Dunstan's, *Monday Evening.*

... I feel so impatient when I think of your solitary walks at Cavendish and mine at Canterbury, and of the impossibility of our walking together—an impossibility too of our own making, so to speak, for I *could* at any moment take the train to London, and from thence to Sudbury, and from Sudbury to Cavendish. The whole journey would not occupy one of my half-wasted afternoons which slip by without my marking their flight, and yet I don't take the train, nor do you. In a certain sense it is not possible. There seems no reason for going, every one would say—and yet what better reason does one want than that which we both have. Well, Cathy, the time will come some day, and we shall sit near each other again. I shall hold your hands,—how well I know their feel and shape, and the look of each finger and nail,—and I shall look into your face, every expression of which is so dearly familiar. The days in our life in which we shall be together we will really live and enjoy and remember. Speed, speed the day! I cry, from the very bottom of my heart. When I think of you I feel as steady as a rock in my affections for you. I feel it so impossible that anything can alter or diminish it in the smallest degree. It is part of myself. If you ever find me wanting in this matter you may feel comfortably sure that I am going out of the little mind it has pleased God to give me.

To the Same

St. Dunstan's, *February.*

... It has come at last.[1] Yesterday morning when I came down stairs, Frank, with a face a yard long, handed to me a letter and rushed out of the

[1] My father's appointment to work in London.

room. I knew what it was, and sat down till the sick feeling which came over me went off. In those few moments I seemed to say good-bye to all my past happiness. Oh, my dear Cathy, I go about with such a dead pain in my heart. . . . Of course it is not yet absolutely settled, but I see no shadow of hope—none. And so, as the days grow long and the primroses begin to bud, I must strip this poor little house and go with my children to live in a London street, and their pleasures must be limited to the worn grass and dirty trees of the squares and parks. It does seem so hard upon them, just when they are beginning to understand the delights of the country. How happy they would have been this year in the farm and orchard and in the dear, dear old garden at home. And what *shall* I do with myself, shut up in a London house, without even a carriage to get about in, and an immense way off from every one. I feel now as if I *could* not go. When I think of London as our *home* for perhaps the next ten years my life seems a blank.

To the Same

St. Dunstan's, *March*.

I thought of you this morning as I was blown violently across the street after morning church to Mrs. Streatfield, and stood on her doorsteps vainly trying to hold up my umbrella and keep down my petticoats. I knew you must still be in church listening to the sermon and the roaring wind,—and I so often think of the chancel and of the poor men who look out of the window while the Belief is said. What rough weather we have and how delicious it is when the lull comes, as it does every two or three days, bringing us such warm bright days. The garden at Harbledown is beginning to look pretty with crocuses and daffodils, and the beds under the window are blue and white with the sweet violets. Barbara and I sat there on Thursday morning and were almost too hot in the sun. The four little ones played about so happily with their spades, carts, and wheelbarrow, and made a little dirt garden in the bushes, into which they stuck crocuses and hypaticas. The carriage took down my three monkeys, who went off singing a hymn at the utmost pitch of their loud voices and to the most extraordinary tune, the proud Tomlin smiling with pleasure at this public exhibition of their learning and piety.

To the Same

ST. DUNSTAN'S, *20th April.*

. . . Agnes looked so pretty the other day as she came down the road on the donkey, her brown curls blown about, and her little straw hat pushed back from her flushed face and ornamented with a great bunch of ferns and celandines. In both hands she clasped a perfect faggot of anemones, primroses and lady-smock. Bernard and Mary[1] ran by the side and behind whipping Jenny with long palm-branches. The other day we went up to Miss Webb's wood, where we sat on the sunny bank, while the five children played with the little stream of water. The children, the lambs, the water, the flowers and the chorus of birds, filled the picture with pleasant, dreamy sights and sounds. At such times, my Cathy, I would have you, and you only, with me. I know no one who can so

---

[1] Mary Lyall.

fully sympathise in my admiration of a green grassy bank with the sun on it, and other people's remarks and exclamations produce in me a sombre smouldering irritation ; I cannot quite say wherefore.

To the Same

ST. DUNSTAN'S, *April*.

It is half-past seven and yet I have plenty of light whereby to begin a letter to you, sitting at this window with my writing book on the ledge and my ink-pot in the flower-stand outside. The strong east wind has also departed from us, glory be! and the south-west breeze, which you doubtless have been enjoying all day, blew before it reached Suffolk over the primroses and budding bells in the woods of Kent. If it only could blow me to Blacklands! It has been a lovely day, but with these spring days a melancholy fastens upon me. I alternately hang my depression upon your absence and our approaching change, but I well know that without these real causes my spirits would flag. Spring is more melancholy to me than autumn. I am always full of self-reproaches and longings for I know not what. I long to be and to do better, but I have no courage to begin. I know too well what is right and wise, but I am unstable as water and cannot excel. My resolution is as weak as my standard is high. I am happy in my pleasant pottering life, and at the same time angry with myself for being happy. A squirrel born in his comfortable little cage, and used to it, and with plenty to eat and drink, is stupidly happy, but, at times, my Cathy, he must have dim instincts and yearnings for the tops of the trees and the open sky. And, at times, I too seem to have a glimpse of heaven opened, so to speak, but it is but for a moment, and I rattle round and round in my cage again.

I know what it is. It is this sleepiness, this leprosy of indolence which sticks to and grows upon us all, and upon me above all. And one day I am convinced it will be a body of death to me, for to me it is like some dreadful body clogging me, from which I cannot escape. And it is not my real body which is at fault. That is well worked and little indulged. Indeed I think I could make my body submit to any discomfort if only that *something* which is neither my mind nor my heart nor my soul but which is *me myself*, could be left at peace, to dream and to sleep, and at last to die, nothing attempted and nothing done. Wretched state, and yet true. And in London things will be worse— there I shall live in a dream. I daresay you will think all this morbid and depressed, but it is not. It is the result of honest reflection. Do not try to argue with anything I say unless you really feel as I do. Your friendship will be and is so precious to me, and I desire with all my heart that it should be sincere. It is possible to have the closest intimacy with independence of thought. Both of us, I think, are too apt to *try* to agree with other people. One ought to try to see what truth there is in what things they say, but not try to warp one's own clear conviction for the sake of agreeing. . . . The woods are charming now, the cutting down this year at Faulkner's has thrown open the prettiest views. When you get to the end of the deep lane, and stand at the point where the old pilgrim's road emerges from its copse, the whole rising ground to the right hand is a blue mountain of blue bells, blue already, though they are not fully out. Yet I agree with you that the cowslip is by far the most delightful flower to pick. There is something so pleasant to touch and eye in the shape of the fragrant and delicate clean stalk—and then to shut one's eyes and bury one's face in a great bunch is a joy indeed. I wish there were more here.

Two days ago, I walked into the wood beyond Mount Ephraim, where there is a pretty little clearing and faggots piled up like little houses. There I sat by the tiny brook, among the anemones and ladysmock, and for the last time leisurely lingered gathering up the threads of my past life and retracing many scenes and sensations. By next spring we shall be quite gone, and the place will know stranger's feet and voices.

To the Same

ST. DUNSTAN'S, *May*.

This is old May-day, and my thoughts revert to the many pretty pastimes in which old England used to indulge. It is as warm as any May-day need be, and a delicious down-pouring shower is just now falling, which would have refreshed the drooping garlands. All last night it rained hard, and the day began with a thick steamy vapour rising out of the earth, which made the whole atmosphere feel like a steamy greenhouse. On going out at half-past two I was astonished to find myself much too warm. The wind is slowly veering round to the blessed south, and I hope and believe warm days are coming at last. As I sit and write in this open window, the rich odour of the lilacs and sweet briars in the neighbouring gardens and the *growing* smell, that indescribable odour, rather essence, of life and spring, are almost oppressive. . . . Ever since

I last wrote to you the trees and flowers have burst out in a wonderful manner as if they knew this rain was coming. The old Cathedral is standing in a garland of beeches and limes,—you know how pretty it looks. . . . I went to the Cathedral on Ascension day, in the afternoon, but coming in very late did not go into the choir, but sat in the south transept on a bench which was exactly placed so as to catch a view of the Black Prince's tomb and St. Anselm's chapel. I could follow the whole service perfectly, and drank my fill of gazing upon the Norman arches and mediæval iron-work gates of the little chapel. In the anthem the sweet boys' voices asked over and over again, "Who is the King of Glory?" and the crash of the organ and men's voices replied, "The Lord God of Hosts; He is the King of Glory." I do not generally like repetitions, but in this anthem it is so very beautiful. As though one side could never weary of asking the question, or the other of giving the joyful answer. It is very singular, and, I am sure, very wrong, that one should feel more devout when alone in a church, or with a very small company of worshippers, or in the dark, or even in a strange congregation. It is surely contrary to the true Christian feeling, but it is so with me. At Winchester, for instance, I generally have felt more struck than at Canterbury, and I am sure it is simply because I do not know the people or the priests.

To the Same

ST. DUNSTAN'S, *May* 1861.

. . . Oh, my Cathy, what weather is this! I am sitting, it is true, with the window open; but the dull white face of the wind-mill is turned due to the east, and the dull thick evening air is raw and cold. The Cathedral bells are ringing, a sound which fills my soul with vain, uneasy longings, and which certainly gives me as much pain as pleasure. Nevertheless, I am sorry when the sweet jangling stops. You need not imagine that we are doing anything more in woods and fields than you are. May-day was the last fine day, and even that evening was cold and black. May "comes dancing from the east" this year with a vengeance. Are we to begin again this life of sullen clouded skies and bitter chill wind.

To the Same

LONDON, *Christmas Eve* 1864.

My darling Cathy — My whole heart goes out to embrace you, and nothing written or spoken can express the love and longing that makes me shed tears of, I don't know what, when I begin to write to you. It is the remembrance of you, and you only, that makes Christmas sad to me. No thought of any one else affects me in the least; but I know that our hearts beat to the same time. . . . Ber held his little revels yesterday, and had a happy day. What a glamour there is in childhood, and how glorious do the most simple preparations seem to their innocent, unworldy eyes. These three children have just the simplicity and imagination that makes it a pleasure to do anything for them. On Monday is our tree. Good-bye, my dear, dear Cathy. In spite of four children my heart-strings all pull towards Cavendish in a marvellous way.

To the Same

LONDON, *1st December* 1865.

I should have written to you from Harbledown, where I thought of you every minute of the day, but for the extraordinary amount of business to be done which prevented any one from sitting down to write anything like a letter. It is impossible to realise that Harbledown is standing empty, and that we have no longer any right or possession in our old home.[1] I almost feel it now more than I did when there. At Harbledown the feeling that papa was gone surpassed every other, and, while most things went on as usual, one did not take in at all vividly that everything was being done for the last time. Very few things in my life have been so painful as going round with mamma to say good-bye to some of the poor people. On Sunday, just as it grew dark, she and I slipped across the road to the Mint, and went to old Bishop's, Partis, Streeter, and others. We were only a few minutes in each house, and did not sit down. Indeed, I went no further than the doorway; but the little fire-lit rooms, the broken prayers and blessings, the burst of tears from old Partis and Bishop, and our dear mother's wan face and tearful eyes have left a peculiar and strong impression on my mind. The whole village feels deeply, and there was a sense of dullness and loss which was quite remarkable. In Canterbury also, where I went to pay all the bills, the tradesmen expressed universal and strong regret, and earnest hopes that mamma should return.

[1] In consequence of the death of her father, the Rector.

II

LETTERS 1869 TO 1876

To her Sister

Fox Holm,[1] *4th August* 1869.

My dear Cathy—This is your birthday, a blessed day for me, and I almost wish that just for the time we could all be children again going over to Godmersham to keep the feast on the top of the breezy hill. On those rare days, at least, the hearts of father, mother, and children beat in happiest unison. We all felt and re-echoed the cheerful and poetic spirit in my father's manner, and sighed and yearned with my mother as eyes and footsteps turned to the corner of the little churchyard.[2] Should your birthday return for a thousand years, my only Cathy, it could never bring with it such a length of golden hours as those Godmersham afternoons contained. And the drive back to Canterbury between the hedges, bringing chance of glow-worms, and the wonder of rattling over the

[1] Till 1867 we had spent the late summer and early autumn months at different places in the country, three of those holidays at Freshwater, in the Isle of Wight. After that year we went annually to Fox Holm, near Cobham, in Surrey, a house built for us by my father's brother-in-law, Charles Buxton, on a clearing in a wood on his property. We went there every year in April, and returned to London about the end of October.

[2] Where two of her mother's children were buried.

St. Margaret Street stones, and the glories of the shop-lighted High Street, and the sympathising manner of Becky, softened by a flower from the babies' grave. Where the governess was on those days I cannot imagine, but my memory holds no trace of her.

B. stays till Monday, and her company is a pure pleasure. She is looking very well, and as usual contents herself with all she finds. She possesses in a high degree the good manners of always appearing perfectly happy and pleased. . . .

On the 24th August 1869, my mother saw her second boy, Alfred, alive and well in the morning and a few hours later lying dead by the bank of the river Wey. He was in the tenth year of his life.

To the Same

Fox Holm, *1st September.*

. . . Miss Pepys has just been over, her poor dear old face all swelled with crying. I feel so much calmer than other people, and have hardly shed one tear for the loss of the dearest of all my children, and the one who loved me the most. And yet it is not that I do not know what I have lost. He has always been most precious. Indeed, had I known how few were to be the delightful years in which I was to enjoy his presence, I could hardly have done more to make him happy and certainly I could not have loved him more.

To Mrs. Stephen [1]

Fox Holm, *3rd September.*

Thank you very much for your letter, and please

---
[1] Now Lady Stephen.

thank your husband for his. It was very kind of him to write, and I shall keep his note.

Just as I wrote these words an answer came to our telegram saying that Frank [1] will be here on the 20th of this month. It is an unspeakable comfort to feel that he is safe, for I had felt as if he and Alfred had disappeared together. It has been a terrible time, and at first I could think of nothing rightly for the longing that all could be as it had been, and then he was my dearest child of all. Looking back upon his life I can remember no serious fault, neither had I ever occasion to be displeased with him about little things. He was the soul of truth, and had a most fine temper. But God fulfils his purposes, and we shall one day see all clearly. And we struggle up again into something like happiness even after the most beating storm.

My brother Alfred [2] writes with great eagerness about Mr. Stephen coming out, and has been reading his book, and hopes great things. I wish that Mr. Stephen would promise to know him and to like him. He will go through his ground on his way from Bombay. He is Commissioner of Berar, and lives at Alkola, a very curious place. But he will surely meet him at Agra.

Pray thank dear Miss Martin for her kind note. I knew that she would be sorry, and that she would write.— Ever your most affectionate   SIBYL HOLLAND.

To her Sister

FOX HOLM, *Sunday 11th October.*

. . . I have been at both services at Hatchford. This afternoon walking alone through the woods I

---

[1] My father, who had been in America.
[2] Now Sir Alfred Lyall, K.C.B.

wished for your company with a strong wishing. The walk is so lovely there these still autumn days. Up to Fox Warren, and along the terrace drive, and through the Deacon's Woods, and out into the old mossy farm meadow, and again through the woods, and then under the great chestnuts and elms into the little churchyard. This is eminently an autumn country, as you know; I noticed this afternoon how heavy the morning dew still lay on the moss along the deep roadsides, and how wonderful are the colours of the fungi, and how thick lay the acorns and chestnuts along the wood-paths. The children, going to church in the morning, counted fifteen squirrels. These lovely days and nights seem to me a sort of mercy. They linger out Alfred's summer. Even his sweet peas and pansies still bloom, and all the flowers are still alive on which his eyes rested. Some morning we shall come down to see them lying burnt by the frost, and my last illusion will be gone.

The children put a cross and crown of flowers on his grave every Sunday morning. Mrs. Deacon sends me the loveliest creamy roses and large lilies. I put moss between each flower and the dew keeps them alive for days. But I wind and twine and arrange the flowers in a dream, my Cathy, out of which I awake to unspeakable anguish. I could never have imagined how sharp and terrible would be the pain of mere absence, for I certainly would not bring the child back, nor do I struggle against God's decree. . . .

To Mrs. Stephen (in India)

BOULOGNE-SUR-MER, 20*th April* 1870.

. . . Will you for me thank Mr. Stephen for writing to me after he met my brother. I thought it so very kind of him, but I was not surprised, for I begin to understand the sort of person he is. Whatever happens you are a very happy woman to have such a husband —tenderness like the great deep, and faithfulness reaching to the clouds. . . .

Boulogne would be unbearable in midsummer. Even now the sun beats down with a sort of white heat, and the Quai is almost impassible for dust and glare. Nor does the sea send up any cool breeze. I rather long for the cool side of a well-watered London street. The great miracle of spring is beginning again, though very slowly. If a few showers of rain would fall, all the world would be green, but the hardly perceptible east wind that accompanies this scorching sun prevents progress. I have often felt such impatience at this sort of pause in nature while the days grow long and time passes, but this year I don't mind. A few dry leaves and flowers in my drawer are dearer to me than the whole of the coming splendour.

To her Sister

Fox Holm, *20th May.*

I wish you could see the deep peace of my Alfred's resting place at Hatchford. The little churchyard is bosomed round with great lilacs in full bloom and rhododendrons coming into flower, and in the old orchard behind the apple blossoms almost sweep the top of the long grass, which is full of cowslips and bluebells, and one can look down into the pretty neglected gardens of Hatchford House, where no one is living. I sat there a long time and there was no sound of any human being, but such a wonderful fulness and sweetness of nature. There are only two other graves there,

Charles Fulke Greville and his wife. The place is all lovely, but it half kills me to know that my boy's bright hair is under the turf.

To Mrs. Stephen [1]

37 SUSSEX GARDENS, 1871.

My dearest Mrs. Stephen—This is only just to wish you good-bye once more. I would come over for one more embrace, but that it would be foolish to take a minute of your time from your nearer friends and children, and I have nothing to say, at least nothing which for me would be speakable.

I seem to have an actual pain in my own heart at the thought of your parting with your children, but the moment you have turned your back on them your face will be towards your husband, and great comfort lies in this. We shall think of you often and with some degree of anxiety till we hear that you and little Rosamond are in his arms again.—Farewell and believe me always your loving   SIBYL HOLLAND.

To the Same.

FOX HOLM, 5th June.

... I quite agree with you as to the impossibility of going through the groundings again with one's youngest children. I began reading "Markham" with Lucy and Frank this summer and found it too sickening. The utter *banalité* of children's history books wearies one to death. And the horrid stupidity of the descriptions!—do you remember in "Little Arthur"

---

[1] Who was returning to India to rejoin her husband, the Legal Member of Council.

" The Druids, my dear boy, were a kind of clergymen ? " Franky's simple comment on this was, " Like papa with no clothes on," for he had not yet come to the robes and mistletoe.

We have been here since the end of April. Frank has not been able to come down much, as he has been short of a Druid or Curate, but the children occupy most of my time, and I garden and teach and dawdle about the bowery lanes. Little Michael too seems to fill up all spare half hours, and I like the weight of his soft little body on my arms as I go about the house and garden. He surveys the blooming world about him with a kindly eye, and stretches his white round arms towards the flowers and children and animals among whom he lives. Why should a Druid be ever forced upon his mind's eye through the medium of the abhorred Mrs. Markham? I hope that you are not teaching my sweet god-daughter anything at all but to love and be happy. She seemed to me wondrous intelligent, and, if you only don't stupefy her with facts about the Druids, she will be the most charming little girl in England.

Every one's attention here is divided between the French news and the Tichborne case, which is really very interesting ; one does not quite see why, for he is certainly an impostor. To-day's papers say that the Legitimist Party are pledging themselves to restore the Pope to his rights—should the Orleanists be re-established. It is impossible to believe in such madness, and if there is any truth in the rumour, one sees no hope of any settled government in France. France might greatly gain by a religious reaction, but then it must be a religion with a dash of Puritanism, not a priest's religion. Druids will not suffice just now. . . .

To her Sister

FOX HOLM, *June*.

... I have just come back from a pilgrimage through the woods to Hatchford for the sake of sweet St. John, but found no service. ...

... This place is like some dream of greenness, and the creepers on the house have flung long sprays in every direction. Every window is the greenest bower, and we look out on green beyond green of waving boughs and brake. But the fulness of summer beauty here is for ever and ever associated in my mind with the fulness of mortal anguish. The thunderbolt came out of the blue that struck both this house and Emily's.

To the Same

FOX HOLM, 11*th April* 1873.

... I have been at Hatchford with poor Emily. The fields and woods and orchards thereabouts are in parterres of primroses and cowslips and anemones and all the other pretty growth of spring. The sides of the little lane leading up to the church are covered with primroses and dog violets, and the birds sing all round. The pansies are out on Alfred's grave, and the rose-bush at his head has put out tender leaves; but when I stood by the little marble cross all the joy of the spring seems to go out. I cannot understand why the pain should be so lasting and sharp, for I do not wish him here again, in this poor world.

To the Same

Fox Holm, 29*th October*.

Ever since you and Robert drove away together on the 6th December 1861 (I think), it has seemed strange to me that days and days should go by and that you should not know how my hours go by, nor I how you are spending yours, or perhaps how yours spend you and spare not. And this feeling grows upon me more every week of my life. Yesterday I wished you could know that, in the absence of Jellis,[1] I spent the morning on a ladder training the creepers myself; not always on a ladder either; as often standing outside on the window ledges, gay as a lark, as I have always felt when on an enterprise of danger and folly. Also I planted all my bulbs, a pleasing task, giving some hope of coming life amid this dying nature. But what lovely death! As I drove slowly along the Hatchford lane in the donkey chair this afternoon the woods were a dream of lovely colour. Gold, and the deepest russet, and the brightest Christmas green up to the top of the high banks, and as far in every direction as one could see.

To Mrs. Deacon

Church House, Knutsford, *May* 1874.[2]

My dear Mary— . . . Time goes very slowly in

[1] The gardener, etc.
[2] In these years my mother paid an annual visit to two old aunts of my father's—long ago dead now—Miss Mary and Lucy Holland, who lived on at Knutsford. This town, not then much altered by the vicinity of Manchester, was the model for Cranford in Mrs. Gaskell's novel. It was sometimes, indeed, alleged that the two Miss Hollands served as the models of Miss Matty and her sister. Sir Henry Holland was their brother.

this little old-world place. The aunts are so worn out and feeble, and the talk is of such far gone matters, that my own affairs bear an air of unreality. Aunt Lucy forgets Michael's existence, but still laments that Aunt Mary would add two feet to the wall on which she used to perch Michael's father, in order that the people on the London coach might remark his fair long curls; and Aunt Mary still blames Lady Holland for dressing the boys in jackets, instead of the green velvet coats, with gold buttons and wide frilled collars, in which they looked so handsome. And Aunt Lucy says that there were many more birds' nests before the Reform Bill, which taught the farmers to trim the hedges so close, and wonders that I have never heard of Romper Low, the highwayman, who lived on the Heath here and had an underground passage to Old Tabley, and who was so civil to the Miss Rumbolds when they met him and asked him to take care of them over the Heath to Church House, and how Dr. Holland met him afterwards and thanked him. It is so strange to hear all this, and the very primroses and lambs look as if they were only a remembrance too, and they are not real to the old aunts, they only remind them of the real lambs of fifty or sixty or seventy years back. . . . We breakfast here at eight o'clock, eat a biscuit at twelve, dine at four, and a *tray* at eight o'clock. Aunt Lucy said to me this morning, "Don't take ginger wine to-night, Sibyl, love; there's not much left, and Mary will not like another bottle opened, as there is no company but you."

This evening we are to read old letters—Edgeworth's, Barbauld's, Aitken's, Darwin's, Wedgewood's, all that old set. Sir Henry Holland always figures as the fashionable young man in the vortex of London Society.

Miss Edgeworth's letters are charming, and there are drawers full of them. . . . Well, good-bye, and God bless you, and your husband, and Mrs. Scarlett, and Pillicoddy, and Fatima, and the bereaved water-wagtail, and the partridge's eggs, and the rosebuds, and the asparagus, and every other creature in and about Poynters.—Your always faithful

SIBYL HOLLAND.

To her daughter Lucy [1]

KNUTSFORD, May.

My dearest Lucy—Thank my Agnes for her delightful long letter, which gave great pleasure to her father this morning as well as to me. It is so pleasant to have daughters who write long bright letters, and who are sorry when we go away and happy when we return. These things make the happiness of life to the poor papas and mammas. . . . I am rather sorry that you have to pick 300 bunches of primroses—it is almost too much work. You must get the whole school to help you, and any maids of ours that can be spared.

The woods near Old Tabley are a miracle of beauty. The old, old crumbling Hall and Church, and the quiet mere and old boathouse, and the lovely budding beeches and limes, and the carpet of wild flowers below, and the blue sky arching over all make up a splendid harmony. And it is such a pleasure to know that all over England, all over Europe, there are thousands and thousands of hearts to enjoy the beauty. Thousands of girls of twelve years old, and thousands of boys of ten and boys of four years old, and thousands of mothers

---

[1] Then aged twelve.

enjoying the happiness. "We praise Thee, O God, we acknowledge Thee to be the Lord. All the earth doth worship Thee, the Father Everlasting." How many times have I cried this aloud when I was a young girl, and felt the beauty of the world! And now I can say it with a deeper feeling still.—Ever thy loving mother,   SIBYL HOLLAND.

To her Sister

FOX HOLM, *June*.

... My flowers are lovely—the tall lilies are just coming out in the long border, and the lavender and pink geraniums and lobelia make the prettiest border in front of them. The house is again a ridiculous mass of leaves, and there is a quiet glory over everything. Then the birds are innumerable, and there is for ever a sound of young wings about the windows. There are nests of wrens, flycatchers, robins, tomtits, chaffinches and sparrows and water-wagtails in the creepers, and the doves have built their second nest in the clematis of the pent. The roses are not what they were last year, and yet they are better than they promised to be, at any rate there are plenty, and very few grubs, owing to the vast army of little birds.

Mamma is very angry with the Ritualists, but this movement reaches far behind the mere Ritualists. Such men as Carter and Furse and others of that stamp are not Ritualists. What do you understand by "Objective Presence" in the Sacrament? It surely means more than a special spiritual presence. Miss Macrae says that she understands by it a spiritual presence beyond that in the heart of the worthy receiver, which would be merely subjective. Is this correct? and does our highest doctrine of the Sacrament differ so materially from that of Rome?

To her brother-in-law, Sir Henry Holland[1]

FOX HOLM, *August* 1874.

I have been thinking of nothing but Margaret all these days, and yet I cannot write to her. I remember so well that when she came to Fox Holm in the midst of all that trouble in 1869, the first thing she said to me was, " There is nothing to be said." This is so true of a great grief; there is nothing to be said. One can only wait till the wave goes over.

And your loss is so irreparable, for Lady Trevelyan was her children's dearest chosen friend as well as their mother. I always liked to think of the immense affection between them—such a pure and perfect bond.

This grief will make you feel as if Pinewood had long been yours. No joy binds one to a place quite as much as a sorrow does.

To her Sister[2]

SALISBURY, *August*.

. . . We got here about 9.45, went to the Cathedral service, and at 2.30 set out for Stonehenge. We sat a long time gazing at the strange great stones and wide

---

[1] Now Viscount Knutsford.
[2] My mother was in constant correspondence with this sister throughout her life, but after this date it has seemed best to give rather her letters to other people.

plain over which the masses of white cloud drove, as they have driven ever since the men who sleep in the innumerable barrows were fighting or worshipping or camping there. A large picnic and various small ones were going forward, a photographer had set up his shabby travelling apparatus, and a well dressed grocer was standing on one of the fallen masses explaining to his dull-faced womenkind his ideas as to the "horigin" of its existence. Flys and carts were drawn up round. Every soul there but ourselves would have been more suitably entertained at Sydenham or Battersea. The only living creature proper to the place was a pretty shepherd boy of twelve years old, with the felt cap and gabardine, holding a wallet and crook over his shoulder and a beautiful collie in a leash. He stood silent and motionless the whole hour we remained there, leaning on a great boulder and watching the picnic, his dog as quiet as the great Trilithon over his head. We came down by a lovely road under the great Roman Camp at Old Sarum. The thought of the skilled dark-browed Romans who had traced these curves and lines succeeded well in my mind to the idea of the mute rude strength which had piled up Stonehenge.

To Mrs. Deacon

LONDON, *November*.

My dear Mary—Thank you for all your kindness and hospitality. The only thing I regret is that the nature of things obliged me to sleep away seven of the eighteen hours spent under your roof. It is very egotistical and boring when one makes unnecessary statements about oneself and then comes wanting to retract and explain, but yet I could not bear you to think that I wish my condition were other than it is, only that I am horribly conscious of my imperfection in it, and of a strong natural crying out for things in which I have no concern, here or hereafter. It is your wish *for a common*, for a wilder and wider outlook, and it was this expression of your wish that made me mention mine. So that it was your fault, and this conviction brings with it the usual relief.

You will let me have a line in a day or two to say that H. is better. I am so sorry for their pain. In this cold weather they will think of the dear little cherished body for which they can do nothing more, and this sort of pain is the less endurable because it is unreasonable. I remember that I could not see without such anguish the bright hearth and closed rooms, nor can I think of it now without terror. Good-bye, my dear Mary, your affectionate SIBYL HOLLAND.

To the Same

KNUTSFORD, *6th December.*

My dearest Mary—It is long past midnight and I have been buried alive in the feathers of the old four-poster with drab curtains for more than an hour. *Two* hot water-bottles were interred with me to make up for the want of fire in the outer world. Such a storm of wind roaring round this old house, and the rain slashing against the window that commands the churchyard where the grave-stones all lie flat and close together. I cannot sleep or read, and I have been lying staring into the dark till my head aches. Below this room is the surgery, to which a long stone passage leads. I can quite well hear the two old doctors moving about and rattling their medicine bottles, making up drugs for the people who have long since been in the churchyard. The two old aunts are just the same as when I saw them last, only more weak and weary of life. They are wheeled off to bed about nine o'clock, but then comes the moment of the companion, who brings out an acrostic of her own making, so vague that there is not the slightest clue to the meaning, and I have to puzzle over it till ten. The evening begins at five, and is only interrupted by the tray of Oswego and bun-loaf. You cannot imagine to what a low ebb of mind and body it brings one. . . . However, I have written away my ghosts, and am so cold that the hot-water bottle lumps look not unfriendly under the quilt.

To the Same

37 Sussex Gardens, 16th December.

My dear Mary— . . . Christmas draws near, doesn't it, with its usual burden of preparation. Pleasing and yet toilsome. Hampers of evergreens, balls of string, blankets, toys, coal tickets, red-nosed and dirty and clean sickly faces, holly-pricked fingers, wax candles, and wire that won't twist, parcels of all sizes, and innumerable secrets always being talked about, boys and their friends, and the servants' relations, crowded London churches, and solemn country churches where the lights shine coldly in the green branches while the parson hurries a little in his afternoon discourse and the children think of nothing but that it is Christmas day. And this I see whenever I shut my eyes.

Don't you sometimes long for the time when the days, the high days, shall succeed in stately splendour, and none of this brown paper, and string, and holly sprigs shall be required? And then I shall find again the fair faced boy who haunts me for ever here, and whose presence elsewhere makes all these things seem so unreal. Will you put some little flower for me on his grave on Christmas morning? . . . This will be rather a sad Christmas for your poor coachman with his pretty boy gone. But it must be borne and there is no way out of it.—Your very affectionate, yes, really your *very* affectionate   SIBYL HOLLAND.

To the Same

FOX HOLM, *Thursday*, 1875.

My dear Mary—We did not get home yesterday till 6.30, and Frank would not then let me go on to Poynters. Indeed it was rather too late and too dark. And then, after dinner, when we thought of a pilgrimage through the soft darkness of your woods, rain began to fall, so I thought of the Palm Branch all the evening, and dreamt strange dreams last night.[1]

The very thought of seeing that Palm and of your having brought it here yesterday gives me a sort of shock. It is curious to feel how great is really the difference between imagination and reality. I often wonder whether the eye of the mind or that of the body is the true one, and what in the next world will be the face to face vision, without the old dark glass to which we are so well accustomed? . . .

[1] The palm branch was that same which was laid on the breast of Bishop Patteson by the natives who murdered him. They pushed his body out to sea in a canoe with hands clasped over this palm.

To the Same

CAVENDISH, SUFFOLK, *May*.

My dear Mary— ... I had half a mind to ask you to befriend Lucy during my absence in some such simple way as asking her to tea, but forbore, not from mistrust of your kindness, for you are always more ready to hear than I am to pray; but because an unfulfilled request haunts your too-gentle spirit, and because it is sometimes as difficult to arrange a very small matter as a very great one.

On Thursday last 600 of the villagers spent the afternoon up here. They are a poor, worn race, but with easy, unsuspicious manners and quick tongues. We processioned from the school to the church, Agnes leading the way and bearing the great banner; tall, grave and meek, and steady as a rock under the weight. Behind her walked the little girls, then the village band and choir, then the boys and then the mass of women and babies and the very old men and women, half laughing and half crying and blessing the Lord, and the weather, and themselves, and Mr. and Mrs. Peter. Among these I walked, and felt for the moment the burden of the poor man's life, which is only bearable because it is so simple. Towards the close of the evening, while the young people were dancing and the children swinging and running races, I proposed to a company of elderly village matrons a game in the meadow. We played "hen and chickens," "drop the handkerchief," and other well-known games, and with extraordinary spirit. Our wit, agility, and good humour were surprising, and our laughter rent the air. "Rin, Loiza, rin, Lor! the poor ouddare's legs fare stiff, and the lady's more nor a match for she. Save us! that's the best play a'se seen yet. Fare round the ring, stiddy Myra, and give we oud widders a turn. Mussy-a-be, a'm wally fully o' pine, what with the cake and stuff and leffing,"[1] and more and more laughter. In short, we had a very good day of it. . . . Write me a line, my dear Mary. It will only cost you a queen's head and a quarter of an hour.

To the Same

Fox Holm, *Sunday Evening, August.*

My dear Mary—You must be at this moment on some heathery knoll watching the splendours, the first splendours, of the sunset that is just over here, leaving the house and garden in a sort of gold green shadow, while the broad lights still linger on the Fox Warren fields. I do humbly trust that you are not at dinner eating hot grouse.

We have had some very hot weather, and this morning the sun smote sore on the heads of the poor pilgrims to Byfleet Church. I did long to have a little camp meeting with Frank and Luce under the big trees by the Manor House wall, but we endured on, and heard a sermon about Naaman, and felt surprise that in such weather he could have objected to dip in the Jordan. . . .

. . . . *The Cuckoo died that night.* It sat on the perch after its supper and went to sleep, the cage placed on a table. Next morning, very early, I found it dead at the bottom, its pretty wings outspread and its eyes

---

[1] I am informed that this is not a very accurate representation of Suffolk dialect, but I leave it as written.

open. Luce is persuaded that it was wrong to cage it, and quotes poetry to prove that a cuckoo has a wild mysterious existence, and that it is hardly right to try and *see* it, even. . . . Have I thanked you kindly, ma'am, for a basket of plums, of very good plums, which came from Poynters some days ago, and of which the boys ate too many? I often think that gifts should always consist of fruit or flowers. I don't mean charities, but gifts. You smell them, or eat them, and are pleased, and it is all over. A permanent gift is a sort of torment in the long run.

My dear Mary, I have been *quite* alone since Friday morning, which is my excuse for prating on, and to write to you staves off painful thoughts. I wish that I could bear it all, and that other mothers were all happy. But I think much of Mrs. Bertram Currie, and I know the terror which comes in the lovely summer afternoon when the sunlight seems empty. But these dear children will never feel the pain of parting—

> Full short his journey was, no dust
> Of earth unto his sandals clave ;
> The heavy weight that old men *must*
> He bare not to the grave.

> He seemed a cherub who had lost his way
> And wandered hither ; so his stay
> With us was short, and 'twas most meet
> That he should be *no delver in earth's clod*,
> No need to pause and cleanse his feet
> To stand before his God.

Is not that pretty ? and true of those sweet lost boys and girls ? Good-night, my dear, and God bless you.— Your affectionate   SIBYL HOLLAND.

To the Same

Fox Holm, 11*th October.*

My dearest Mary—It is very disappointing that you cannot go to Winchester on Thursday. I should so love to pilgrim in your company. Perhaps in another life there will be long joyful pilgrimages through wondrous landscapes to noble shrines, where choirs of angels will sing, and Paul himself will preach and expound things unimaginable, and p'raps and p'raps, as children say, I shall meet you there; and the time will neither be short nor long, but the fulness of life and joy. And with these imaginings I shall console myself as we fly along on Thursday through the dim October fields towards the old stones of Winchester, and I shall leave the scene of the Conference, and the heavy pratings of —— on "elderly married members" and hie to the great Church to the tomb of William Wykeham, where I will make a humble prayer for myself, and for you. But could you not possibly so arrange that I might have one little walk with you next week? Could you be put down here in one of your rounds, and let me walk you home through the woods? Is this quite impossible? Is an "elderly married member's" life (I speak of myself) to be for ever spent in arranging for other people? Before —— decides that it is, do let me arrange for one little bit of pure pleasure. If you will do this for me I will expect nothing more till next October, but will remain all through the year, and through all mortal years, your true and loving friend,   Sibyl Holland.

To the Same

FOX HOLM, *October.*

My dear Mary—With the greatest pleasure I will be ready any time after two o'clock to-morrow.

Agnes and I came here on Tuesday night. Nature greeted us with a surprising burst of tears, and still sobs amid her faint smiles. Let us hope that to-morrow autumn's deep smile may be here again.

> The soft October days are with us, Mary!
>   Broad lies the sunshine on the quiet land,
> Autumn's *deep smile* is here, and fingers faery
>   Flushing the woods that wait for death's chill hand.
>
> I cross the lawn and gain the upland meadow,
>   Lingering, I turn, and turning linger still;
> The warm light floods the vale, and the deep shadow
>   Rests on the southern slope of George's pine-clad hill.

The local poet, who is apparently on his way to take tea with a friend, proceeds to describe the various emotions, patriotic and domestic, aroused in him by the distant prospect of Windsor Castle and the near view of his own humble abode. He describes his further walk, the moor, the wood, the farm in a little lonely meadow, the old gate into the home field, until "once more he stands beside the friendly door." He remarks upon the peculiar form which a friendship takes, contracted between persons of middle age, ignorant of the childhood and youth of each other. He supposes that this friendship is, in consequence, of a loftier nature, and that the one common object of the friends (as of travellers who meet half way on a pilgrimage) must be the *end* of their journey. The past is past, the present is a waking dream; they have learnt to take little pleasure in the mere incidents of travel. Therefore the life which will be after travelling days are done forms the staple of their discourse. This is all set forth in two or three stanzas of more or less merit. The friends, having taken their tea together, separate, and the poet makes the best of his way home. Unseen, he meets friendly wheels steadily moving towards the house he has left, and utters an unspoken greeting. He reaches the wicket gate of his own garden, where he pauses awhile and sees many ghosts. He feels a wondrous peace and gratitude, looking upon the roof which covers so much love and innocence. "My heart's own temple, my Jerusalem," and he ends by exclaiming—

> And I am grateful! oh, my Lord, Thou knowest
> My heart's glad throb before Thy throne doth pass,
> Clear as Archangel's song, or as the lowest
> Faint hum of insect in the trodden grass.

I am sure you *long* to see the whole poem. You will get this farrago at breakfast, and I laugh to think how you will try to hurry through it, while Mr. Deacon is wondering at your puzzled absent look. I am supposed to be making up my accounts, and am sitting surrounded by weekly bills. I tear myself from Woodbury's red book to answer your note. "*L'esprit de détachement* is the great thing," Fénelon says. There is no more writing paper in the house, hence these scraps. Ah, madame, *la sainte pauvreté*.

To the Same

FOX HOLM.

My dear Mary—Here is the book, and on the back of this sheet is the prayer as nearly as I can remember.

It comes out of Bishop Andrews, and Greek collects, and Solomon's prayer, and I don't know what else. Words run so much in my head, and I don't always know how they came there. There is nothing more than you could find yourself; but you are pleased to like anything your friends do, and this spoils your judgment, although, no doubt, it adds to your enjoyment. On the whole, however, I am disposed to think that the truth brings the most pleasure, and I hate illusions and interchange of compliments. . . .

To the Same

2 GLOUCESTER STREET, *6th January.*

My dearest Mary—At this time of year we have generally exchanged salutations, and I hardly know how I have allowed Christmas to slip by without writing some sort of greeting to you. The thought that some good fortune might bring us face to face while I was at Fox Warren made writing seem unneedful, but I got no nearer to you than your seat in church on New Year's morning. Lucy came flying to show her pretty book and note,—" Look what Mrs. Deacon sends me," and she kissed both book and note. " *Mr.* Deacon, you stupid thing," says wiser Agnes; and Lucy, acknowledging her mistake, renewed her kisses with fervour. I wish that you could have seen the play that the girls acted for the amusement of the servants, etc.

We nearly killed ourselves with laughing; the children did astonishingly well, and the audience *roared* applause. . . . I hope that the New Year will bring you nothing but good—good days and nights, good friends and books, good health and thoughts, good songs and sermons and shooting, and good roses, and a few good talks with your loving poor friend

SIBYL HOLLAND.

To her daughter Lucy

CHURCH HOUSE, KNUTSFORD, May.

My dearest Luce—You will not really want a letter on Sunday morning. You will be as happy at Poynters as a cowslip; but I said that I would write, and you shall have my only spare half-hour. Aunt Lucy is lifted into the pony chair every morning at 11.30, and I drive her about the lanes. These lanes are all cobbled, that is, they are paved with round stones. The hedges on either side are planted on the top of banks, which banks are covered with primroses and woodsorrel and mosses, and June will see them adorned with thousands of lofty fox-gloves and many kinds of ferns.

The roads are broad and beautifully kept, and are mostly bordered with great beeches, whose branches sweep over the wide footway. The cottages look like small homesteads, and many of the labourers keep a cow in the little croft which is nearly always added to the garden of the cottage. The hedges of the crofts and gardens are full of plum and damson trees in full bloom. The older women wear short petticoats, wooden soles or clogs, a little plaid shawl pinked across, and a large white frilled cap. They stand knitting at their garden gates, and laugh pleasantly when you speak to them, answering with a loud voice and with the strong clipped accent of the country. I do so love this loud voice, which gives one the feeling of independence. You would not understand the children a bit, if you listened to them talking and playing, nor can I understand what the maids say among themselves, unless I pay great attention.

There are a great many Irish in the town, all very poor and very merry. Just at Easter the Roman Catholic priest died. He was quite a young man, and very well educated, but no one in Knutsford knew him or had ever spoken to him except his own poor people. He was ill for one week, and died in his lonely little room, with an old Irishwoman sitting by his bed. His body was taken over to Ireland; all the Irish here accompanied it to the station with loud lamenting, and all the village in Ireland came out to meet it, carrying his poor old mother with them. When the respectable Protestants of Knutsford heard all this, they wished they had done something for Father Casey; but it was all too late.

A few days ago an Irish boy died who belonged to the Society of Good Templars. The priest performed the service for the dead in the Catholic Chapel; then, as he was to be buried in the churchyard, the body was brought, and Mr. Barnacle, the clergyman, read our service. Before the grave was filled up, a man rang at our gate and asked leave to stand on our wall and read a prayer and make an address in the name of the Good Templars. Aunt Mary gave leave—or rather her old maid did—and so the Good Templar talked away, while the clergyman walked crossly off, and the priest, who had come to look on, leant against the churchyard gate with rather a melancholy face. I watched it all from the window, and could hear every word, and I thought how far away the boy's spirit was while his poor little body was carried about. The grave was soon filled up, and the people clattered away.

Bernard comes here on the 10th, and then goes with his two friends *viâ* Harwich to Amsterdam, and then to Rotterdam, Brussels, Waterloo, Ghent, and the Forest of the Ardennes, on the French and Belgian frontier, where they will fish and talk for three weeks. Bernard used to know all about that country when he was a little boy of seven, and he and I used to read Froissart together.[1] Won't it be delightful?

Farewell till we meet, dear girl of my heart. Give my love to the dear lady of Poynters.

To Mrs. Deacon

KNUTSFORD, 22*nd May.*

You said, my dear Mary, that on the 29th you should leave home. Can we meet before that day. I must thank you with a living voice for all your kindness to little L. V. She has written me such a happy letter from Poynters.

Shall you be driving in our direction on Friday, or may I come over on Saturday to the Verandah. Only I am half dead, and feel as if none of us would survive the thunderstorm which is crashing over the town at this moment. Aunt Lucy neither hears it nor sees. She is recovering from a fit of choking into which I sent her, *me miseram!* by a mild little joke at tea, and, as has often been remarked, the disturbance of the

---

[1] My mother read to me in those early years, before I was ten, the whole of Froissart, De Commines, De Joinville, Herodotus, Plutarch's *Lives*, besides a great deal of poetry. I think she read to us as children the whole of the *Iliad* in Lord Derby's translation, most of Chaucer, all Spenser's *Faery Queen*, and Milton's *Paradise Lost*, besides much else. At a rather later time she read to me the whole of Gibbon's *Decline and Fall*.

inner man is more terrible than all the convulsions of nature.

I thought of you all on Sunday morning. The old ladies, though dissenters,[1] and even on bad terms with the parson, keep a rigid hold on the house pew, which is situated in the N.-E. aisle of the church, under the great ten-tiered gallery, and in a line with the Three-decker. It was re-lined with baize in 1801. Date in brass nails on the door. The corners are wide and the hassocks large, and I am ashamed to confess that the seclusion was not uncomfortable. Not a soul could I see save the parson himself. I think that these surroundings made me quicker to remark the virile and Protestant character of the cvi. Psalm and the vi. Deuteronomy. A family religion, in which the master of the house is the teacher, and where each man fights his own way out of his own Egypt. Nothing mystic is here. I wonder who is right ; but I think that real English Protestants are rather like the old Jews. That is a blessed text, "If any man do My will, he shall know of the doctrine," and we had that too.

Are the rhododendrons out, and the azaleas in the woods? Lord love them! You can't imagine how glad I shall be to go home. I think I could run all the way and not be tired.—Yr. loving

SIBYL HOLLAND.

P.S.—It is so difficult to get paper here, for one cannot stir without waking an aunt, and then one has to talk or read. I was ten minutes trying to hook this piece of paper noiselessly on to my knee.

[1] Unitarians.

To the Same

FOX HOLM, 31*st August.*

My dear Mary— . . . The weather here has completely changed, and the golden days seem already at an immeasurable distance. Rain has fallen in floods all day and the wind is roaring in the trees. I have been since yesterday on that old red sofa upstairs, but am all right again and enjoying this quiet room below. I am writing on the sofa in the corner—the air is sweet with the fragrance of the wood fire and the last bunch of roses and the leather of books. Bernard is leaning against the sofa reading *Daniel Deronda*, in which he sees a thousand deep things; Lucy absorbed in Boswell's *Johnson*, Agnes harassing the company by reading aloud bits of *Madame d'Arblay*, the two boys [1] at chess, and Michael above sleeping as though he would never awake. I feel a deep content. One advantage, among many disadvantages of having a sensuous nature (don't mistake the word) is that outward harmony of things soothes so much. In no conceivable circumstances of life could I fail to be influenced by the weather. Is this the case with you?

Mrs. Kingsley [2] has been making me read her husband's life in the proof sheets. It is extremely interesting, and of course all the more so from reading it in this way chapter by chapter and talking it over with her. The public will think it rather too long. She puts in too many of his youthful productions, and it is curious but true, that the youthful productions of a man of genius differ very little from those of other clever boys. Byron did not write better poetry

---

[1] One of them Digby Lyall, a cousin.
[2] The widow of Charles Kingsley.

at sixteen than many clever boys do. I almost wonder how, with her intense feeling about him, Mrs. Kingsley can go through it. There would be something to me so awful in the gradual resuscitation of the past, the slow building up of the figure of the lost until the whole man appears—must be given to the public, himself and not himself. But, perhaps, in the case of an already public character, the strong desire that he should be known would perfectly overcome this. What do you think?

But you won't answer—you see other things in the moors and in the wild eyes of your Highland girl. Fair fall you all . . . Vale.

To Bernard Holland

November.

I read your stanzas and the note which accompanied them with indescribable feelings, and at the end found myself suddenly blinded into tears. Idle tears, perhaps, for I don't know exactly what they meant. What you write must always give me a peculiar pleasure, for, in some respects, you are the very echo of my own mind; no, echo does not do, for you substantiate in words, thoughts, and feelings that have hovered disembodied in my mind. I have never felt it to be the least generally necessary to salvation to dwell upon the doctrine of eternal punishment. At the same time I do believe in the downward tendency of the soul of man, and, as also I believe in the immortality of the soul, I cannot put away the thought that many souls may wake to a sense of misery and with a clear recollection of neglected opportunities, and, as Dante says in his famous lines, there can be no greater misery . . .

III

LETTERS 1877 TO 1882

To Mrs. Deacon

2 GLOUCESTER STREET, *8th January* 1877.

MY DEAR MARY—'Tis not my wont, you will allow, to leave any note of yours unanswered, but I do not like to write to you otherwise than cheerily, and 1877 has opened rather gloomily to us. On Christmas Eve some subtle poison errant in this heavy air caught Michael by the throat and laid him low with an attack of diphtheria. Then the doctors say that Lucy's kind and eager little heart is radically diseased, and the whole way of her life is to be altered. No running, or dancing, or riding, or excitement. This is hard on her whose very life is motion. Then we have had every sort of disaster at the hospital, where everything is disorganised by the division of opinion. This culminates to-day in a great Governor's meeting, in which our side is likely to be smitten hip and thigh, our virtue availing nothing against the crafty and unscrupulous foe. . . . Fair fall your roof this year, and long may it cover your dear heads, and long may your memory abide there after we are all gone to the place where we shall verify whether indeed " the sayings learnt on this dark earth be true."

To Bernard Holland

2 GLOUCESTER STREET, *February*.

Write me a good long letter to-morrow to give a change to my ideas. All this week we have had frightful illness in the hospital, and such scenes of bodily and mental distress that I feel quite stupid about other matters. I seem to hear and see and smell nothing but sick and dying people. But it is quite impossible to say how much one learns in going through these things. I always feel that these poor people teach me so infinitely more than I can teach them. The power of religion is certainly great, and the soul seems in some cases to cling to the idea of God as though to some actual tangible help. The decaying of the outward man and the living brightness of the inward spirit is often quite wonderful.

. . . Oh! yesterday morning we went to Holland House. It is of quite extraordinary interest and beauty. I longed for you, but you will see it one day.

To the Same

2 GLOUCESTER STREET, 20*th February*.

Thanks for your letter and for the very pretty, more than pretty stanzas. The ring and the rhyme, and, to a certain extent, the reason of them make an impression on one, just about the impression you intend no doubt. But I have not the feeling which lies at the root that our faith is dead, nor do I believe, nor do you I am sure, that the mind of man, however developed, can ever form a fairer or more perfect scheme of peace on earth and goodwill than is contained in the Gospel. What *is* dead, and certainly a good deal *has* died since

the Middle Ages, is the belief in such doctrines as the
essential sanctity of the priesthood, with its peculiar
power of binding and loosing, and the efficacy of certain acts of devotion as separate from the spirit of the
inner man. But then I do not seem to find these
things insisted upon in the Gospels, or in the Epistles
either, nor does the hand of Science clash to any
serious extent with our Scriptures, and to Christians
the Gospels suffice. I begged your uncle Alfred to
mark me out a course of reading, which, if I followed, I
should track the way by which the intellectual men of
this younger generation have arrived at the point
whence they perceive that the old creed is lifeless. He
replied that it would be very difficult, etc. But why
should it be difficult? I have an entire desire for the
truth, and I am not afraid to enquire. If prayer and
a firm belief in God and a future state is no longer of
avail, why should not a woman of average understanding be enlightened if she *can* be enlightened demonstrably? It is this reluctance or difficulty in giving
grounds for unbelief that makes so many women suspect that the true reason for the leaving of the former
ways is a dislike in the minds of men to the exercise
of prayer, and to the irksomeness of trying to live by
spiritual rule, and it *is* irksome. Also to a certain
pride which has overflowed men's hearts in consequence
of the progress of science. But we may be wrong;
only I should think there ought to be some explanation which I could be made to understand.

I should think you were a Benthamite, at the same
time I should be sorry to think that you could not
understand the other side of the question, and as I
have no great faith in intuitive knowledge but think
that all knowledge is imparted I will send the Coleridge.

It would also comfort your poor mother did she know that you read every day half a page in the Book of Books. I think the happiest part of my life was when I could hold my Father with one hand and my son with the other, and so it is with our ideas. Let us hold our new ideas, the children of our youth, without letting go the author and guide of our own childhood. In any case I love to know your mind, and may God in His mercy keep you from the slough of materialism in which a man is given up to follow his own heart's lusts and left to his imagination without a sting of conscience. This, and perhaps this only, would break my heart; in all other courses I should find much in which to hope and to rejoice.

To Mrs. Deacon

DOVER, 3rd May.

My dearest Mary—With all the desire in the world to see you before I left London, I could not do it, but there is a " Broad-stone "[1] of happiness in the knowledge that you will presently be at Poynters, and that I shall find you in the verandah some sweet May afternoon when the *thorn is white with blossom*. But I begin to feel rather old and grizzled under the hawthorns, and I am conscious of a horrid dependence on an armchair and a teapot in enjoying natural beauties after a long walk. "The outward man decayeth," is rather a heavy sound in the spring light. Strengthen us so much the more continuously in the inner man. These are our "waters of Jouvence," my dear, which as a child I did long to find, not knowing how near the fountain was.

[1] Kenelm Digby's book is called *The Broad-stone of Honour*.

Have you read your Harriet Martineau, and did you read Florence Nightingale's letters? And have you ever read St. Beuve's *Port-Royal?* I have been reading it for the second time, and cannot find any one to talk to about it. Luce was confirmed last Friday. She and Meta Holland knelt together, and the Bishop laid his hands on two very innocent heads. She makes her first communion on Whit Sunday. I am here till the 10th, and the rest is very pleasant. My mother is fairly well, and Barbara full of ideas and laughter. Bernard is very happy at Cambridge. I write to him, and he sometimes takes what his poor mamma says, and weaves it into sweetest verse, and returns it, to her great pleasure. . . .

Farewell, my only Mary. Heaven send we may soon meet and all may be well.

To the Same

Fox Ghyll, Ambleside, 16*th August.*

My dearest Mary—A vast budget which I saw Agnes despatching to Miss Mildred will have contained any possible news that there was to give you. But you desired me to write, and my pen, after hovering uncertainly over this sheet of paper, has turned north like the needle of a compass.[1] Frank and my sister Mary arrived on Tuesday evening, and Miss Macrae and her pupil are lingering on, so that we are a large party. The house is full of laughter and chatter from morning till night. The country is perfectly lovely, quite beyond my expectations, and it is quite delightful to be in Wordsworth's part of it. I stood long by his grave yesterday. He lies with his wife and sister, the eager-

---

[1] Towards a Highland moor.

hearted, wild-eyed Dorothy, under the yews of Grasmere church. He was such a true poet of the Lakes, born and bred here, and living out his whole life. He has always been my favourite poet, and every turn of the road, every rock and bush, seems to expound him and his writings. If you have his poems in the house, do, for my sake, read again his lines written at Tintern Abbey. There is no Wordsworth here, so we have to fall back on our recollections. The Matthew Arnolds arrived yesterday, but we have only just seen them. The Miss Arnold of Fox How is very pleasant—very unworldly, very little luggage of any sort to go through the world with. I like her much, and I like the swift Rothay which runs below the garden, and the little stream which rushes from the hill above to join it, and the soft green mountains which surround the house on every side. The garden runs up into the Fell and is full of flowers. It is like a jewel hung on the mountain's breast. Yesterday we had a lovely long day out among the hills by Easedale Tarn. Lucy *wept* as we returned. "It is so beautiful and we shall perhaps never see it again."

To the Same

FOX GHYLL, AMBLESIDE, 3*rd September*.

My dear Mary—It is delightful to hear that you are going south about the 12th. So are we, and in my heart I have already bade a cheerful "farewell to the North, the birthplace of valour, the country of worth." To me these virtues avail not where the sun never shines, and hitherto we have subsisted on gleams, occasional gleams. To-day is dry, with a very cold wind, and Frank, Bernard, my sister Mary, and Agnes, have set out to walk over Grisedale to Ulleswater. This sort of exercise is very pleasant, and we have made several, but I cannot share the long walks. It is about twelve years since we were all together away from home in this way. It does not seem so very long ago, and yet, when I remember that I was then twenty-eight years old and our eldest child eight, and that I used to scramble down the cliffs with Agnes on my back and Bernie in one hand, and that I ran and rowed and swam, and went into places where Frank did not dare to follow, it is certain that no other twelve years can make so much difference again either to the children or to me. Now I am glad to be left at home to read and write and to join Mrs. Matthew's teapot.

Lucy and Nelly Arnold are the most amiable girls possible, with plenty of sense and decision, and the more we see of them the better we like them. There is an overflowing tenderness in the whole family. It is lovely to see Edward Arnold, in whose eyes there is already " the light that never was on sea or land," with his brothers and sisters and son and nieces. There is an expressed tenderness which would be too much to be borne, so like it is to the tenderness of parting, were it not the outcome of a whole life of goodness and affection. The Poet [1] was talking of you the other day and said, " If you see them first give them every message of affection you can think of. He is the dearest man and she the dearest woman in Surrey." He said this so suddenly and heartily. We see very little of him, nor do we go much to Fox How. They are plagued by an incessant stream of visitors, who call on the faintest possible pretext of acquaintance, and to avoid this, he shuts himself up, or goes out fishing.

[1] Matthew Arnold.

Mildred Whitmore wrote **Agnes** a quite beautiful little letter about her brother's death. I do so wish that she could have been spared such a grief. There is something so particularly melancholy to the young imagination in a death alone and far-off, and a girl may so reasonably hope to have her brother's friendship all her life. It is a great loss.

Nothing interests me more in this country than Grasmere Churchyard, where Dorothy and William Wordsworth lie side by side, exactly as they chose to lie, having lived their whole life out in the place dearest to them on earth. Did you ever read her *Tour in Scotland?* It has long been a favourite of mine. Their spirit seems to dwell on everything here, and, after all, the change since their time is not great. A few more hotels and lodging-houses, and public vehicles. You might sweep them all away in a day, like the tawdry ornaments in some great cathedral.

I wish that we were within hearing of your preacher on Sundays. Here the church privileges are few. The seats are agony, the singing miserable, and the sermons long, much too long. Matthew Arnold sits facing the whole congregation, in a small square pew under the pulpit.

To the Same

2 GLOUCESTER STREET, *1st November.*

My dear Mary—Barbara tells me that you are laid up with a bad cold, while we have been imagining you at Lythe Hill. . . . Shall I come and take the night-school for you on Monday? Shall I?

Frank has been wanting me all the week to fix to go down with him to Fox Holm on Monday to see what Umney is doing, and after sitting a while with the guinea-pigs and musing with the donkey, I could lunch at Fox Warren and drop in upon you about five o'clock with a bag. Then, if you were well enough, I could night-school with you; if not, I could read you a sermon, say one of South's or Butler's. All this is only supposing that you are at least thoroughly convalescent and alone with the man of your heart, and in the humour for it, and fifty other supposings. There is nothing really to do at Fox Holm, so that any other day of any other month would do as well, only distance never lends enchantment to *my* view. So, Mary, send me a post-card. Mary, Mary, send me a post-card.

We have a fog this morning, and probably there will be one to-morrow. Last Sunday was what words can't tell. The thickest smoke imaginable. We felt our way to church. Inside the sacred edifice a dense fog,—all the gas lit and flaring through it, everybody there because they could not sit at home, seal-skins and woolly veils exhaling a miasma. Quite a little purgatory below, as Dr. Watts says. Let me know how you are in any case, and believe always that I am, your affectionate   SIBYL HOLLAND.

To the Same

2 GLOUCESTER STREET, *Sunday Night, November.*

My dearest Mary—It is cold to-night, and the horses' hoofs ring on the road outside with a frosty sound. Here it is very warm and silent, the girls are reading under the lamp, and I have been sitting at least twenty minutes in this armchair, pen and paper in my lap, trying to think of any more reasonable excuse for writing to you than that I hope to get a note in return. Next Sunday is Advent—how the year swings round—how short all time is, and yet how far we seem already from the sweet lost summer of 1877. But Agnes avers that a touch of its fragrance still hangs about the houses and gardens, and she brought me a handful of mignonette and violets and leaves to show that she said true. The poor little sprays looked wistful, and I thought of the pencils, and half-written notes, and bits of work which a child or a servant will collect in the room of some dear soul that is gone, and bring to one with an awe-struck face.

This is very sentimental, but we are a sentimental family. . . . I am very busy all day with one thing or another. Schools this winter rather than hospitals. I have been going about to some of the great High Schools to see their system of teaching. The whole education question is excessively interesting. When one has acquired a certain practical knowledge of a subject, it is delightful to theorise, and it is so much more satisfactory than getting the theory before the practice. And one distinct consolation in growing older is that one makes fewer mistakes—we act with more certainty, and have no need of that eternal going back in our minds about things which used to occasion such loss of time. We have settled how much we can carry, and we have humped the burden on to a comfortable place on our back. It is this, or perhaps it is that it is so long ago since we stood on the threshold of life and cast a "level glance at pleasure flying from afar,"[1] that we have forgotten the lovely dawn. . . .

---

[1] From a poem of W. Johnson, the Eton master.

To the Same

Fox Holm, *June.*

My dear Mary—Before we had left your gates yesterday Barbara's weak spirit failed at the thought of playing lawn tennis, and she has persuaded me to tell you how infinitely she would prefer to assist at the tournay from the heights of the verandah. . . . I do feel so extraordinarily happy in this weather. I wish that there were not always the feeling that perhaps this perfect sense of enjoyment is not quite right. On a fine summer's day I cannot help feeling that all is forgiven. I wish we could spend seven or eight hours on the downs all together. B. and I would meet you at St. Martha's chapel at any hour mentioned.

To Bernard Holland

Fox Holm, 19*th July.*

. . . I think you are right in the main as to the unadvisability of making the Old Testament so much a part of religious education as Protestants are inclined to do. At the same time the Old Testament has done very good work. Some years ago it was the history, geography, and poetry in one, of all the English poor, and I have often been struck, in talking with old people, to find how deeply they have meditated the stories of Joseph and David and Ahab and Ruth. Too much has often been said, as you remark, for the purpose of palliating the crimes of the Old Testament. But, on the other hand, those crimes, as of Jacob and David, have been too triumphantly pointed at by anti-religionists. I own that I am always irritated by the way people speak of Jacob and David. They seem to miss the point altogether. No one could palliate David's crime, but to a mind at all experienced in spiritual life it is a distinct comfort to know that even such a sin can be repented of and fully forgiven. It is almost impossible to teach religion as a separate part of education. It is like poetry. Children learn what poetry is by being with people who *truly* feel its influence, and in whose nature it forms an important part, and so also they learn religion. Only, as few people pretend to poetic sentiment, the world is spared a mass of false sentiment and inconsistencies, and there is consequently no active opposition.

I think that we ought to be able to do something for our schoolgirls by selecting a set of really cultivated and high-toned schoolmistresses.

To Mrs. Deacon

FOX HOLM, *July*.

My dear Mary—Do not fail us to-morrow, for I must talk to you about the Guild before you go. . . . Do come early and stay as long as you can, so as to give time for some serious discourse with me as well as for a laugh with Barbara. I cannot bear to think how near the time is for your departure to Scotland, and when you return the summer will have gone for ever. However, my dear Mary, beyond all summers and winters, and in whatever state of existence, while memory and feeling last, I shall love you.—Your affectionate SIBYL HOLLAND.

To the Same

Fox Holm, *29th August*.

My dear Mary—Thrice has your coachman left a basket of superb fruit at this door. It is so good of you to think of us when far away in this manner.

There is little news stirring. . . . The Frosts came over to tea last week and brought a very sharp Downside babe to lead the donkey. He looked at our gray parrot, who was standing on one leg on the top of a chair eating a lump of sugar, and observed, " That ain't a howl as sets there?" I liked this cautious and masculine manner of asking for information. We have rain off and on, and there is a premature whiff of autumn in the early morning air. We lead a quiet life, neither grave nor gay. Miss Macrae is with me, and we teach the children, walk and botanise, and read much and talk a little.—Good-bye, dear, and very dear Mary.

To the Same

Fox Holm.

Dear Mary— . . . The sight of you did me a world of good, and I had such a pleasant walk home, owls hooting and pheasants chicking and chestnuts bobbing down through the soft darkness. I thought of the many poor, honest men and women trudging back to their old doors with tired backs and thinking of nothing particular, and, with my waterproof, which seemed as heavy as a faggot or a peck of potatoes, I felt quite like one on 'em, and a thought about the Squire's lady as ad been a talking to, and a nice lady she is, bless her heart, and that were a pertikler good cup o' tea, that were, and a injaed it too, a did, but lor, a never let one of *my* childer stan' and pick the peel out o' the cake. Take an' eat it, an' eat what's in it, or let it be; what's the odds whether ye eats cake or no? but, heart alive, talk o' eddication and give 'em a knife to pick out the good peel! That's a larning on 'em wrong.

To the Same

Fox Holm, *October*.

My dear Mary— . . . It was so pleasant to be at Poynters last night, and I wish the minutes were to come over again. Is it not delightful to have this cheer of beauty and sunshine before we enter the dark cavern of winter? You must let me come to you one of these afternoons.

I do not like to think of Mrs. C. going back to town when fogs have begun already. Why should she not sun herself a little longer in the sweet air? I often think how eager people are for some things, and how chary, even to themselves, of pure leisurely enjoyment.

To the Same

2 Gloucester Street, 30*th October*.

My dear Mary—I cannot let this evening pass without sending you one word to say that I shall remember you, together with many other blessed ones, living and departed, at the early service to-morrow morning. I know that you feel exactly as I do about All Saints' Day, and that to us it is more, perhaps, than to many who keep stricter vigil and more solemn Feast.

Most dear and blessed you have always been to me since I first knew you.

I could say many things, but that it is not easy to write in bed. A catarrh, which is, I suppose, an aggravated cold, caught me two days since. My intellect is completely submerged, but my affections survive. . . .

To the Same

2 GLOUCESTER STREET, *1st November.*

My dearest Mary—The day comes round again, and with the day comes the special remembrance of the saints above, "the solemn troops and sweet societies, that sing, and singing in their glory move." May we and ours in the end of all things be numbered with them in glory everlasting!

But as there is a great gulf fixed between us and those blessed spirits, and as we must spend our *meanwhile* on the "firm opacous globe of this round world," I long for fuller communion with the saints below, and feel it hard and strange that a few damp meadows and misty autumn woods should so completely cut me off from your dear presence. Agnes brought a pleasant breath of Poynters air back with her, and I listened with understanding ears to her exact and detailed account of how every quarter of an hour had been spent. She had "never been so happy in her life," and this is really saying much, for her life has flowed serenely enough.

To-morrow she and I mean to go to All Saints' early service. Last year it was lovely with white and scarlet flowers and long processions of holy women, really endless files, black and gray and disembodied-looking in the twilight, the November twilight, of the church. We have unpacked and settled ourselves among the four million of neighbours, and I have run round to the hospitals, and seen the site of the new school, and undergone the congratulations of the principal parishioners on our safe return. It is pleasant, but tiring, and I always feel so tired and tender from the parting at Fox Holm. The little house looks so desolate the last few days, so in harmony with the decay and death going on in the woods and garden. The play is over, the lights going out one by one, and the house left at last dark and empty, the voices of the actors gone as though they had never been.

This afternoon I went into the old flower shop in Crawford Street for a flower. "Indeed, ma'am," said the girl, "you cannot have one, we want them all for All Saints." I said "Your flowers were lovely last year there." "Oh, ma'am, you should see them this year, it's splendid, and we have done it all. The great cross is magnificent." "Well," I said, "you must give me a church flower; my saint is alive but dying, and your saints must spare her one." "Oh," said the girl, "and to think how I've been complaining of my legs aching all day, and she never to get up again; you shall choose what you like, ma'am." There were tears in her pretty eyes, and I kissed her smooth cheek as I took the flower. Many of these London girls are so quick-witted and generous. If I had nothing to do I should take a large house and look after a hundred of them. And they are so pretty.

When I saw you last week I did not know of Mr. Deacon's kindness about the school. Frank is much cheered on his way, and I have hopes that the school will do much. It is such a great undertaking, so much greater than anything else I have had to do with that I have never had courage to talk to you fully about it. I have the responsibility for the idea, and this rather weighs upon me. . . . My dearest Mary, yours always, and at all times, and in all places,

SIBYL HOLLAND.

To Bernard Holland

2 GLOUCESTER STREET, 2nd December.

I have been thinking of you all day and am glad to know that at this moment, 7.30 P.M., you are not at work. I shall be glad when next Friday is over and you out of it all. I particularly enjoyed my quiet two hours with you at Cambridge, and had a very easy journey home to the Wen,[1] flying steadily through the flat fields, over which the darkness was softly falling. There is a sort of attraction in the very desolation of the country at this time of year. I suppose it is the seasonableness that half pleases one. I thought of Milton's sonnet about the dark afternoons and miry ways.

Yesterday, in London, was too terrible, really a day of wrath, a dreadful day. Fog and drizzle, and thick mud and dinginess indescribable. This was our Advent portion to drink. The sound of the Advent Collect was the only cheer. From my earliest days the words "now in this mortal life" have stirred my heart, and the "armour of light," and the "great humility." In thousands of children's minds these words have been associated with the deepening into winter, and the light and mirth of Christmas seen afar off.

[1] Cobbett's name for London. See *Rural Rides, passim.*

I am sorry that Mr. Gladstone has spoken so long and so vehemently. I often think of the lady who said that he made her weary of the cardinal virtues.

To Mrs. Deacon

Fox Holm, 24th June.

My dear Mary—The blessing of Saint John be with you, and may many midsummer days shine and burn themselves out on dear Poynters, and many midsummer night moons look down on the cigar of its master, and what I want to say is, will you send that Downside maiden to see me as soon as possible. . . . Have you heard that M. our good and brave M., is seriously ill. The oculist fears congestion of the brain, and has sent her away to-day to Brighton. The good Priest sits with all his feathers drooping.

Emily and I went to see her yesterday. She was most sweet and cheery, thankful for all the years of hard work she has done, and ready to conform her will to the good pleasure of Heaven. She is a good, *good* woman.

To the Same

Cavendish, Suffolk, 23rd August.

My dear Mary—The time seems long since I heard of you. . . . There is no news stirring, at least nothing of interest, and when I try to think of anything I can only remember that Frank is gone to America. We came up to town together on Saturday morning, and he jumped out of the cab and disappeared, bag in hand, among the crowd of people at the Oxford Circus, and

I came on here, stopping by the way at Cambridge, where Bernard met me. We had six quiet hours together in his rooms, and among the old chapels and libraries and gardens. The place was so solitary and silent that it almost seemed to exist only in the mind and eyes of the tall low-voiced boy at my side. He is penetrated body, soul, and spirit, with the feeling of the place. . . .

. . . Oh for Paul of Tarsus! If one could preface the word of rebuke with his full and tender recognition of all, and more than all, that is well done in others, how great would be the increase of faith, hope and charity! The older I grow the more strongly I feel how much happier one ought to be, and how far happier we could make each other. The troubles that God sends are certainly not those that spoil one's life.— Farewell, your loving   SIBYL HOLLAND.

To the Same

My dearest Mary— . . . I can think of nothing but Cabul. In Barbara's last letter she said that she had had a long letter from Cavagnari describing his friendly reception and his beautiful house and garden. He has been all the time with them at Simla, and went off in joyful spirits. It stirs one's whole being to imagine the Englishmen charging out of the burning house and among the masses of dark faces in the court. I think there must be a sort of joy in such a death. I cannot pity them. But we are in a fine mess. My brother Alfred will feel it keenly.

When are you coming home? You have been away an enormous time, Mary!

To the Same

FOX HOLM.

My dear Mary—We shall be charmed to come. . . . D. really has a kind heart. She is more elfish than selfish. What a jest!

Hers is a nature that would all turn to gold if once she could be touched by the "folly of the Cross." You will know what I mean. No other words seem to express it. I envy her her visit at Poynters.—Your loving, your very loving   SIBYL HOLLAND.

To the Same

2 GLOUCESTER STREET, *November.*

Dearest Mary— . . . I took Mildred to Sandroyd on Tuesday. How splendid the great stretch of woods looked from the top of Fair Mile, and, as we drove along the road between Silvermere and St. George's Hill, the air was full of myriads of softly falling bright leaves, though not a breath was stirring. The hoar frost lay like silver in every shady corner, and the spruce firs were of an astonishing vigorous green. Their Scotch brothers of a deep blooming blue. You are living in the midst of this sunset of the woods, but I want you to know that I saw it too. It made me happy on Tuesday morning to be sure that you were somewhere out and about seeing and feeling the same things. It is a superb autumn and winter country.

Gertrude Frost died quietly on All Saints' Day, and

was buried last Saturday. The church was full of the innocent tears and sobs of her pupils.—Your loving

SIBYL HOLLAND.

To Bernard Holland

VEYTAUX, *20th April.*[1]

... This afternoon we walked to Glyon, on the road to the Col du Jaman. We came down through loveliest pastures in which the crickets were chirriping madly. Mrs. Chave says that May is the month for Switzerland, and that the spring is three weeks earlier than usual this year. The blossom of the fruit trees will be over, I fear, when you come on the 3rd May. I can hardly believe that a fortnight hence the country can be so charming as it is now. And the weather is like summer, only with more vigour in the air. Yesterday we spent the day at Lausanne, and saw the Cathedral, which is considered the finest in Switzerland, and it is in good repair. It is *never* used. Within is neither altar, nor font, nor pulpits, nor seats. It seems to me that there is no sort of sign of outward worship to be discovered in this country. Anything more miserable than the afternoon service which we attended in the "Stattliche Kirche" of Montreux cannot be imagined, a sort of service so much better suited to a white-washed meeting-house, in which it certainly finds its natural expression. ...

[1] My mother went to Switzerland to be with her daughter Lucy, who had spent the winter at Algiers for health, and could not return to England till May.

To Lady Stephen

VEYTAUX-MONTREUX. 22*nd April*.

My dearest Mary—I can hardly believe that in the full tide of the London season and the coming and going of people and things you will have time to read a letter from me, but you made me promise to write. I had not seen Paris for twenty years, and it looked to advantage about six o'clock on a fine April evening, the streets crowded with merry, well-dressed persons, and the trees on the Boulevards just bursting into leaf. We went on to Lyons next day, and I did not find the nine hours' rail too long, so absorbed was I in looking at the country as we flew along. I never imagined such cultivation. The whole country is like a hand-cultivated kitchen garden. England is a wilderness in comparison. France certainly gives one the idea of an immense prosperity.

At Lyons I waited a day and a half for Lucy, whose ship had been driven out of her course towards the coast of Spain. On the second night she arrived just at dawn, when I had given her up and gone to bed. She is looking very well, eats and sleeps and is for ever talking and laughing. We came on here about a week ago, and have hitherto had the most perfect weather.

This hotel is a few hundred yards above the lake, and the view is much the same as that from Vevey— the blue lake below us, the mountains opposite rising straight out of the water, the little gay bays and villages, with the soft circling line of the Jura to our right. On our left the head of the lake and the gigantic snow-clad Dent du Midi, filling up the opening of the Rhone valley. Behind the hotel the pastures and wooded heights rise above 2000 feet. Beyond these we see the granite and snowy peaks of the Dent du Jaman, over whose green "Col" I hope to see Bernard descending on the 3rd of May. Little paths zig-zag gently up through the pastures, which are knee-deep in lovely grass and flowers, and the wild cherry throws its garlands of blossom in every direction. Chillon sits solemnly in the blue lake below.

Yesterday we took our work and book and sat the whole morning on the slabs of gray stone on which the Castle of Chillon is built. The water lapped all round us; shoals of fish, great and small, swam to and fro, and beyond the blue shadow of the castle the lake glittered like silver. The afternoon we spent high up under the cherry trees, where the grass is full of cowslips, and orchises, and large blue forget-me-not, and the large grasshoppers chirrup quite madly in the warm sun. I enjoy it, but I am a little too old for many of these idle, happy hours.

The company in our hotel is vulgar, but of a passing away sort. It serves to whet the blade of Lucy's criticism. She is severe, as only youth, with its as yet unlowered standard, can be. Later on in the day we waste fewer blows, and live and let live far more easily.

My little Michael goes to school next Saturday, and I cannot think of his departure without tears. The older I grow the more I feel partings of all kinds. I seem to understand more fully what they really mean. Partings are a dead loss, however much one may accustom oneself to live without the creatures who are so dear.

Our newspaper arrives here in an uncertain manner. There is much political talk at one end of the *table d'hôte.* It is very funny to hear six quite ignorant people talking confidently and arrogantly of great affairs. They are all exactly on the same level, and so cannot detect one another.—Always, dear Mary, your very affectionate   SIBYL HOLLAND.

Please give my love to Kate, and remember me with respect and affection to Sir James.

To Mrs. Deacon

2 GLOUCESTER STREET 15*th November.*

My dearest Mary—Please thank Mr. Deacon for the goodly gift of game. A brace of birds has gone on to a family more friendless and remote from pheasants than ourselves. Luce has come home, and when I told her of Mr. Deacon's contribution to the school library, of which she is to be librarian, she exclaimed, "Oh mamma, mamma! He *will* be clothed about with glory."

This weather is an enormous gain upon the winter. One forgets how near he is' at hand, in this beautiful smiling departure of all that made summer and autumn. On Saturday morning I went down to Mortlake, and took Micky out of the large cage where Mr. —— keeps him along with 122 other small English singing birds. We went into Richmond Park, and struck across the grass among the herds of deer and the old trees till we came to Richmond Hill, above the Thames, and not a soul did we meet all the way. From the terrace we went down to the water-side, and sat on some large clean stones to eat a provision of white cake and grapes. And at this point I had resolved to open a conversation with Michael on his besetting sins, of which his schoolmaster had sufficiently warned me. But the design was hindered by a party of geese, who were balancing and bobbing against the current, and who at once landed expressly to join us and to partake the meal. Micky wore a little gray coat with a large hole in each elbow, a small red cap on his fluffy head, and a pair of odd socks. Cake in hand he crouched easily on his flat stone, and sat motionless all but the wild look of pleasure in his eyes, and surrounded by the noisy geese who wobbled and screamed in stupid agitation, while the shining, flowing river threw it all into good relief. Afterwards the sun set so splendidly from Richmond Hill. The river was like steel inlaid with gold flakes, and the immense landscape drowned in purple softness. We drove back to Mortlake station, and then poor Mick said good-bye with a sudden blanching and trembling, and in twenty minutes I was at Vauxhall, with all my reproof unspoken. This was feeble.

I always remember a story your brother Maynard told me at Canterbury, years ago, of an old woman in his parish who used to say to him, " Ha-a! *nice adwice, nice adwice.*"

We went to St. Paul's on Sunday. They sang " Rock of Ages " and " O God, our help in ages past." An immense sound of voices rose under the dome, as the vast congregation heaved themselves slowly and firmly into the tune. I suppose there is no congregation in the world like that. It is London worshipping, and worshipping in its own way. My dear Mary, I have given you no news. I always seem to write to you about nothing at all, and desperately to post my letters. That Lady Alice Fortescue, who died on Saturday, was for some time with her sister at the High

School. Such a tall, beautiful, spirited girl, and as kind and simple as possible. She was hardly ill three weeks, and has been broken off just like a flower in a wintry storm in spring.—Ever your loving

SIBYL HOLLAND.

To Bernard Holland

FOX HOLM, 2nd October.

Your Venetian letter was welcome as flowers in spring. . . . I have been reading the Mendelsohn family memoirs. There are many letters from Florence, Rome, Venice, and all those places. Did you go through Monselice between Padua and Venice? F. Mendelsohn calls it "lovely Monselice." Write me more and more descriptions of what you see. Nothing gives me more pleasure than your descriptions. Some day I may see those places, and I shall see them with the thought of you uppermost in my mind.

In reading about the Mendelsohns it strikes me that music, sculpture, or painting does more for a man than poetry. I think a great musician or painter is a happier man, and makes others happier, makes a much more lovely life for himself and others than a poet does.

I suppose a poet is a more solitary person, or that the expression of his talent is more difficult than that of a musician. There is less joy about it. Then a musician or painter forms a school and takes delight in his disciples, while a poet always dislikes his imitators, rather unjustly, I think. A poet in the long run gives incomparably more pleasure, and his work is more immortal, at least in his own country, and this must be his consolation.

We are pushing forward our winter preparations in Gloucester Street, but we may be detained in these woods till all the leaves have fallen but those of the oak. Those oaks that were cut off in the early spring have contrived to cover themselves with a supply of large, vigorous, dark green leaves, which may remain on till after Christmas.

To Rosamond Stephen (her god-daughter)

2 GLOUCESTER STREET, *Christmas Eve.*

My dear Rosamond—'Tis true the jug is small, the smallest of small jugs.

But it holds as much cream as mothers allow to a little maiden while she dwells in her father's house.

And if my Rosamond should marry to please me, I swear by the font of her baptism to give her a noble silver jug, that shall hold a good pint English of English cream.

Meantime the years will swing round, and the Xmas Eves, and you will grow tall and blooming to behold, and *within*, like the King's daughter, you will become all glorious with the wrought gold of wisdom and kindness and pure and precious thoughts.

I rarely see you, but I hear of you, and remember all I hear; besides, I know the rock whence you were hewn. You will wonder some day to find how well your god-mother understands you, and how easy it is to get on with her.

Our whole family salutes your family with good wishes for 1882—and, my dear Rosamond, believe, that all thro' the year, and thro' all mortal years, I shall ever remain your loving god-mother,

SIBYL HOLLAND.

To the Same

2 GLOUCESTER STREET, 24*th February*.

My dear Rosamond—I am delighted with my sunflower and with all the neat little sketches in it, which I examine with pleasure. I shall keep it for ever on the sofa in my own room, and I shall have many thoughts about you when I look at it. It makes quite a cheerful appearance on the old striped cover. I like the bud and the empty calix and the two large blossoms. —Ever your loving god-mother,

SIBYL HOLLAND.

I have this moment come back from twenty-four hours at Fox Holm. The daffodils and primroses are coming out and the birds are singing as if their hearts would break.

To Bernard Holland

FOX HOLM, 20*th September*.

... We are having lovely weather, only too advanced for the time of year. The Virginian creepers are blood-red and already dropping. The mornings and evenings are extraordinarily mild and the mid-day sun very hot. On Sunday not a breath was stirring, and the air was quite transparent. I had a strong sense of the great change beginning; the beauty was like the beauty that slowly settles in the face of a beloved friend after life has ceased. I hope that there is a future for the fine Italian race, but it may be that some peoples will never be able to fit themselves to the modern civilisation, at least never for themselves so as to become great in it, just as England was nowhere at all in the days when art of every kind exalted a nation. I am sure that what you say of town and country life in Italy must be perfectly true. No doubt all the delight of life there has always been in towns. I think that before many years are gone by, things in London will alter, and a Boston or Weimar will form itself somewhere in our provinces.

IV

NOTE AS TO THE LIFE OF THE WRITER OF THE LETTERS AFTER THE YEAR 1882

IN the year 1882 my father was appointed to be a Canon of Canterbury, and gave up both his work and his house in London. For a time, however, he kept his Surrey house, and, till the end of 1885, my mother continued to live there for three or four months in the later summer and autumn. The rest of the year she spent in the Precincts of Canterbury Cathedral. In this age of perpetual motion, it may seem strange that, except for a few days now and then spent on the coasts nearest to those of England, my mother was only abroad three times in her life. Her first journey was to Switzerland, in the early days of her marriage, her second to the shores of the Lake of Geneva in the spring of 1880, her third was with me to Italy in the autumn of 1885. We went to Milan, Bologna, Florence, Orvieto, Rome, Subiaco, Siena, Pisa, and thence drove along the lovely road from Spezia to Genoa, staying two days at Sestri Levante on the way. Between Spezia and Sestri the road winds to a considerable height, and then descends again to the sea. At the summit we made the carriage pause, and I went to the edge of the slope to pick some arbutus berries. As I turned to the carriage I saw my mother gazing backward, southward, toward the beautiful outline of the Carrara mountains which would, in another moment, be lost to sight for ever. I know not why her look struck me so much, but I see it now. It seemed an eternal farewell to that southern land of which she had thought so much and seen so little.

Returning over the Mont Cenis we drove from Chambery to the monastery at the Grande Chartreuse. Here I spent two nights, while my mother lodged at the adjacent hospice, where ladies are entertained. On our way homewards in October, we stayed two or three days at Paris. Thence to Fox Holm for, as it proved, the last days she was ever to live there. Among the following letters a few relate to this journey.

In the following year, 1886, my mother had to meet the great sorrow of her life. Every tender tie of the deepest affection and most intimate sympathy had intertwined her whole being with that of her younger daughter, Lucy Verena. I need say little of this singularly sweet and beautiful relationship of mother and daughter—the letters speak for themselves. In 1876, when Lucy was fourteen, it was discovered that her heart was diseased, and her gay and active nature was condemned to a life of restraint. In 1879 she all but died of a severe attack of rheumatic fever. This time, however, she recovered and lived to be for seven years more the charm and delight of her family. Lucy was by nature wholly free from worldly ambitions, and her malady still more concentrated her affections to her home. Her life was always precarious—she knew this and so did her mother, and this knowledge gave to their love the pathetic charm attached to all that is most beautiful and most transient. My elder sister went to India in the autumn of 1883 and stayed there till the summer of 1885, and Lucy became during this time my mother's sole constant companion. Between her first illness in 1879 and her second illness in 1886 the winters were mild. But in January 1886 a winter began which proved as severe as that of 1878-79. With it returned my sister's illness, and in the middle of February she was again attacked by rheumatic fever. Her native vitality was great, and my mother had to watch her darling fighting against terrible sufferings for more than six months. At the end of June the life of Lucy was altogether despaired of, and she received the last sacraments. She rallied, however, in a wonderful way, and towards the end of August she was moved to Harbledown Lodge, two miles from Canterbury, a house, then empty, taken for the purpose. Here she seemed better, though very weak, and for ten days she was able every morning and evening to lie out of doors, in the fields or garden. But on the afternoon of the 3rd of September, as she was being taken out, she became insensible, and died two hours later. She was buried in the lovely churchyard at Godmersham. Lucy was twenty-four years old when she died.

After this we went no more in the summer to Fox Holm, in Surrey, and that long chapter in my mother's life, so full of her joys and sorrows, came to an end. At the beginning of 1887 my father bought Harbledown Lodge. Here, every year till her death, my mother came from Canterbury in June and stayed till the middle of October. The house stands on a southern slope, with fields above and orchards below and around it. On the north, at the top of the hill, begins the forest of Blean; below, the undulating depths of the valley are rich with fruit plantations and hop-gardens. Shakespeare makes Lord Saye and Sele say of Kent—

> Sweet is the country, for 'tis full of riches.

a line one thinks of in the valley of Harbledown.

On the further, southern, side of the valley is a steep wooded hill, along the top of which runs the ancient "pilgrims' road," whereby the pilgrims from the southern and western shires used to travel to visit the shrine of Thomas à Becket. To the south-east, beyond the opening of the valley, rises the chalk range, yellow in July with wheat-fields, expanding at this point into the wide, rolling, open country of East Kent. In this part of England the air is pure, strong, and clear, and the skies are usually of a peculiar pearly blue, thus mirroring, as my mother used to say, the pale seas which lie north and south and east around the Kentish peninsula. Here, and in the Precincts, she spent her remaining days, in the sweet country of her childhood and girlhood, and the early years of her married life.

> Ah! that hamlet in Saxon Kent—
>   Shall I find it when I come home
> With toil and travelling well nigh spent,
> Tired with life in jungle and tent,
>   Eastward never again to roam?
>
> Pleasantest corner the world can show,
>   In a vale which slopes to the English sea,
> Where strawberries wild in the woodland grow,
> And the cherry-tree branches are bending low,
>   No such fruit in the south countree.

So her brother, Alfred Lyall, wrote in the days of his youth on the dusty, sunburnt Indian plains.[1]

At the end of June 1889, my sister married and

---

[1] See "Verses written in India," by Sir Alfred Lyall.

departed to live at the other end of England, in Cornwall. All my mother's children had then left the home. In the following August my mother was received into the Roman Catholic Church. This was a step towards which she had for many years been tending, led by her innermost nature.

> Cosi vuolsi la dove si puote
> Cio che si vuole, e piu non dimandare.

It would, perhaps, be enough to use these words of Dante, but I will mention some circumstances relating to this great venture of her life. Her father was a philosophical and learned clergyman of the older school. Her mother was a sound English Churchwoman, but always had a strong taste for the great French religious writers. This she transmitted to her daughters, and my mother all her life was a great student of the French divines, especially those of the seventeenth century. In history she was much influenced by Bossuet and the great work of Fleury. At one time she was absorbed in the controversies connected with the Port Royal movement. Newman ascribed to the novels of Walter Scott the first impulse which started him upon his line of mental development. This and the like literature, especially the romances of La Motte Fouqué, appealed strongly to her young imagination. My mother told me that once, when, as a girl of fifteen, she was staying at the house of her uncle, the Dean of Canterbury, she stole down to his study one night when the house was asleep, took possession of his cathedral key, fearfully let herself into the dark, empty, vast and mysterious church, and passed almost the whole night prostrate before the altar. At another time, half in play, half seriously, she horrified her most respectable

North German governess by informing her that, in consequence of a vow, she must walk barefoot up the long and dusty ascent of Wingate hill, on the London road, and carried out her resolve in spite of remonstrances. In the earlier years of her marriage, however, she made, I believe, a serious intellectual effort to adopt what is called the "evangelical" view. On one occasion, at St. Dunstan's, she rebuked her sister for turning eastward during the Creed, on the ground that the ceremony was not justified by sufficient reason. My mother was not at any time, I think, in very real sympathy with the modern "High Church" party, although she may at times have thought that she was one with them. Perhaps she was never at any time free from doubt as to the claim of the Church of England, and it may be said, in one sense, that a doubt is a suppressed or resisted conviction. Those who knew her best, about half-way between 1870 and 1880, think that she then found it difficult to resist the conviction that the Church of Rome was justified in its claim to the allegiance of the Christian, or, at any rate, of the whole western world.

About the same time, however, she turned her attention towards the question of the higher education, on strong and decided Church principles, of girls in the upper and middle classes. Her interest in this matter had first, I believe, been inspired by the study of the foundation and history of "St. Cyr," the creation of the sensible and practical Madame de Maintenon.

The rapid progress of the "undenominational" high schools for girls had made it necessary that something should be done if the Church of England were not to lose all hold upon this immensely important branch of education. At my mother's suggestion, my father organised a Church School Company, which founded, in 1878, the very successful school in Baker Street, and, some time later, a second school in Graham Street, near Eaton Square. My mother was extremely interested and occupied in the creation and start in life of these schools, and became also one of the chiefs of a guild or association founded in order to combine teachers and others interested in the education of girls on Anglican principles. This office she held until she resigned it nearly a year before her change, in consequence of her growing conviction that she must join the Roman Church. These affairs, added to her constant labour for the poor and sick, so much for a time occupied her mind that they delayed, perhaps, the step which she finally took.

The change from London to Canterbury in 1882 made a great alteration in her way of life. An intimate friend who knew her mind on these subjects better than any one else, writes, " From the time she went to Canterbury in 1882 I felt it " (the change) " to be only a matter of time." The Cathedral was a great pleasure to her, and no one at Canterbury more constantly attended its daily services, or more deeply felt their beauty. She delighted in the constant hearing of the English Psalms and Lessons, and, after she had joined the Roman Church, spoke sometimes of the loss which she felt in this respect. But Canterbury is a place very especially associated for many pre-reformation centuries with a form of worship and doctrine in substantial accordance with that of the present Roman Church, and very unlike that of the three and a half hundred years of the reformed Anglican Church. The Cathedral and City are full of relics of the "old Religion," and must produce a singular impression upon an imaginative soul haunted, as my mother's so long had been, by the idea that the Roman may be, what it claims to be, the true, or, at least, central Catholic Church, to which is paid perpetual homage in the Creeds. Whether she was right or not, certainly she was led to the Church of Rome by a most ardent desire for reality.

In addition to its historical associations, Canterbury had in those years a modern Roman Catholic atmosphere derived from other circumstances. About the time of our return there in 1882, the Jesuits, driven by recent laws out of France, had bought as a school for French boys a large country house, called Hales Place, on the outskirts of Canterbury. The boys were numerous and belonged to the best families in France. During these years many French people of distinction visited Canterbury, and several took houses or lodgings in the town. Among these came from time to time the eloquent and chivalrous Catholic leader in the French Assembly, the Comte Albert de Mun,[1] who had two boys at the school. Occasionally he dined at our house. The Jesuit Father at the head of the College was himself a gentleman of good birth and noble breeding, the well known Père du Lac. For some reason the school was closed in the year 1890, much to the grief of the people of Canterbury, who had good cause to like their French guests. The building is now used as a seminary for French and Belgian candidates for the order. It was bought by the Jesuits from the mortgagees of Miss Hales, the last representative of a very ancient, and once great, Kentish Roman Catholic family. Miss Hales herself had retired to a house called Sarre Court, amid the Thanet marshes,

[1] Better known perhaps to some English readers of the *Récit d'une Sœur* as the son of Eugénie.

about nine miles from Canterbury. As a girl she had been a friend of the Lyalls, and after our return to Canterbury my mother frequently went to see her at Sarre Court, or entertained her at the Precincts. Mary Hales died at Sarre Court, at the age of forty-five, in April 1885, and was buried in her father's vault under the Chapel of Hales Place. The presence of the French School and of the Jesuit Fathers lent a certain splendour to the ceremony, due to one who was the last of an ancient and honourable race.

I have mentioned the Roman Catholic elements in Canterbury life, but I do not think that any one person had much to do with my mother's step. Her own nature had long been leading her to Rome. The speed with which she moved towards her destined goal was much quickened by the illness and death of her daughter and circumstances connected with this. A subjective reaction attends the sudden cessation of a long fight against death; a soul-solitude follows a great loss; and she had, besides, a doubt as to the long continuance of her own life, or rather a firm belief that she would not long survive her daughter. Yet it was a hard thing for one in her position to take the step. It is a difficult pass that leads from thought to action. She had also, perhaps, the "Lyall repugnance to decisive action," of which she speaks in one letter. She waited till August 1889; then, on the 20th of that month, saw a Father Gordon, whom she knew by name only, at the Brompton Oratory, and on the following day made her profession of faith.

A few days after her change some one at Harble-down sang the touching old Jacobite song beginning "Farewell, Manchester, noble Town, farewell." She listened with emotion, and said, afterwards, that the words expressed her feeling. Did she feel, for the moment, as she listened, that she too, after all, might have departed "shadows to pursue"? It was her venture. I remember that she said once, after her change, "Well, if the Roman Church is not the true Catholic Church, there is at any rate none truer." She often said that Roman Catholicism was Christianity *au grand complet.* This view does not deny, of course, that essential, or fundamental, beliefs are held in other Churches. Those who hold it feel that, for themselves, the Roman Church offers the most complete or adequate expression of Christian devotion.

It is possible, I hope, neither to condemn nor to praise beyond others those who find in the Church of Rome that which satisfies their reason and feelings. One result of the long and undecisive religious contests of this century is that there is now more tolerance in opinion. Certainly, people are not condemned so severely now as they were fifty years ago for choosing the form of religion most in harmony with their mature disposition. It is impossible that there should not be some modification in relationship to other persons for one who has crossed a gulf so wide, or rather, perhaps, so deep, as that which separates the Church of England from that of Rome. To a disposition so sensitive in regard of friendships as that of my mother such modifications were painful, but she found, I think, that they were not nearly so great as she had at first apprehended.

A change of this character, even by one who leads a private life is, in a sense, a public act of importance, and requires explanation. For this reason I have given rather numerous extracts from letters relating to it; a few also from a journal kept by my mother. It will be seen that she took the step by no means lightly, but most reluctantly, under an irresistible conviction or attraction.

After August 1889 my mother became a faithful attendant at the Roman Catholic church of St. Thomas, in the Burgate at Canterbury. It could not be said that any mere external allurements attracted one who exchanged for this very humble place of worship the stately aisles and beautiful chantings of Canterbury Cathedral. Yet still sometimes, on a dark winter afternoon, she might pass with her quick, decided step across the Precincts, enter by the little south door into the dim transept of the Cathedral nave, and, from below the steps, listen to the English psalms and anthems, so delightful to her, chanted in the choir above. She gave, at this time, as a gift to the Cathedral, psalm books to be kept in the nave, and in the beginning of each she wrote words of deep meaning from some divine author.

My mother had always devoted much of her time to the service of the poor and sick, and, after she had become a Roman Catholic, her zeal in this direction seemed even to increase. Naturally, in these last years, she gave special regard to the Roman Catholics in Canterbury, mostly Irish, and the poorest of the poor. By these, and by many others, she is still remembered in Canterbury with gratitude and affection.

I do not think that, in these closing years of her life, she could be better described than in words used by Mrs. Craven[1] in her account of the later years of Lady Georgiana Fullerton :—

"Sa charité déjà si vive devint plus tendre, plus ardente, plus également distribuée entre ceux qui réclamaient ses aumônes et ceux qui demandaient ses

---

[1] Pauline de la Ferronays, better known as the writer of the *Récit d'une Sœur*.

conseils, son appui et sa sympathie. Elle avait toujours compâti aux peines d'autrui ; elle en avait toujours écouté le récit avec attention, avec intérêt, avec patience. Mais plus elle avançait dans la vie, plus cette patience devenait tendre, pénétrante, sage pour conseiller, habile pour comprendre, puissante pour soulager. Il est presque permis de dire que ces grands cœurs unis à Celui qui est l'Amour lui-même participent à sa puissance, et obtiennent le droit de dire comme Lui ' Venez à moi, vous tous qui souffrez et qui êtes chargés, et je vous soulagerai.' "

It remains to say that she found in the Roman Catholic church the full satisfaction and consolation which she sought.

The following letters extend from her return to Canterbury at the end of 1882 to her death in September 1891. In 1882 she was in the 46th year of her age.

V

LETTERS 1883 TO 1885

To Rosamond Stephen

THE PRECINCTS, CANTERBURY, 5th January.

MY DEAR ROSAMOND—I have never written to thank you for your good little letter, which pleased me quite as much as the silly little sugar-bowl can have pleased you.

You see my words were true, the year has swung round, and the great clock of the world has struck once more.

You are taller and wiser, I am older and not more foolish. You are climbing merrily up the hill with the sunshine on your face, while I have rounded the top and have turned my face to the shadows. There is a long distance between us, but I shall always send back a cheery voice to my god-daughter once a year until my trudging ends, and I disappear into silence and darkness, and you will say, *my poor old god-mother is gone.*

This sounds gloomy to you, but not at all to me, so much I hope to join the great company of happy souls elsewhere.

I wish very much that you and Dorothea would come to see us here. You would like the ancient places, Becket's Shrine full of splendid old windows, and the great High Altar in front of it, and you would like to see the Black Prince with his fine Plantagenet face carved in bronze and his coat of mail and helmet hanging above him, and the cloister door where the four knights burst in to murder the Archbishop, and the Pilgrim Inn, and then to go to the top of Bell Harry Tower, and to see Archdeacon Harrison come into Church with one eye open and one eye shut, and a nose just like the beak of the jackdaws who fly for ever round the towers, and are almost as regular at Church as he. All this you shall see if you will come next week.

Michael salutes you.

Greet the mother of Ajax with a holy kiss.[1]

Lucy salutes Helen.

Salute Katharine the elder sister, Agnes's friend and mine.

Salute the Judge!

Salute Herbert, James, and Harry, the beloved brethren.

Be wise unto that which is good.—Your loving godmother, SIBYL HOLLAND.

To Miss Arnold Forster

CANTERBURY, *18th March.*

I had quite forgotten my own birthday until your kind note and Agnes's warm embrace reminded me of it, at the same instant. Forty and six years have I wandered in this wilderness, and returning to this par-

---

[1] Reference to the part of Ajax, taken by James Kenneth Stephen in the Greek Play at Cambridge.

ticular spot in the desert has made me feel the times past so far off that I should hardly be surprised were I to discover that I was born a hundred and six years ago. I think this is partly owing to the fact that all my contemporaries have left the place, and that those friends who remain are indeed between eighty-five and a hundred years of age. They welcome me warmly and treat me as an equal in years and in wisdom, and this gives me a strange decrepit sensation.

Bernard came down yesterday to our great pleasure. We sat round him and asked him a hundred questions as to people and things in London. You cannot imagine how little interest the Canterbury folk take in public affairs. The blowing up in Westminster Street is never mentioned, nor have I heard the names of Gladstone or Forster *once* since we have been here. They are really dead to the world on the side of politics. I sympathise much with Mr. Forster's speech, but you see that all the world has gone mad about Mr. Gladstone; whoever opposes him is thought wrong; people have ceased to consider the subject on its own merits, and it will be the same thing with every other question. I begin to understand the mingled fear and dislike with which many persons regard the Prime Minister.

I rejoice that F. looks so fair and happy. This will go far to reconcile you to the step she has taken. Certainly the one thing we desire for our beloved ones is that they should be happy, and this at whatever enormous cost to ourselves, and in this noble and natural desire we can trace the great image in which man was created.

We think constantly of you all. Our own changes make us realise other people's changes. My dear Frances, all these changes and chances of mortal life are figures of the great change that must come to us all. There is a wonderful sense of awe and love and hope when one fixes one's thoughts thereupon.

To Lady Stephen

CANTERBURY, 17th May.

My dearest Mary—This is good news indeed! solid, pure, good news, without spot or wrinkle or any such thing, and I rejoice with you from the bottom of my heart.

My brothers have often talked of Sir Robert Egerton, and I now marvel that nothing ever prompted me to ask what he was like ; why did I never inquire as to his height, his voice, his hair, or want of hair ; his temper, turn of mind, and a hundred other particulars which are now of deepest interest ?

What a pleasant shifting of the scenes . . . But this was *the way of the wilderness* by which your sister was to be led; by doubtings and murmurings and plagues and serpents and rocks and streams and manna, she was to be led into a land flowing with good things, and there may she dwell for ever, and may God bless her and keep her. This is my hearty good prayer. If she is now with you, embrace her for me. I have always loved and admired her since the time I first saw her a great many years ago.

We are looking forward to seeing your James on Saturday, and we hope that Harry will come also. The weather is perfect, and the stately old church rises finely from among the young green of the trees into the transparent air.

But life in these ancient places is other than elsewhere. One either *dreams* or wakes to a sort of pain, an "aching void" as it were. Perhaps it is the old life that is gone and is not replaced by the new.—Ever your affectionate   SIBYL HOLLAND.

To Miss Cunningham

FOX HOLM, COBHAM, 14*th July.*

My dear Miss Cunningham — It was very good of you to write to me. I had thought that letters would be troublesome, which was the reason I wrote to your sister and not to yourself. I do approve your marriage theoretically and actually. I like the idea of the strong and solid alliance of friendship and large common interests into which you are entering with Sir Robert Egerton, of whom I have long heard a thousand good and charming things. You should have burned the old letters without reading them. It was with a shock that I remembered (Sir James's face seemed to appear to me with a menacing expression) that I had ever advised you to become a Roman Catholic.

The step is never, in my opinion, a wholly illogical and unprofitable one, but as matters have turned, it would have been a false step for you, for whom other good things were laid up in the days that were coming.

All the kind things that you say of remembrance and affection I fully return, nor could I possibly cease to think tenderly of you as long as memory lasts. I wish that it were possible to you to come and spend an evening and morning with me here before you go away. You know we are only half an hour from Waterloo. You could come down in the cool of the evening, and go back before the day grew hot. There are many days when no one is here but the two girls and myself. And it would be such a pleasure, just "as though one put a rose in my hand," as the Germans say. In hope of this I do not say farewell, but God bless you.—Believe me, always your very affectionate   SIBYL HOLLAND.

To Bernard Holland

CANTUAR, *27th November.*

... I am reading Carlyle's letters drop by drop, and learn much from him every way. He satisfies me about many things more than any one. He is the finest of all pessimists. But I find it very difficult to imagine what, on the whole, he would have the mass of ordinary human beings to do. If a hero were to arise, then they must clearly follow and obey him; but, if no such person is anywhere to be discerned, I suppose then we must all do our day's work as well as we can? He is not a teacher, but a prophet and a seer, speaking only to those who have ears to hear, and multiplying the deafness and blindness of those who think they see already. My soul conforms to his remarks on dull Mill and his " wooden set."

To Miss Arnold Forster

CANTERBURY, *16th March.*

... The real sorrow felt for the babe that dies as soon as it breathes shows what a world of love and joy and hope belongs to the very idea of motherhood. It is a wonderful thing. There is all this idea of motherhood, and then there is the love for the individual child, and then there is the noble sense of bringing up a soul in the faith and love of God. All this love and high purpose is now broken, and we can only say it is the will of God that it should be so.

. . . The loss of children has been much in my mind for the last week. I went with Bernard to Fox Holm on Saturday week and found our man there and his wife in the deepest distress, their only child, a lovely little girl of four years old, dying of sudden inflammation. I went again on Monday, and the child was dead; the beautiful little body lying on a bed upstairs with some primroses and violets on its innocent little breast. The grief of the poor parents was terrible; the child was all the world to them. It is hard to see these buds and blossoms perish so untimely; just too when all the world seems so full of life and promise.

These warm spring days are pleasant here, and I wish you would come down and see us. As I write, the Cathedral is standing bathed in sunshine from end to end; the rooks are building and quarrelling. Bernard and Lucy are slowly walking across the grass towards the south door, and I hear the boom of the organ, which warns me that I must stop writing and put on my cloak and bonnet.

To Mrs. Deacon

Fox Holm, 8*th September.*

My dearest Mary—I ought to have written to you long ago to offer thanks for excellent grouse. . . .

... Yesterday, Barbara, Luce, and I went to Hatchford. All the quality being away there was plenty of room, and we enjoyed the service in spite of the astonishing clanging, crashing, and whooping made between Miss ———— at the organ, the choir, and the congregation. I was in an exalted frame and felt above it all. B. suffered a little. Mr. Benham preaches very well, and there is something touching about his manner. The wind blew so soft from the south-west as we jogged along to church. The lanes, the common, the woods all seemed so lovely, and so *well-known*. Something in this country at the turn of summer into autumn goes to my heart. It is partly that I have gone through such things at this time of year, and the remembrance of them gives expression to the landscape, and in this there is nothing melancholy. It is like the face of some well-beloved friend with whom one has passed through good and evil days, and who has always been faithful and kind.

Bernard is in the Shetland Isles with a man who lives there all the year round, shunning human intercourse and weaving the most wonderful dreams. I knew him as a romantic youth years ago at Canterbury. Bernard writes extraordinarily well, and his letters seem to come from fairy-land. When we meet I must tell you about the dreaming Laird of Burravoe. The two Franks have been away in Norway these five weeks, and are coming home to-day. They have been very happy together. . . .—Ever, my dearest Mary, your loving   SIBYL HOLLAND.

To Bernard Holland

CANTERBURY, 18*th November*.

Do bring me the Carlyle. I long to read it. The lines[1] are very beautiful and, as you say, they express all that can be said by reason or emotion alone. St. Paul's teaching of striving to become worthy of this nobler existence by communion with the mind of God in Christ consolidates the natural idea. I *must* believe in another life. That we do not live by bread alone, that the life is more than meat and the body than raiment, is a belief to which my whole soul adheres. . . .

It is strange that Kent should have as much hold on you as it does on me—almost. You are the child of my youth. Years and years ago I used often to dream of nights that I was an active young man lightly descending the slopes of some lofty mountains towards a sunny plain, which I took to be Italy. Now for some time I perceive that it was not myself but you of whom I dreamed. And I dreamed it long before I married.

To the Same

PRECINCTS, 29*th November*.

Our letters crossed. . . . The dinner at the Club was rather brilliant. Oakley is an interesting person, but, looking at the way in which our country is arranging itself, I doubt whether any satisfactory career lies before him. Certainly more lies are taught than were taught fifty years ago. The Radical sham, which Carlyle thought the greatest sham of all, is in full bloom and

---

[1] Lockhart's lines, beginning, "It is an old belief."

has yet to produce its fruit. I wish I knew why Carlyle was so convinced that all Catholic worship, as a true thing, is completely and hopelessly dead. If he had thought that it never had been a true thing I should not be surprised, but, in his remarks about the churches abroad, he says that it died 300 years ago. What was there more real in it *then* than *now* to the common half-educated priests and poor good women—and did it then have any more hold on minds like Carlyle, and Froude, and J. F. Stephen, than it has now? I should so like to know this. I was extremely touched by Carlyle's almost break-down of feeling in the majestic silence of Ely Cathedral. That, and a thousand other things, was so honestly and beautifully felt and expressed. . . . Our old country town here has worn a cheery look these mild winter days—Harbledown and St. Thomas's hill peering clearly over the old gables, and Kentish village people coming in to buy and sell for Christmas. . . . G. C. P.[1] came back for a night to procure a relay of books, but retired again to Folkestone next morning. "Master is forced to go away," says Stickels, "because he can't take any fresh air in Canterbury. If he goes out he meets ladies and they will stop him—so he has to set indoors till it's dark. At Folkestone, bless you, he's out all day long, amusing hisself *by* hisself."

To the Same

PRECINCTS, *23rd December.*

If you do not come home to-night here is a word of greeting for your 28th birthday. I see more and

---

[1] A cousin of my mother's, much older than her, who lived at Canterbury, and died in 1894.

more, as time goes by, how different a mother's love is to any other in the world, how abiding and without possibility of shadow or change, and yet how hardly necessary to the children as they grow beyond early youth.

I often think of my mother's words the last day of her life as I held her head against my shoulder. She said, "It seems strange that I have no more to say"; and I answered, "It has been a long friendship and all has been said"; to which she replied, "That is quite true, all has been said."

And I feel this in writing to you. It has been a long friendship, and there is no more to say. I could never put into words all that you have ever been to me, nor can I cease to hope and believe that the God and Father of our Lord Jesus Christ will keep you all your days, and guide you whither you go. My prayers will follow you as long as I live.

To the Same

PRECINCTS, *7th February.*

I cannot wish you at the Nile to share in our disaster. What a strange thing is the desire of quiet souls to be present at scenes where, at any moment, the whole being may be blotted out for them. I have no doubt that this, like many other strong instincts of the soul, might be traced to the eager anticipation of death, which is really the desire of more life. Because I suppose that a man is never so much alive as when all care and anxiety for his living body ceases, as it must do, in battle. . . . Gordon makes a wonderful figure just now, whether he is alive or dead; his joy no man can take from him. He has overcome the world, and is of good cheer. His little book on Palestine pleased *me*. He is like the centurion in the Gospel. He knew what it is both to command and to obey, and has absolute faith in his Master's word, and such a soldierly simplicity as never was. His whole career redeems the life of the "so-called nineteenth century." After all, at no time of the world have such men been anything but very rare indeed. It is a comfort to feel that they are still possible.

To Francis Holland

CANTERBURY, 20*th April.*

I have only time for a word to you to wish you many many happy returns of the day. I went to London on Thursday, and came down on Saturday, and went straight to Sarre Court, where I found poor Miss Hales dying. She died a little before midnight on Saturday, and I and Lucy had to perform all the last offices for her. I came home an hour ago, and have to go back again to-morrow, and am so tired that I can hardly see. The last few days have been so tragic and strange. Miss Hales is the last of a great Kentish family, and there are many curious and unnormal circumstances, of which I will one day tell you.

[The following letter is one written, not by my mother, but by my sister Lucy. I insert it because it relates an incident which many people at Canterbury, and some in France, may remember with interest :—]

Lucy Holland to Bernard Holland

PRECINCTS, 26*th April.*

... I can hardly believe it is only a week since last Sunday; it seems at least three. My thoughts have been ever of Mary Hales. Nor can I ever forget this week. Mamma and I left Sarre Court on Tuesday evening about seven o'clock; and, for the first time, neither she nor I were in that house. We drove all the way home, arriving after dark. Next morning we drove first to take up G. C. P., who wished to go to the funeral with us. He got in, and we drove on down the High Street; but, before we reached the Westgate, cousin G—— began to mutter something about "not going on," "a long service," "getting out," etc. We took no notice of these mutterings. Mamma told me, in a whisper, this was always his way at family funerals. As we turned into North Lane, we saw close in front of us the hearse, followed by a single carriage; we had arrived exactly at the right moment to follow it down the road to St. Stephen's. At every house, all down North Lane, the people were standing at their doorways; the men all with their hats in their hands, silent and interested. Arrived at the gates of Hales Place, the hearse stopped outside, and a messenger was sent up to tell Père du Lac that it was there. The bell of St. Stephen's Church was tolling, and we heard the boom of the Cathedral bell in the distance, but there was no feeling of gloom; there could not have been a more lovely spring morning; everywhere "green were the leaves, and sweet the flowers," and the warm bright sunshine over everything. All at once, after we had waited about ten minutes, down the drive from the house came a long procession of boys and priests. Twelve of the senior boys, clad in scarlet cassocks, white surplice, scarlet shoes, and broad black sashes, headed the procession, carrying the Cross and candles. Behind them walked all the rest of the boys; then came all the Fathers in surplice and barretta; and, lastly, some of the Benedictines from Ramsgate. Never, as long as I may live, can I forget that which I saw then. "How strange to be here," mamma said to me; and, indeed, it did seem strange. At the gates the procession turned, formed again in perfect order, and preceded the hearse up the avenue to the chapel, the Fathers chanting psalms as they walked. The coffin, followed by Father Ephraim,[1] Mrs. Trueman, mamma and I, was carried up the aisle, and laid on trestles, close to the altar step; round it stood six great silver candlesticks, with lighted candles, and on the coffin mamma and I put a beautiful cross and wreath of white flowers we had brought with us. The mass was sung by Father Swithbert, the Superior of the Benedictines, and a great friend of Mary's. Besides us, the few intimate friends, there was no outsider at all in the chapel, only the French boys. As mamma said, they know nothing of Mary Hales's troubles and difficulties; they only thought the former owner of Hales Place was come back to lie where her father was buried before her.

After the mass the coffin, covered with flowers and incense, was carried round to the back of the chapel, and was lowered gently and carefully into the vault, the Fathers chanting the last sentences. I threw into the open grave some lovely white pea blossoms that had been gathered the night before out of the walled garden at Sarre Court. Some one put into my hand,

---
[1] Miss Hales's chaplain, a Benedictine.

as I stood there, two white flowers, and told me they came from the wreath Mary had worn the day she became a Carmelite.[1] . . . Father Ephraim wished very much that I should go back to Hales Place, after lunch, to go with him into the vault, " to have one last look." So we drove back to Hales Place, and went right down into the vault, where, by the light of a candle, we saw the three coffins lying there; an old looking crucifix lay on that of Sir Edward Hales. Afterwards we walked a little in the woods. Père du Lac was walking up and down a path in the woods reading his breviary. I thanked him as best I could for all he had done. He turned quickly away, his eyes full of tears.

To Bernard Holland

Fox Holm, 5th July.

. . . I agree with you about Mrs. ———. She is the most charming young woman I know, save for her ill health. This, perhaps, adds an interest, but takes away a charm. I wish I could see more of her. She is very sweet to me always, but, perhaps, she is so to all elder women whom she likes, and she must know so many. If I were sure that to know me better would give her anything like the pleasure it would be to me to love her and her little children more freely, I would take a good deal of trouble. As it is, I never can believe that people care for me as I care for them. It does not seem likely.

To Francis Holland

Fox Holm, 18th July.

I missed you much in returning here on Tuesday,

---
[1] Miss Hales had once belonged to this Order.

after a tiring day in London. My visit to —— was very pleasant. She is serenely content with her lot, and I really think that she has done very well with her life. After much variety, amusement, travel, and freedom, she finds herself exactly where other fortunate women of her own age are. I like Mr. ———. He has all the ease of a perfectly unpretending gentleman born in fairly good circumstances. There is much more interest in country life when the country is not treated as a toy, but where good or bad land, fair or foul weather, health or sickness among beasts, is a quite serious matter affecting an owner's pockets, and those of his poorer neighbours. The house and grounds I like particularly. No odd turns or surprises, or artful points of view within or without, but everything very comfortable, and exactly what one expects. Lofty rooms, large high windows, thick walls, polished doors shutting off passages and staircases, an excellent temperature and solid quiet, frightful ancestral portraits. A great yew hedge and long sunny wall enclosing a garden full of fruit and flowers; plenty of books, new and old. Witley steeple and Black Down visible, so that you know whereabout you are. We are going on here in the ordinary way—Arnolds, Leafs, Tennysons,[1] Buxtons, Miss Blunt, and so forth. Herbert Stephen comes to-day, likewise Ellen Macrae. Herbert and L. V. are to dine at F. W., where are Christine Fane and the Sydney Buxtons, and E. O. Bouverie. Bernard and Agnes dine with the Egertons; the Tennysons with the Arnolds. We are all going to tea at Pain's Hill this afternoon—and to float on the lake—with Walter Leaf. To-morrow the Tennysons come to tea and

---

[1] Lionel Tennyson and his wife had taken a house near there this summer.

supper, bringing with them Miss Maud White and Mr. Dawkins.

Michael is happy with the Dreaming Laird. Bernard is rather sad at heart and so am I. Agnes is as usual "nor grave nor gay." Luce goes about particularly untidy and cheerful—reads all day—and wanders through the "long gray fields at night," bringing back from the river bank faggots of purple loosestrife and ladies' bed-straw. The garden is drier than ever, but the tall white lilies brave the sun and throw back the light from their petals in quite a dazzling manner. "*They too must die.*" I may come to Cavendish in the first days of August. Will you be at Cambridge? Is Mr. Goodhart[1] there, and how does he fare? We miss him in the accustomed seat. There will always be a place for him under our roof as long as I cumber the earth, and this, should he appear to-morrow, or next summer, or not for twenty summers.

To Agnes Holland

LOCARNO, *7th September.*

... The valley began to widen and chestnuts appeared, and then vines, and then maize and vines and mulberries planted together, and enormous pumpkins lying in the green meadows, each with its own little heap of manure devoted to its special use. The churches are countless, high up on the loftiest buttresses of the mountains and on the lower ledges and in the valley itself. Also many little shrines and tiny chapels, with great wooden porches larger than themselves. Everywhere women labouring the earth, poor mothers of children who must be fed. I feel a sym-

---

[1] The late Harry Chester Goodhart.

pathy with the peasant life, hard though it is. What days of toil and nights of deep, dreamless sleep! But think what Sunday is to these people. One day in seven in which they all forbear to work, and when other ideas are suggested to them, ideas of life, and death, and rest, and Christian charity and sacrifice, and consolation in trouble and warning in prosperity. I believe that we often measure church work wrong. It is too much to suppose that people will be improved visibly by going to services, but we may fairly hope that what they already hold of good and true may be preserved to them. There is a tradition of Christian conduct which is learned at home and confirmed by religious teaching and offices. The idea is preserved in the minds of the people, however short they may come of it.

To the Same

SUBIACO, *27th September.*

We left Rome yesterday at 3.50, and went by tramway twenty miles across the Campagna, to Tivoli, where we arrived at sunset. The last half-hour the road winds up through fine old olive gardens, and the views over the Campagna, with the dome of St. Peter's in the distance, are very striking. We walked in the twilight to the bridge on the other side of the town and saw the Anio leaping over the rocks, and the little circular temple of Sibylla on a point of rock overhanging the stream. There are winding walks and grottos all the way down, but it was too dark to go. . . . Next morning we went to the D'Este gardens. The entrance is through the courtyard and flight of steps belonging to the Villa D'Este. The garden is on the steep slope of the hill and commands a wide view of the Campagna, with Rome in the distance. The garden is really not very large, but produces a great effect. It is artfully terraced and planted with cypress and bay and tall box hedges, and everywhere clear water falls or springs up in jets, or lies quietly sleeping or gently trickling in huge stone tanks and circular basins —a real pleasaunce for the great people of the place. At 10.10 we left Tivoli for this place, and drove for about twenty-five miles, arriving here at 5.30. The road runs all the way along the banks of the Anio, and for the first two hours it reminded us much of some parts of Scotland—bare strong hills on either side with very little cultivation. There are no enclosures and no scattered dwellings, but every six or seven miles one sees little towns perched upon the very summits of the hills, the houses so much the same colour and material as the rock on which they are built that it is sometimes difficult at first to perceive that a town stands there at all. As we drew near Subiaco the valley became fruitful, and the hills richly wooded, and there are plenty of picturesque figures, men riding on asses and mules—women too, astride. The women walk barefoot and carry heavy loads on their heads. They are beautiful people, so well shaped and well featured.

Subiaco stands at the end of the long valley, and the mountains close softly in behind the town, fold over fold, leaving only a deep wooded gorge of wonderful beauty, through which the Anio comes rushing headlong. This is the gorge where St. Benedict, as a boy of fourteen, hid himself in a cave, and afterwards where the great monastery of St. Scholastica was built, and still stands. It is the cradle of all the monasteries of the West. If you and Luce will look back in Fleury, to the middle of the fifth century, you will see about it. The streets are as steep as those at Clovelly. At the very top stands the Palace which used to belong to the Popes. We walked through the main street of the town, and over the high bridge, and along a beautiful road shaded with ilex, and by a rough but not fatiguing path which led off the road and up the side of the gorge, and past Nero's villa, and up again till we came to the gates of the first monastery. There we sat a long time, and we both agreed that, taking the extreme beauty of the scene and the historic interest together, it was worth all Switzerland and America and Scotland. About three hundred yards to our right, and below us, lay the ruins of Nero's villa, on a rocky promontory overhanging the river and commanding both sides of the gorge. A hundred yards to our left, and above us, lay the monastery with its Norman tower and soft-sounding bells; from our very feet the broken precipitous ground, planted thickly with old olives, went down right to the Anio, of which we could see the glittering moving line, and opposite us the mountains rose soft and majestic, with groves of beech and ilex, and green lawns to the very summit. . . .

To E. M.

SIENA, *1st October*.

My dearest E. M.—You will be at your work again to-day, and I hope in a good vein, in spite of a somewhat troubled holiday. I am sure that you are right in determining next holiday not to suit yourself to other people. There are some forms of self-sacrifice that seem to lead to no useful result, and among these may be classed that of helping other people to amuse themselves.

I wish that you were with us here to see the superb Cathedral. It is full from end to end of marbles and pictures, even the very floor is all inlaid with beautiful figures of Sibyls and prophets. Much the most religious place that we have been in was Florence. There is a sort of life and affection in the expression of the Florentine religion that does not seem to exist at Rome or anywhere else that we have been in Italy, except perhaps at Subiaco, where we spent last Sunday. It is the most beautiful little old town on a steep hill, quite away from railways, and almost untouched by the stream of time since Benedict first took up his abode in the neighbouring mountains. We did not much like Rome, although one learns there more than in any place in the world, but the weather was very hot and the air languid. St. Peter's I cannot like, and the Colosseum and Forum are melancholy.

The truth is, that at Rome the old Pagan world still clashes with the Christian. In all the churches the most beautiful columns and marbles are of ancient Rome. They were the most beautiful, also the newest looking, things in the churches. What I liked best at Rome were some of the little ancient Christian basilicas, and the gardens on the heights round the town, from which one gets the most beautiful wide views of the Eternal City. The Campagna spreads like a sea all round Rome and gives one an isolated feeling. . . . The weather is quite splendid, and here the air is cool. I am glad to have seen Italy in the autumn. The vines and figs and mulberries and peaches are in full beauty, the vintage just beginning. Large white oxen drawing low carts laden with purple grapes. We drove this afternoon about four miles out, through the vineyards, to a large old Palazzo which the Government school of Siena has bought for £400 as an occasional country home for the boys. It was such a nice place, on the side of a hill, with great pillared winding staircases, stone floors, and great loggia, or open verandah to the upstairs rooms. Woods of chestnut and beech stretching away behind, and an untidy old garden full of rosemary and lemon and orange trees. No furniture except some beds stuffed with beech leaves, and some chairs and tables for the boys to dine. One old man to look after it. A little church with campanile tower close by. . . .—Ever, my dearest, dearest dear E. M., your loving   SIBYL.

To Francis Holland

SESTRI, *Sunday, 5th October.*

You will have thought that I was never going to write to you, but at first you were away, and this last week I have had several letters to write besides those to Fox Holm. I cannot remember whether I wrote to papa or Agnes from Siena. We took one pretty drive there to an old chateau called St. Colombo, about five miles from the town. A large old house with marble winding pillared staircase and great loggia to all the front rooms, standing in an old garden and surrounded by vineyards. The municipal school of Siena have bought it as a country resort occasionally for the boys, and only gave £400 for it. The views from the ramparts at Siena are extremely beautiful, just such as you see in Poussin's landscapes. Fine undulating and broken foregrounds of vineyard and olive gardens, and then soft lines of mountains, fold beyond fold, into the farthest distance. Into this beautiful valley we descended on Friday, and were soon in the fat Pisan plain not so far from the sea, the Apennines pearly blue in the morning light all the way on our right. Pisa is a walled city standing in a dead flat— six miles from the sea. The Cathedral, Baptistry, Leaning Tower, and Campo Santo lie all close together in a quiet open green space in the north-west corner of the enclosure. All of white marble, glittering in the clear air as though fresh from the sculptor's hand. The Cathedral and Campo Santo are filled with pictures and frescoes. The Italians may know their whole Bible by eye and by heart if they take the trouble to look at their pictures. The Old Testament is painted from end to end at Pisa and everywhere else. While we were in the Baptistry, admiring the immense marble font, carved as fine as if of ivory, two babes, twins, of good family, arrived to be baptized. They were held at the font by their elder sisters, girls of thirteen or fourteen, and went off afterwards covered up in white silk chrism robes embroidered with gold and flowers. We stayed four or five hours at Pisa, and then went on to Spezia, the bay whence Shelley sailed to his death. . . . Spezia is now a large port and a busy place. We took a carriage there yesterday morning and drove up and through the Apennines here. Such a heavenly drive. The road is the old high road from the province to Rome. Julius Cæsar used to do the distance in eight days, riding and dictating to his secretary as he went along. The views of the Carrara mountains looking back towards Italy are most lovely. We were sorry to pass the summit and come down the northern sides among fir-trees instead of the charming myrtles, rosemary, lavender, arbutus in full fruit and flower, rue and many other sweet smelling plants. We shall find all these again in our drive towards Genoa. This place is so pleasant that Ber wishes to stay till Tuesday. Sestri is on a large bay. The town runs along the shore and out on to a narrow promontory terminating in a rocky hill with castle, church, and cypress. Our hotel is built on the narrow neck of the promontory, and the sea comes up to the garden—from which a little flight of steps descends to a narrow strip of sand, so that bathers can walk out of their rooms into the sea. A little Franciscan church and convent stands prettily on the first platform of the hills on the mainland—and commands a view of the whole bay. . . . We have this large hotel entirely to ourselves as far as visitors go. The proprietor is a rich old gentleman who lives on the first floor with his daughter, an officer's wife, and her children. Cats, doves and pigeons live harmoniously in the court among the orange trees and geraniums. We hear no sound but the short plunge of the waves, and see little but sea and mountain and sky, and the peasant women climbing up the winding path to the little church at the sound of the bell. It is as quiet as Guernsey, but with more colour in everything,—in language, manners, and religion, as well as in sea and sky and growth.

To Agnes Holland

CHAMBERI, *8th October.*

. . . I stayed some while in the Cathedral,[1] and was pleased to see the women come in, hot and breathless from their work in the market, and give

[1] At Genoa.

themselves truly to their prayers. I think that I shall
never forget the figure of one elderly woman who knelt
on the step of the altar rail, her face bowed on her
hands, quite motionless and absorbed from the beginning to the end of the Mass. A sweet girl of seven
or eight years old stood on the step, and leaned on the
balustrade, her soft eyes attentive to every movement
of the priest, but not otherwise joining. The beautiful,
careless, and not irreverent attitudes of the children in
the churches are so evidently the origin of the groups
of cherubs introduced by the great painters into their
sacred pictures. We went up to the top of a high
church in Genoa to get a true idea of the city. I
thought of my dearest mother sketching it years before
I was born.

To Francis Holland

Fox Holm, *23rd October.*

We ended our journey at Paris, where we spent two
pleasant days at the Hotel Voltaire. Certainly nothing
can be gayer than the view from the upper window.
There was the excitement of the elections going on
while we were there. I was struck in Paris by the
way in which the Republic has effaced every trace of
its kings and its ancient government. Except the
statue of Henry IV. and that of Napoleon I. they have
erased every line of royalty. Paris is a most beautiful
city, but I could hardly keep back my tears as I
walked in the Tuileries gardens and remembered the
terrible things that had been done there. The innocent
blood seemed to cry out from the ground.

From Lucy Holland to Bernard Holland

PRECINCTS, 3*rd November.*

... I took the white chrysanthemum wreath to Hales Place yesterday. Père du Lac was in the chapel when I went in, showing it to a French parent; so I had no difficulty, and he let me lay the flowers exactly where I wished. I was glad they were white flowers, for there—before the altar—was laid a small coffin. It was such a beautiful, bright, sunny afternoon, with a sky as blue as in summer. I remembered, as I came away down the long avenue, that the yellow and red leaves lying on the ground were the same as I saw in their first tender green loveliness last April. Then, and yesterday, Hales Place looked very beautiful, but spring is the best. I think Admiral Maxse is right. Come as soon as you can.—Your loving sister, LUCY VERENA.

To Bernard Holland

PRECINCTS, 6*th November.*

The weather here is cold and dampish. I often think of Italy, and, like Digby,[1] have a difficulty in believing that it is not heaven. There is certainly a great pleasure in remembrance, and I can see in my mind's eye nearly every place we visited, especially the points where we stood or sat and gazed at the prospect. I often sit on the low wall of the Casale Rotondo and look towards Rome, and see Soracte in the distance, and the aqueducts striding across the Campagna. Also I haunt Nero's villa, and the ilex grove by the Bene-

---
[1] Kenelm Digby, in *Mores Catholici.*

dictine monastery, and the little terrace of the Franciscan church at Sestri, and St. Columba in its vineyards. I only regret the crowd of little affairs which prevents me from fixing my mind more frequently on these ideas; and I fear lest they may fade. The more I think of Rome, the more I feel how much less cheerful it was than Florence and other places. It would never suit my temper of mind. I like neither ancient, nor mediæval, nor modern Rome. Neither the Colosseum, nor St. Peter's, nor the railway station. What is really pleasing in Rome is to be out of it, as one was at the Casale Rotondo, and at St. Pietro Montorio, and in the Medici Villa.

To Rosamond Stephen

PRECINCTS, CANTERBURY, 23rd December.

You see, my dear Rosamond, that what I foretold has come to pass. The years have rolled on, and you have become taller and wiser and more loving and beloved.

I also have become older and more grizzled, but not, I hope, more foolish. We are both bound on the same journey, but you are stepping lightly up the hill in the sunshine, while I have rounded the crest, and am plodding downwards.

> 'Twere sweet to pause on this descent,
> To wait for thee and pitch my tent,
> But march I must, with shoulders bent,
> Still farther from my prime.[1]

For I must still keep far ahead, and all that I can do is to send you back now and then a cheery voice till the day comes when I shall disappear altogether in the

[1] From "Ionica."

deep shadows of the valley, and you will say, "Ah! my old god-mother who gave me the sugar-tongs is gone—*poor old dear.*"

This sounds melancholy to you perhaps, but not in the least to me, for I hope to join a great company on the other side and to see again many dear persons from whom I have long been separated. This I hope to do, and, even if this were uncertain, yet it would make no difference to me now, for I see nothing better to do in this world than to lead a Christian life. But, in my belief, it is not uncertain.

I should like to hear how you get on at school, and whether you like girls more or less now that you see so much of them. Tell me also whether the lessons are dull, or hard, or too long.

Will you take some notice next term of two little girls, Margaret and Edith Furse? their father is a new Canon of Westminster. Their mother was a very good and beautiful woman, and she died four years ago when their youngest brother was born; they are very spirited children. Michael is come home from Eton. He arrived soon after eleven in the morning, having left very early, and entered playing *Home Sweet Home* upon an instrument called a zither. It was quite the exile's return.

The household here salutes you. Lucy salutes Helen. Greet the mother of Ajax with a friendly kiss. Salute Katharine, Agnes's friend and mine.

Michael sends greeting to Dorothea. Salute Herbert and his brothers.

Salute the Judge.

The Canon salutes you.—Your affectionate god-mother, SIBYL HOLLAND.

VI

LETTERS OF 1886

To Bernard Holland

PRECINCTS, *4th January.*

A kind note and carriage came down on New Year's evening to take us to Hales Place, that I (especially) might see the boys act their French play for their parents. It began at seven o'clock, and was a pretty sight. All the French papas, headed by Comte de Mun and Père du Lac, entered together and were saluted with salvos of cheers. The orchestra, composed of boys, masters, soldiers, and one or two cathedral men, and conducted by a Father, was excellent, and the acting was fair. The second piece was *Gringoire*, a little altered, and was rather touchingly rendered. Père du Lac received an address at the end, and made a serious but charming speech on the situation of things, family life, etc. He and Comte de Mun came round to speak to us, and it was altogether pleasant.

To the Same

13th January.

I have also sometimes regretted a very little that we did not see the Pope, but only a very little. I wish that we could have got into his gardens, and have surveyed him from an upper terrace. Sestri does appear like a dream, but it is pleasant to know that it does lie there in that lovely fold of shore, and that by an effort of will we could arise and go to Sestri. I often think of Kenelm Digby's words—" Beneath Ausonian skies all these deeds of love are practical, and Catholic manners as of old, and this I know to be so true from what I saw and heard that, at this distance of years, long separated, I feel there is danger of mistaking Italy for Heaven."

I also have seen and heard, though we visited Italy too late to receive Digby's whole impression.

To Mrs. Deacon

PRECINCTS, CANTERBURY, 24th January.

My dearest Mary—I am very much shocked to see in to-day's paper the death of Mrs. ———. It is terrible to think of the young girls and their poor father. They all seemed to take such delight in one another that there was a pleasure in seeing the group. *She* always surprised me. Such a full tide of life, project, and talk; no silence, reflection or isolation of spirit, but a sort of joyful worship of the ideal they had themselves attained. To such souls death must come indeed as the "pale King of Terrors," and the desolation of their grief does not bear thinking of. One can only hope that God, Who made His creatures, will in some way comfort them. There is as much help in the thought of His justice as of His mercy.

We have been anxious about Luce, who went ten days ago to her aunt's in Brook Street, and had to go to bed at once with rheumatism and fever. She has

I

just come home looking very shadowy, and says she will make no more feeble attempts after pleasure. . . . Tell me if Mr. Deacon is well, and if you are. The last Sunday when we all came over to Hatchford, and the service went so well, and we said good-bye to you at the gate, is as clear in my mind as though it were yesterday. The autumn woods and sunshine, and the kind eyes and voices.—Ever your loving friend,

SIBYL HOLLAND.

To Bernard Holland

PRECINCTS, *2nd February.*

What touches and excites R—— and others like him is politics, and literature with a political aim. They *have* a sort of sentiment about this, but otherwise are of adamantine bowels,—no romance, no silence, no isolation of spirit. I have been amusing myself, as I go about the house and city, with imagining the effect on various minds of a very prolonged existence which should not at the same time decline but rather increase in force. Give Gladstone another fifty years, and one's imagination dares not follow him. Give Carlyle fifty years and he would wear a halo round his fine old head. Give the same to —— or to —— and they would be found uttering words full of sound and signifying nothing. Give it to —— and he would be found with eyes hermetically closed, a mutter on his lip, and a half-sarcastic smile fixed for ever.

To Francis Holland

CANTERBURY, *12th February.*

Mr. Bradshaw's death is a great shock, and will be such dreadful pain to Mrs. Oxenden. Will you, my darling boy, do this for me? Will you write me a good letter telling me anything you hear about his death or his last days—or the feeling manifested in his University —anything in short that I may send to his sister abroad, Mrs. Oxenden, who is a great friend of mine? She loved her brother with extreme tenderness, but knew very little of his Cambridge life, and I know that every word about him would be precious, and like a cordial in the midst of her deep pain.

To Miss Arnold Foster

CANTERBURY, 23*rd March.*

. . . All my time is taken up with Lucy, but I must send you a word of thanks for your dear letter. Your sympathy and affection are very much to me. I do think that young friends are one of the greatest pleasures of the autumn of life, and to feel that one's children's friends include oneself in their affection consolidates one's position. . . . What months of anxiety you have had; there is something so exhausting in the concentration of one's thoughts on a sick person. Whatever else one is doing, one's thoughts fly, and wheel, and settle round that one person, and there is the perpetual effort to recall and resume. I have thought so much all along of your mother and her beautiful patient face.

To Francis Holland

PRECINCTS, 8*th April.*

I wish, indeed, that Lucy were with you, to gather primroses and taste the sweet air that blows so lightly over the wide wolds. I sometimes feel here, as though she would never be well and out again. And yet Luce is better—rather stronger—eats a little more, and is lifted in her blankets every day on to a couch for a few hours. But her progress is very slow and it is still entirely a bedroom life. I have been unwell also with neuralgia, but am better again now.

To the Same

PRECINCTS, 20*th April.*

Many, many happy returns of your birthday. I can hardly believe that my "little Frank" is twenty-one years old. The years roll back and show me the fine April day on which you first saw light in Sussex Gardens. You were a great pleasure to me as a babe —and at twenty months old you showed a sort of serious vivacity that gave me great pleasure. The summer after you were born I brought you and all the others down to Harbledown for three weeks, just in the hay time, and I used to carry you up to the high meadows behind the Rectory, and sit by my father on the hay-swathes, looking down over Canterbury. Thence we went to Lyne to a charming old farmhouse Uncle Henry lent me. Papa and his father went to Norway and I was alone there with you all— except that Cathy came for a bit. Thence we all went on to the Isle of Wight, and I was summoned to Llangollen, in North Wales, to my dear father's deathbed, and came to Harbledown for his funeral. Then we all assembled for the last time in our old home. The year after that we spent at Hatchford, and the following—1867—at Freshwater, where Lucy fell ill of her first rheumatism and laid the foundation of her present illness. The year after that we went into

Fox Holm in the month of May. You were a darling boy of three, Lucy was six, Alfred nine, Agnes ten, and Bernard eleven. I am so glad that you enjoyed your time at Porlock Weir. I must go there some day. It is an immense gain to be able to derive so much pleasure from nature. . . . This is the first Easter in all your twenty-one years that I have not had you by my side on Easter Day. I hope you will not desert the altar whence your mother and father draw all their consolation and hope. One we all are, however widely separated, while we eat of one bread.

To Bernard Holland

THE PRECINCTS, *3rd June*.

. . . How difficult it is to hold the balance between the over-powering feeling of the nothingness of life below, and the feeling which is really almost as vivid of everything being of importance. It is one of the difficulties of the religious life, that, while one is minutely to attend to every detail that affects one's neighbour's comfort and well-being, one is to regard the whole spectacle as nothing. I suppose it is really best to do as well as one can, and not to think too much about the eternities and infinities. . . .

To Mrs. Deacon

PRECINCTS, *16th June*.

My dearest Mary—Thank you *much* for your little word of kindness. I often and often think of you, and always with unchangeable affection. There is now no hope that Lucy will ultimately recover. A dreadful enlargement of the heart has set in, and this must sooner or later be the end. She suffers not much pain, but her weakness and emaciation are very great. She has had 120 days of fever; never six hours without it. She is very courageous and steady, and has, I think, had the great parting in view all along, but the length of time tries one's resolution. She is invariably gentle, as all my children are. This is all I can tell you, my *dear*. Your too tender heart will easily guess all the searching, essential pain, and also the thousand consolations of which the greatest is the firm belief that all that happens is the will of God for Luce and for us, and that all that happens now, and will happen as long as she draws breath, was known to Him and designed by Him with regard to her from the moment of her birth. There is a sort of comfort to me in writing this down. At these times how great and healing are the commonplaces of religion!

Lucy asks to whom I am writing, and says, "Ah, send my love and say how I wish I were walking to Hatchford, and could see her in church." Her mind has always run upon Fox Holm and Hatchford.—Ever your loving friend, SIBYL HOLLAND.

To Francis Holland

CANTERBURY, 20*th June*.

I am glad that your suspense is over. Your degree is almost what I expected it to be, taking all things into consideration. I should not have been surprised if it had been higher, because one always hopes for the best as regards one's children. I should have been vexed had it been lowest, and I shall be delighted to see my dearest boy when he comes home. Luce is a little better these two days. . . .

To Bernard Holland

THE LODGE, HARBLEDOWN, 23rd August.

We are fully established here, and Lucy has been lying out of doors on the couch the greater part of the day. She enjoys it, but is very feeble, and Mr. Reid says that she has not yet got over the move of Saturday. We moved desperately, for she was very ill on Thursday, partly from the check upon her great longing to get away. Mr. Reid took the greatest care and trouble. She was laid upon a hospital stretcher in my room at 6.20 A.M. by him and the hospital porters, carried down stairs, and out into the old street, lifted high in the air and put into the open brake. Mr. Reid sprang in by the fore-wheel and took her head on his knees. I jumped into my brougham, and off we went. Lucy lay in her brown and white Carmelite dress and little parted hood, exactly like a pale nun on a bier, only her large eyes moving. I looked out now and then and always saw her face, and the young, grave doctor's bent over it, intently watching. We drove out of the silent town into the fields. Agnes and Amy were on the "perron" watching for us, and Lucy was soon in the house, and on a couch eating some breakfast. This place is perfect for us. I am thankful to God for giving us this pleasure, and hope whatever may be His blessed will for us hereafter . . .

To the Same

THE LODGE, UPPER HARBLEDOWN, 31st August.

I am sitting on a hassock beside Lucy, whose wheel-couch is drawn up outside the garden fence in the airy meadow, overlooking the flower-beds first, then the orchard, then the hop-oast, and then the pretty stretch of hop and wood beyond. There is a splendid shadow from the house and great elms all the afternoon, and we have our tea here, and watch the broad lights lengthen, and drink in the pure air, which is most delightfully sharpened by the smell of the hops. Lucy is drinking her new milk, and quietly looking out under her white hat. I hardly dare count on her, but there is such a blessed repose in this cessation of pain and sickness, and I am thankful for the present moment. The place is pleasant in my eyes, and I wish it were ours. I should like to own this southern slope.

Your letter from Limerick came this morning and gave great pleasure. I am so glad that you are keeping a few days for us here, but I wish you had had more time for Ireland. I agree with you about religion. I could not live in Ireland or in Italy without being a Roman Catholic. It is something also to be of the religion that you find at Nemi and again at Limerick. We *are* of the same religion really, but are so cramped in some directions and so unbridled in others that it don't seem to be the same. . . . Lucy sends her dear love and says that she is very happy and comfortable. We hear from where we sit the tumultuous voices of the hoppers returning and assembling near the Plough.

To Lady Holland[1]

THE LODGE, HARBLEDOWN, 10*th September*.

. . . I felt sure that the next great assault would break down the already shattered citadel of Lucy's frail

---

[1] Now Viscountess Knutsford.

body, but it might not have come for many weeks, she was so wasted and worn out. But, after death, her dear little face recovered its soft oval, and she lay with such a careless grace, her head a little turned, a smile upon her lips, and her eyes quite bright under the half-closed lids. She looked careless of all things here, but smiling and attentive to something else. One could hardly look long upon her without smiling also. Her hair had never been cut, and was drawn loosely to the top of her head, and a little just waving on her forehead. I wish that Meta and Sybil could have seen her. The Warden of St. Augustine's, who often visited her while she was ill, came and looked at her, and wrote afterwards to the old Archdeacon, " It is not possible to imagine death more beautiful."

I did not go to her burial, but Bernard drove me next day eight miles through the woods to the place where she lies, close-cradled against the south chancel wall of the old church which my father served about fifty years ago. She, and I, and Bernard, and Richmond Ritchie spent a long afternoon there last year, at Whitsuntide. Lucy sat trimming her hat with the flowers she pulled from the long grass, and said, " Ah, Ber, here will I be buried ; *promise* to bring me here" ; and she reminded him of this several times lately. He was passionately fond of her, and wrote when she first fell ill, " I have long known that Lucy is the dearest thing I have on earth." Indeed, we all adored our sweet, sprightly girl. She was made for her home, and her home for her. I am comforted by many things in spite of the searching grief. Your dear words are a great pleasure to us. All my children love you truly.

To Sydney Holland (her nephew)

THE LODGE, UPPER HARBLEDOWN, *17th September.*

It is indeed a true, solid pleasure to hear that dear Mary's pain and peril is over, and that you have a sweet little daughter, who will one day trot by your side and call you "Father." We all think that Mary will make a delightful mother, and I quite long to see her and the babe in her arms. It will be such a deepening and widening of life for you both. All the hope of the world lies in the children. They are not, thank God, *born* Radicals, or agnostics, or worldlings. They are born fresh and fresh, the precious little souls and bodies. Every new-born child is a new chance for the world to be better and brighter.

It was good of you to write to me about Lucy. She fell in love with Mary and would always have loved her and understood her. It will always endear Mary to me more than ever that she liked Luce. I cannot write of my loss. Lucy and I were, perhaps, too passionately attached to one another, but we all loved our sweet girl, and all expressed our love.

She was so gentle and courageous in her long illness. We had often talked of death, but neither she nor I had ever imagined that we should have to face it for so many months, and to make what we *knew* were such vain endeavours to avert it. Yet such was God's will for her, and for us, and I believe that what He wills is not only good, but best, the *very best*.

Give my dear love to Mary. I shall remember her and the darling babe in my evening prayers.

To Francis Holland

HARBLEDOWN LODGE, 24*th September.*

It is one of those perfectly still autumn mornings rather peculiar to England—a light mist and gossamer flying in every direction—hop-pickers making their way down through the woods to the gardens, a squirrel leaping noiselessly across the lawn, and a wood-pecker in the elms breaking the silence. What a different scene from the ceaseless gaiety of your brilliant metropolis![1] I like to think of you there. . . . Agnes is going to write to you on Sunday, and will give you any news that there may be; I have none though I *feel* as if events were taking place. It is six weeks this morning since we brought our sweet Luce here, and looking back the days seem crowded with great events: so much does life consist in the emotions of the mind.

To Sydney Holland

HARBLEDOWN LODGE, 26*th September.*

Tell your dearest Mary that it will be a real pleasure to me if she calls her little daughter after mine. I shall take a particular interest in the darling babe, and will never forget her in my prayers. I can really wish nothing better for Mary than that this child should be the same source of joy and love to her as Lucy was to me; that there may be the same willing obedience and docility as long as childhood lasts, and the same tender love and friendship on either side as years go on. . . .

[1] Paris.

To the Lady Mary Holland

HARBLEDOWN LODGE, *Sunday*.

We all thought of you and your darling babe, and of dear Sydney, on Saturday. With us it was a pouring wet day from dawn till dark, but I hope that you had a gleam of sunshine among your Welsh hills and meadows. Sunshine in your heart I am sure you had, notwithstanding all the pain and peril you have gone through, and notwithstanding your present bodily weakness. What a shifting of the scenes it all is for you; you have always been so active and well, and are now obliged to make a long pause. And now, too, you will lay aside some of the sweet carelessness of youth, and must ever bear in mind and heart the little child whose life is for ever interwoven with your own. I shall think so much of you and of her; we are all so much pleased that she is "Lucy," and we all like "Katharine" also. What you say of your feeling about our Lucy gives me much pleasure. I am quite sure that you would have loved Lucy more the more you knew of her. She had so much courage and gentleness and originality.

I am sure that you will let your little Lucy lead a free life, and that you will plant good and noble ideas in her mind, as soon as she can understand anything. I am sure that she will be a charming little girl. Do you know Wordsworth's—" Three years she grew in sun and shower "?

To Bernard Holland

HARBLEDOWN LODGE, *Michaelmas Day*.

You were good to your poor mother, and may God from whom descends all fatherhood in Heaven and earth receive you, and bless and reward you a thousand and a thousandfold for it. I have had so much more than I deserve of all good things. It is quite right that our sweet Luce should go. The world could do nothing for her. I loved her passionately and so did you, and she returned our love. It was Heaven to me to see you together, and when, that morning, I heard her voice and yours mingling in the Confession and Gloria in Excelsis my heart overflowed with sad joy. I had longed for that so often, and it came as things longed for do, only in far different ways from what we imagine. Lucy *was* the heart of the family. She was the living expression of all that is truest and best in us. You are all dearer to me when I think of her, and God knows with what unspeakable tenderness I carry her in my heart, and how gladly I would suffer all things could I spare you suffering. You must suffer, but your life is before you, and more kinds of happiness than you think are to be found. Lucy was the charm and solace of your early manhood; she loved you and loved everything you said and did, and your very name was delightful to her ears and lips, but nevertheless her heart was drawn above. She walked with God, and is not, for God has taken her. It is not for nothing that souls have early in life so strong a hold on things invisible. My sweet girl! it is not at all surprising that she is not here; what should she do here much longer, and why should she grieve, and suffer partings and loss? she was fit for other things, and has them. . . .

To Francis Holland

HARBLEDOWN LODGE, *8th October.*

I began a letter to you on Wednesday, but my pen and spirits failed. I have felt so unwell all this week, and begin more and more to miss my darling girl. Then the plan about —— makes me rather melancholy. But she is literally wild with pleasure. I suppose that always in service people look towards ultimate independence—most old servants seem glad to go if they are sure of means of support.

All change is painful to me, I think. I wish you were here for some of these quiet October days, dim dewy mornings, broad sunny middays and afternoons, and, towards evening, a delicate mist partly formed of the motionless cottage smoke, lying across the dismantled hop-gardens and woody slopes. But I doubt not that in Paris, beautiful blood-stained Paris, the days are also beautiful. I should like to wander with you in the solemn avenues of Versailles. We shall go back to Canterbury in the last week of this month. I often think of Lucy's saying, "Oh mamma, never take me back to Canterbury; take me further on." And we did take her further on; through the woods and by the clear stream. That road seems to me now a sort of *via sacra*. The railroad crosses it just opposite to Chartham. . . . The Duc d'Alençon has taken a house in Canterbury, and there is considerable going and coming across the water.

To Bernard Holland

HARBLEDOWN, *8th October.*

Your verses touch me very much. I seem to miss my sweet girl more and more. I have often in the last few years considered with a sort of astonishment *what* Lucy was to me, every hour of every day, from week to week, from year to year. Sometimes I thought it was too much, then again I remembered that she certainly would not live for many years, and I abandoned myself to the dear delight. I have often wept, knowing that I was destined to weep this darling child, and she has often with smiles declared that she gladly believed that she was not destined to weep me.

All that remains for us now is to enter into God's design and to carry it out. Lucy preserved her baptismal innocence, and lost it not, for God took her, as He took Alfred. He speaks to you also in a thousand ways, my dear son, and it is the wish of my heart that He may speak with the efficacious voice of grace to your deep, tender, and faithful soul, and then you must hear and follow for ever.

To the Same

THE LODGE, *19th October*.

The mist drew up at 10 A.M. yesterday, and revealed a lovely day of still warm sunshine. Mrs. Reid and her little boy to lunch, and G. C. P. afterwards, occupied the golden hours, so that I hardly got out till after tea, when I mounted the hill to the little group of Scotch firs. The air was perfectly warm and still, though the dew of the night before was yet in the grass. There was a streak of light lingering in the west—otherwise the landscape was wrapt in soft October darkness. The nibbling of the sheep, and the cough of one afflicted in the flock, and the occasional deep sighs of Sandy[1] stretched at my feet were the

---

[1] A collie dog.

only sounds that broke the silence. In Surrey, at that season and hour, I should have heard the acorns and chestnuts patter to the ground, and the uneasy movements of the game in the covers or on the trees. Long I remained there, leaning against the centre tree, as against a pillar in a little unroofed temple.

To the Same

THE LODGE, 29*th October*.

Yes, dear Ber, that is so. When I think of Alfred and Lucy I can say with poor Cowper

> Yet, oh, the thought that thou art safe, and he,
> That thought is joy, arrive what may to me.

Every one follows his own temperament or humour. This nothing ever really changes. So hearty, practical people remain cheerful and doing through tremendous reverses (except here and there a *very* practical person shoots himself), and people with whom ideas and affections hold the foremost place receive a deep impress of a melancholy sort. Not melancholy, quite; but of course, if your turn of mind is such that you cannot see anything beautiful or beloved without at the same time remembering that *tout passe*, then, when it *does* pass, the thought is a hundred times deepened, and so one proceeds loving and weeping from loss to loss, from shore to shore, till at last it all ends. And yet I would not be the hearty person. I think I see deeper and truer than they do, and that I am far more capable of mentally stretching forward, and almost laying hold on things out of sight. But I am not so useful to my neighbour as the hearty one is.

I drove this afternoon round by Thanington, and by

Chartham Hatch. The line of bronzed woods against the clear, pale blue sky was very pretty. Plenty of Kentish men and boys at work in the fields, filling sacks with large potatoes, or burning bines, and the plough going steadily from hedge to hedge.

To Francis Holland

PRECINCTS, 5*th November.*

The reason that I have not written is that I have been very unwell with neuralgia, etc., and also that Agnes and I have been engaged upon the uninteresting, and, this year, the sad work of resetting ourselves in this house. And there has been more to do than usual, because for so long before I had neglected all my household concerns, and had left in a hurry in August, thinking of nothing but our sweet girl. Agnes and your father went to Godmersham on Tuesday, All Souls' Day, taking some flowers. It was a day of still, broad sunshine, and they said that the beautiful beech woods along the high park and down the steep side of the hill looked like a glory. The ash tree that hangs over the stream was also pure pale gold, and Lucy's grave lay warm with the full sunlight on it against the old chancel wall. Your uncles in India write that they are so glad that we have lain her there.

To Lady Stephen

THE PRECINCTS, 8*th December.*

My dearest Mary—Thank you for your kind words. I have often thought of you, and wished to write or speak; but then again I have thought, why should I renew her old grief by recounting mine? And it seemed easier to be silent. The thing that has been all along in my mind to say to you is that I shall ever remember all the kindness which your elder children always showed to Lucy. Herbert and James were as kind in word and manner to her always as if she had been their sister, and she was always so delighted to see them arrive. She was disappointed that I would not let her see Herbert when he was last here, but she was too ill. And one day in August she said to me, "I should so like to see James, he has always been so good to me. How happy I was to sit by him, or walk about at Fox Holm with him!" And I wished, as she spoke, that James could have seen her sweet face, so pale, pure, and bright—"like a spirit," as Bernard said. . . . Will you give my love to Herbert and James? the thought of them is bound up with the memory of so many pleasant days; the like of which can never come again. I am sure that they will always remember Lucy among the friends of their quite early youth.

And my love to Rosamond, and even to the Judge. He always makes a great figure in my mind, as of a person without whom the world would be ever so much poorer. Long may he live and judge mankind!— Your very affectionate friend, SIBYL HOLLAND.

To Bernard Holland

PRECINCTS, 15*th December*.

Père du Lac wrote me a note on Monday (St. Lucy's Day). In my reply I referred to the day, to which he made answer, "j'ai prié pour Miss Lucy toute la journée d'hier; nous faisions le si bel office de sa douce et vaillante patronne. Puisse-t-elle l'avoir reçue au ciel."

To Francis Holland

CANTERBURY, *17th December.*

I should love to hear you arguing with the Décadent. I suppose he would be a sort of Pater; I own to a profound dislike for that turn of mind, and I should shriek with the majority were I seated at your dinner-table. I do not wonder that *Notre-Dame* seized you. So it did me when I read it. It is the most powerful of Victor Hugo's novels; but there is great power also in *Les Misérables*, which is his longest book. I quite agree with you about historical novels; next to them comes the philosophic novel, which I always like also. I think that poets are generally inclined to write a novel or two—*vide* Göethe, Victor Hugo, Alfred de Vigny, Cervantes, and many others. In most poets this inclination finds its expression in drama. Shakespeare would have been the greatest novelist ever created if he had not written plays; and this, perhaps, goes to support Matthew Arnold's definition of poetry as the "criticism of life." Victor Hugo is a seer, like Carlyle; he really seems to reproduce the past, and he tears down a good many shams. I do not know whether I ever remarked on your observation as to your reluctance to express great admiration for established triumphs of art, such as the Venus of Milo. I am sure that you ought not to have that feeling, any more than one should resist saying what has pleased one, even if no one else has admired it. Nothing can be more hackneyed in poetry and description than the Vevey end of the lake of Geneva; but when I had been there a short time, I felt all the force and beauty of Byron's lines, and Coleridge's, and was pleased to feel as they felt.

... I shall be glad to be over Xmas, though I linger in mind in these days when I can say,—This day, last year, Lucy did this or that with me. When February comes I shall be forced to begin again the sad round of her illness. Sometimes I wonder how I could have gone through all those things.

To the Same

CANTERBURY, *21st December.*

Do you remember our conversation at Harbledown, in the high meadow, on the Sunday evening before you went to Switzerland, about immortality and the death of the body and the resurrection? I have often thought of it since, and of the Communion in Lucy's room. Only ten days later we again gathered in that room for Communion; Lucy's sweet face was hid for ever in this world, and Bernard was with us instead of you. . . .

Our weather has been rough, and so piercingly cold. I feel as if Lucy were well out of it; her spirit moving and living in some regions of peace and light; her delicate body turning indeed to dust, close cradled against the south wall of the old chancel.

To Bernard Holland

PRECINCTS, *22nd December.*

Your father says that you are coming down to-morrow, which is good news; but, in case you do not come till Christmas Eve, I write this word to say that if, thirty years ago, your future was all the vaguest dream to me, I could not have dreamed of a dearer son than you have been to me. I could have wished you stronger, merrier, and more buoyant, but then my son would have been less tender, compassionate, and meditative.

Thirty is a middle point—thirty years' back I was ten years younger than you are now; thirty years hence I shall have gone elsewhere, long gone, and perhaps in some still region shall be waiting again for you. And, if the joy to a woman of her first-born is unspeakably great, how much greater would it be to see him again new-born to a greater life and light.

You have shared the sorrow of this year with me. You would have felt it much less had you been married; but, although the pain has been hard for you, yet I cannot be sorry that you are still ours—mine, and no one else's. But I hope that this year may bring you pleasure and prosperity, and no more pain.

To Rosamond Stephen

CANTERBURY, *Christmas Eve.*

My dearest Rosamond—Such a stupid gift this Christmas Eve, only another little jug! but from a stupid and rather melancholy god-mother you must expect stupid and melancholy jugs and letters.

I believe that I ought not to feel sad, remembering what a sweet daughter lived close to my side for twenty-four years; so gentle, merry, compassionate and contented; so loving to her poor mother, and so adored by her brothers and sisters; so detached from this world, and yet pleased and interested by many things in it; so cheerful in company, and yet such a born lover of solitude and solitary places.

It is a great thing for me to have had such a

daughter, and that she should have lived long enough to be entirely known to us ; and entirely loved. She was so long ill that we had time to talk over many things ; we knew that we must part, and we believed that we should meet again, and that wherever we met there would be Paradise. So there it is, my dear Rosamond.

Tout lasse, tout passe, tout casse, except love and work ; this is all we have to do in this wonderful world. —Ever your affectionate god-mother,

SIBYL HOLLAND.

To Francis Holland

CANTERBURY, 30th December.

Many, many happy New Years to you. I begin to feel what Byron did when he wrote, " There's not a joy the world can give like that it takes away." Still, with three sweet sons and a dear daughter, I am still rich ; and, indeed, should a thousand woes betide, I have had much more happiness than falls to the lot of most women. . . . I am very sorry, indeed, that you did not go to the midnight mass, and were only at the stupid charades instead. I have always wished to be present at that service, and I know how ancient and touching it is. I agree with you, on the whole, about the Roman Catholic services. I am quite satisfied with our own services, when they are given with all the fulness allowed by the Church of England ; and when I was abroad I often longed for some service which should answer to our daily evensong and matins. But constantly, in deference to the general Protestant or Puritan feeling, our services are heaped together, so as to make them tedious and unmeaning, and stripped of their real beauty by total negligence of ritual. I think that the Anglican Church, *as she might be*, could hold her own against the world; and I still wish that I could see you a priest in her Communion—a fair and free career in my opinion.

VII

LETTERS OF 1887

To Miss Arnold Forster

CANTERBURY, 18*th January.*

... I do not know how this note may find you, and whether, even while I write, our Father may not have broken down His child's frail earthly tabernacle, and set the radiant spirit free. But any way, whether the sweet boy is here or elsewhere, I feel that you are firm and ever firmer in faith and hope and love, holding fast to the absolute certainty that all that happens is the particular will of God, and that His will is not only good but the best—the very best. I do feel for all your pain from the bottom of my heart; for great pain there is and must be, notwithstanding the deep and true consolations of religion. The comfort is that He knows. I so often think of the words, "And Jesus groaning in Himself cometh to the grave."

To Bernard Holland

PRECINCTS, 22nd *February.*

I will keep good care of the pretty, melancholy lines, but do not read Leopardi any more. He is too beautiful and sad, and will draw you down under the waters when you might mount into the sunshine.

I wish you had been here this fine, clear February day. The Cathedral towers looked as if drawn in fine lines of air against the pale, clear blue this morning early, and the rising sun just flushed Bell Harry,[1] giving a warm tint to the gray stone. We have been for the last day or two entertaining a gentle English Jesuit, staying at Hales Place, out of health, and interested in archæology. I like the company of the S. J. Fathers. They have a finish that is wanting in the modern Benedictines and the secular priests. They all seem to know much of men and things, and are quiet and observant, and therefore humorous.

To Francis Holland

CANTERBURY, 12th March.

We are through the mission, and have not yet recovered our equilibrium in household and other matters, and I have a mass of correspondence to get through. . . . Papa was at the levee yesterday, in gown and bands and three-cornered hat under his arm, and met Uncle Harry[2] in velvet and star and sword. Rather comic, although satisfactory. Imagine meeting Michael under similar circumstances. We have a storm of wind and snow this morning. The wind has gone right round from south to north in half an hour. These are the sudden gusts and whirls that wreck sailing vessels. Yesterday the Brines brought an Exeter paper, which had copied Mick's Jubilee verses from the *K. Gazette*, referring to the author as a gentleman residing in the archiepiscopal city.

[1] The central tower of the Cathedral.   [2] Lord Knutsford.

To Bernard Holland

PRECINCTS, 28*th March.*

The Archdeacon[1] is to be buried at Thanington to-morrow, at one o'clock, by his own request. He has been a friend to our family to the third generation. I never remember the Cathedral without him, and I remember it for forty-five years. He has said to me since we came back this winter, "I miss Lucy's light figure hurrying across the Oaks every morning." I shall never forget his voice in church, nor his look and way when he came up and stood by Lucy's fair corpse, and blessed her, and went to the spot in the meadow where her breath failed, and looked silently round, and wiped away a slow tear, and went quietly away without speaking.

There is a very great and quite unanimous feeling in Canterbury about him.

I feel very much interested in Henry Dillon.[2] He has done wisely to slip his shoulder from the coil and burden of things which he could not remedy, and to be born (as Gregory the Great said of himself) naked into the monastic life. I should like to see him again.

To the Same

PRECINCTS, 30*th March.*

Yesterday was a proper Canterbury day—bright sun, sharp wind, and every one on foot and astir about

---

[1] Benjamin Harrison, Archdeacon of Maidstone.
[2] A friend of mine who had recently become a Franciscan.

a matter of local interest, the Archdeacon's funeral. There was much to be done, because the determination to bring him once more into the Cathedral had only been reached in the afternoon of the day before. The shortness of the notice given, the day altered from Thursday to Tuesday, prevented any very large assembly of diocesan clergy, and at Matins none but the usual two or three gathered together. About twelve o'clock people began to collect in and about the Cathedral, clergy were hurrying round the old corners bag in hand, King's School boys in surplices standing about in groups, and choristers running across the Oaks after a hasty dinner. A great number of wreaths and crosses were sent to our house, and at 12.15 Agnes went up the Lane to fetch the little Blue girls who were waiting ranged round their school-room, saying the burial psalms to pass the time. They looked very demure and nice in their black ribbons, ties, and crepe bows on their little shoulders, and Agnes marshalled them, and made them carry across all the flowers. I watched them from the window as I had watched them last May, and then Lucy was kissing her hand to them through her tears, and the old Archdeacon and his wife were waiting on the grass to walk with them to the bowling green. Then, also, they carried flowers.

When every one had gone through, I followed, and went into the Cathedral my usual way, coming out on the top of the nave steps. The children were seated in rows on the steps, the Cathedral families were on the nave floor at the foot of the steps. A wide lectern dressed with black, and a bier, were placed in the centre of the first bays. The middle was kept clear, and the people lined the aisles. I went with Agnes and stood at the corner of the gate to the Martyrdom, on the lower landing. This commanded the whole centre of the nave.

The clergy came in procession down the North Choir aisle and North Nave aisle, and stood grouped at the West end till the coffin arrived at Christ Church gate, where the Mayor and Corporation and King's School were waiting. When it arrived they went out to meet it, and we soon heard the sweet strains of the psalm. Then they re-entered, the whole body together, and came up the middle nave in good order, and so ranged themselves on either side while the purple-palled coffin was settled on its lofty bier. Then the Dean read the lesson, then came an anthem, a prayer and a hymn, and then, as the march out began, the choir sang softly the Nunc Dimittis, at the close of which the organ broke into Chopin's Funeral March.

Nothing could be more beautiful than the effect of the moving mass of people, the splendid south sunlight, the scarlet robes of the Corporation, the purple of the Mayor and his officers, the long line of pure white robes, the strains of music, and, high above all, on the men's shoulders, the coffin, with purple and silver pall. With my whole heart I said, "Farewell, farewell to him," and it seemed as if he replied, "*Ah, yes! farewell, farewell* to Canterbury—to the Cathedral, to the priests, the friends, the choristers, the children, the old houses and gardens and flowers and budding trees and building birds, to the sun and the air and all that makes up this mortal life." At his hands I have received nothing but good, and his memory shall ever be dear. Canterbury truly mourns for him. For forty-five years he has gone in and out among us, and among those who were before us. His little youngest friend, who saw things with something of his eyes and mind, and who would have wept for him yesterday, has gone before him. We shall never find any one again in the world like the Archdeacon. There was no one (as it says in Chronicles) who kept the law of the Lord, and walked in the ways of his fathers all the days of his life, like unto Benjamin the Archdeacon.

To Francis Holland

CANTERBURY, 21*st April.*

Many, many happy returns of the day to you, and a thousand blessings on your dear head and kind heart. There is no earthly blessing that I do not wish for you, but more than all I wish you a heart above the world. This I think you have by nature, and may God preserve it to you by grace. Spring seems come at last, and a light veil of green begins to show itself in the old gardens. A few more showers would change the face of the world. . . . Mr. Pearson, the architect, has been spending the day here—planning the improvements in St. Anselm's Chapel. Darling Luce would have taken such interest in all this. These soft spring days make me miss her cruelly—but the time must come for us all.

To Bernard Holland

PRECINCTS, 2*nd May.*

. . . I think that you are right about Fox Holm, and that it is time to part, but oh, my Bernard, what has not that little house been to me. It would be ungrateful were I to part from it without a deep pang. You see it was the frame in which my children's lovely

childhood was set. I see you all there in cold early
springs, in splendid Junes, and, above all, in the broad
autumn sunshine. But so I could never see you again
were I to live 100 years at Fox Holm, so I am content ; and I think myself happy to be at Canterbury,
where we have some other links beside your father's
Canonry. And no place is home like Kent.

To Sydney Holland

CANTERBURY, 3rd May.

I do not see my way to coming to you this month.
. . . Bernard will be very angry with me. He wants
me so very much to see " how lovely Llangattock is,
how kind and easy the hosts, and how sweet the little
new Lucy." But I cannot come, dear Sydney. I
don't think that I can go anywhere at all this year. I
feel much more inclined to hide myself away from
everybody till I have been a year without my Lucy.
I am cheerful enough at home, but directly I go away,
and my occupation ceases, memory brings up her hosts
remorselessly.

You don't know what this is, and I hope you never
will. You never need feel it, if God is merciful to you,
as I pray Him to be. . . .

To Bernard Holland

THE PRECINCTS, 12th May.

Your letter from Fox Holm affected me very much
—too much. I saw you standing lonely in the horse-
shed, and my Lucy there too, her little brown shawl
wrapped round her shoulders, and her sweet dim face
in the spring twilight. Sometimes I can hardly believe

that she ever lived; sometimes I cannot believe that
she is gone. No one can imagine what my girl was
to me every hour of every day—really no one could
believe it. I often used to say to her that it was too
much; and now often when I think of her I feel as if
my heart would break or my head go. Still I have
many things left, and nothing seems more certain to
me than that beyond this life there is another, and
that not in vain do we love. Perhaps, after a few
more years, I shall look back to my life up to 1885 at
Fox Holm as one looks back upon a long happy day.
I used to think that the wound of Alfred's death would
never heal. Perhaps it is best to come away. The
place is sweet, but it was the life that we led there
that was the sweetest. I, too, have spent thousands of
delightful solitary hours in those woods and fields.
When all my little children were in bed, I used to
wander out in the twilight, and remain long on the
high ground, within sight of the house, "my heart's
own temple, my Jerusalem," and I have felt such an
overflowing tenderness and love and thankfulness.

To the Same

PRECINCTS, 22nd June.

I have been sitting absorbed in the decorated
columns of the *Times*, and have missed the midday
post. London must certainly have been a wonderful
sight yesterday.[1]

Here we had a fine service in the Cathedral at 11
A.M.—the whole building filled with soldiers. The
standard-bearers, veterans, grouped high up on the
steps in front of the altar, surrounded by drawn

[1] Queen's Jubilee of 1887.

swords held upright. The Cross, flanked by clusters of roses, appearing beyond. This seemed to symbolise all that we have to live and die for. Handel's coronation anthem was very well sung, and "God Save the Queen" was sung in excellent time by soldiers and choir and organ, producing altogether a great rolling volume of sound. In the evening I took a carriage, and went with little Bruce Barter and a school friend who is also here, and Mrs. Trueman and her children who had been spending the day, to a meadow at the top of Tyler's Hill, the opposite side of the road to Hales Place. On this spot a large bonfire had been erected. All was soft darkness when we arrived, but presently the hill above Chartham lit up. Then a wide ruddy glare opened all along the sky in the direction of Dover; then St. Martin broke out opposite to us; then we fired on Tyler's Hill. Then a blaze of rockets went up from the dark woods behind Hales Place (the friendly and cautious Jesuits have held services, waved flags, and sent up *feux-de-joie* these two days). Then a great fire showed itself above Fordwich, as far as we could guess. Then we saw the Boughton rockets go up behind the ridge of forest which lay between us and Herne Hill. Then five great flaring spaces of sky were discernible towards Reculver, Margate, Ramsgate, Deal, and some other place. One of these, towards Deal, shone with great splendour, and at the same time Minster began, like a great distant steady burning lamp. And the whole time the great flare at what we took to be Dover continued. Charles Trueman strode about over the hay swathes, eagerly trying to settle exactly *where* every blaze arose, and interrupted and put out every moment by the screams and wrong guesses of his wife and children.

The deep little lanes were full of Blean natives, and the clergy orphans were careering round their bonfire. No one really tried to see all that could be seen but Colonel Charles and myself, both old natives. We counted thirteen bonfires all at once, and thought of the crowds in London, and of the thousands and thousands of English faces all over England lit up on the high grounds in the midsummer night.

One feels that it has all happened very well, with a good Conservative Government in, and no war anywhere in Europe, and the loaf very cheap, and perfect weather and plenty of roses, and only another six weeks of Parliament sitting. We illuminated this house very prettily for both nights; rows of small lamps and tall candles in each window, a big flag across the street, and little ones disposed about. Mercery Lane was really beautiful, and the High Street good, everybody out and in good humour.

To the Same

THE LODGE, 26th *July*.

Everything looks brilliant this morning, and all beyond the immediate dark green of the garden is of a pearly gray. This is the prevailing tint of East Kent distances, and it is a sort of reflection of the pale Channel colours, clear but pale. The sea, the chalk, the wide cornfields, the great open sky above the northern waters, all combine to produce it.

To the Same

THE LODGE, 4th *August*.

Your letter from the Bains du Lavez has just come to hand. You may imagine with what emotion I read of those places which in all their loveliness are indelibly imprinted on my memory.[1] I am glad that we were there. I often regret that I have not made more excursions with my children since you all grew up. One remembers nothing so pleasantly and distinctly as expeditions with those one loves. I wish we had taken our sweet Lucy to Italy with us. But all this is nothing to her clear spirit now, and almost nothing to me at times. "That immense sad charm," which you so truly describe, is shed over these lovely earthly scenes by the mind of man, and would be terrible and intolerable did our stay end here.

> God who hath power to put our love asunder
> Also hath power to re-unite us all.

This is my Rock and Refuge; in these ideas I rest, and am a little comforted. . . . I am reading Evelyn's *Diary* because of the large print. How well he describes sweet Wotton, with its woods and watered park and old church, in the porch of which Evelyn learnt "his rudiments of one Friar." I like also his account of one John Wall, an Irish Friar, who had become a cavalier, and was going to serve in the German Horse, whom Evelyn met in Paris, and whose delight was to go and argue in public with the Jesuits and other ecclesiastical doctors, and overthrow them in argument. Of quite surpassing powers and eloquence, Evelyn says. This is the sort of character whom a clever novelist introduces with such effect.

To the Same

THE LODGE, *25th August.*

All goes quietly here. The days slip along in blue

---
[1] The shores of Lac Léman.

and gold and purple and the fine white linen of the hour before dawn. The roses are coming in again and the mignonette holds out. Last night, after dark, the firwood balcony sent forth an astonishing aromatic perfume, which filled the dining-room when I opened the window. G. C. P. drove up on Thursday evening with a bag and stayed the night. He fenced cheerfully all the evening with Aunt Emily, betraying much activity and knowledge, some of it surprising, such as a minute acquaintance with the butterine question, and the exact derivation of a slang word, and the genealogy of some fashionable lady; easily, also, unrolling to us the position of the Jesuits with regard to the Orleanists since Égalité, and their quarrel with Charles Xth.'s ministers. Every one's information appeared so hazarded by the side of his. He took some trouble to talk well, and never said "more or less" or "waste paper basket" at all. He explained very neatly all about buck-jumping horses, though he had not seen Buffalo Bill. He sat all yesterday morning in the garden with a book, and says that the place is perfectly delightful. He likes the house and garden and meadows and everything.

St. Anselm's Chapel is begun. We must very soon get the designs for the windows. I wish you would read his life and see what comes to you of it, and go on considering in what form we should commemorate him, and in what our blessed Lucy.

To the Same

HARBLEDOWN LODGE, 21*st October*.

. . . The woods are in full autumn colouring. I walked with Frank this afternoon to Chartham Hatch and then along the brow to the right, and down through a very pretty wood by a path which brought us out at that solitary hop-oast at the foot of the "camp." The fruit gardens are not at all deserted ; men and boys tying and cutting, and burning the "evil" trees and unfruitful branches in heaps outside the grounds. Hoppoles are quickly stacking, and ploughing is begun. It is all good and quiet and touching in the still autumn air. One feels the circling of the seasons in this country. All our walnuts are thrashed and the boughs spread naked against the sky. One of the elms, on what Chaney calls the "hanging level" of the park, is brilliant pale yellow, and the beech and wild cherry are burning red in the Halhed woods.

To the Same

THE LODGE, *27th October*.

I did read Lord Randolph's speech and admired the ending. It is a fine peroration, but he has not been idle and ill-behaved for nothing, and although he may turn a period like Burke, yet his words carry immeasurably less weight than if they had been conceived and uttered by that man of pure and heroic heart. Burke touches one so deeply because his word is himself. Lord Randolph sees what he says, but I doubt whether he really feels it. Still he is far beyond —— and Co., "who neither hear nor see, rolled round in earth's diurnal course."

I am glad that you agree with me that the real worker wants little positive amusement. All the world over theatres exist for the comparatively idle classes, or for those who have not family life. I think the Germans wisest with their music, beer and pipes.

To Mrs. Deacon

CANTERBURY, *7th November.*

My dearest Mary—Barbara wrote me such a delightful letter from Poynters, but it made me shed many foolish tears, just to think of past days. It is not that they are not always in my mind, but when some one else puts one's thoughts into words, all the freshness of sorrow revives. I wrote to you when you lost your brother, but my letter seemed so melancholy to myself that I burnt it. I have thought of him and of you a thousand times. I shall never forget him. I remember quite distinctly each time that I ever saw him, and something that he said or did. I think that his must have been one of those characters whose natural gifts grow into virtues. Some people have delightful qualities, but let them float and waste, but your brother's kindness grew into love, and his good taste and love of art into zeal for the House of God, and so on—and this seems the best and happiest thing that can come to a human soul, and it must come only to those who are pure in heart, and can see and follow the lead that God gives.

And how happy for him, and for my Lucy, and for many other sweet souls to be taken while their whole being tends to God and to the work He has set. But what an unspeakable loss to us!

Often and often in spirit I traverse those woods and arrive at your door, and cross the quiet dark hall, and open the drawing-room door, and find you at your tea-board with one friend. One day I shall come in body. If only I could see your sweet face without bursting into wild tears—that is what I fear.—Your loving

SIBYL HOLLAND.

To Bernard Holland

PRECINCTS, 24*th November*.

We were very much amused by your account of your Sunday in Trafalgar Square. The circumstances hardly justified calling out the constabulary, I think, and I doubt whether the moral effect was needed, for it must be clear even to the most deluded section of the mob that there is *more spirit* in the classes than in all the masses put together. Their gymnastic training is not given for nothing throughout our great schools.

Canterbury is as usual. The stream of affairs is narrow, but runs full to the banks and contributes, I suppose, its contingent to the great ocean of things, and also to the "waste paper basket" about which G. C. P. is for ever muttering and murmuring.

As I write I see the three backs of Archdeacon Smith, Harry Austen, and a "Cathedral Chap" surveying the porch of the Archdeaconry where, perhaps, a spout is gone wrong. Papa, with trenchered head, is hurrying up the path with a Receiver's book under his arm. Mark is arriving from Harbledown with a load of wood and vegetable produce. Bell Harry and all the rest of the vast building is shining white in the southern sun against a black leaden northern sky. We sang just now "In Jewry is God known, the shield, the sword and the battle"—very well rendered.

To the Same

PRECINCTS, 9*th December*.

I like our weather, the south wind always blows, and this morning at six, opening my windows, the dark soft air blew in quite warm. The Cathedral reared itself huge in the light of a low waning moon, and all the constellations looked as if they had wheeled over and were plunging westwards. A blackbird sang, perhaps the same " Early bird, early bird," that John Starr heard, for birds live long. Deus, Deus meus, ad te de luce vigilo.

To the Same

PRECINCTS, 17*th December.*

The morning is charming here—a south wind and bright ascending sun, which, as I write at 9.30, illuminates the whole Cathedral east and south. We have had many such mornings lately, and also beautiful clear evenings. Yesterday, at evensong, I observed the great west window of the nave's south transept, which I can see from my seat, shining like pale amber in the gloom of the great church, and, coming out, saw the wide west clear as crystal, while the south wind was driving up the clouds in masses from the left.

To Francis Holland

CANTERBURY, *St. Thomas' Day,* 21*st December.*

This is the shortest day of the year—the very point of entrance of the deepest cavern of winter, and we really have arrived at it without feeling much of the hardships of the journey. No winter ever seems really very hard or long if we reach Christmas mildly. We have had a sharp north wind these last two days, but bright sun and blue sky, and starlight nights as the watchman has duly informed us. The middle and lower population of Canterbury has been stirred by the report that the Star of Bethlehem has re-appeared in the east. This turns out to be the planet Venus, who rises most fair and effulgent just before dawn and still shines beautifully long after the eastern sky is rosy with the rising of the sun. . . . Sarah Bernhardt's immense gains are surprising. That an actress should make so much money seems rather to equalise things. The world certainly pays good salaries, and He who said My kingdom is not of this world, also pays His servants, but in quite other fashion. And I am sure that it is a fact that not one woman in a thousand envies Sarah or would change lots with her. Hardly would she excite a moment's envy in a poor cottager or little maid-servant. Things are so much more equal than they appear.

To Rosamond Stephen

THE PRECINCTS, CANTERBURY, *Xmas Eve.*

My dear Rosamond—I do not know whether the ugly little tea-caddy with a sliding top will yet have reached you. It was chosen in a great hurry between the trains, and I have a decided impression of having sent a frightful object to be engraved with your pretty name. But I know that Rosamond will receive it kindly as a sign of tender remembrance on the part of her god-mother.

I hear of your dancing at Eton, dancing on the very brink of womanhood, which is wonderful when I remember the tiny bright-eyed girl I first saw fresh landed from India. And I hear that you dance very well.

And from another person that you learn very well, and from another that you talk very agreeably, and from another, a very small person, who appears to speak the exact truth, that "Rosamond Stephen is *such* a kind girl." All this news of you has reached me within the last week, and I feel that such a sweet god-daughter deserves more than an ugly caddy. So she shall have besides it her god-mother's love and blessing and prayers, which last either are worth nothing or are worth more than all the gold and silver of this poor world.—In haste, dear girl, your most affectionate

SIBYL HOLLAND.

In December 1887 my mother began to keep an irregular journal, and from time to time continued it until the spring of 1889. The following extracts are taken from the beginning of it. A very few more will be inserted later on.

Extracts from Journal

1st December.—On beginning a work. Far be it from me to will, and much less to undertake, anything whatsoever in this mortal life that has not Thee, oh my Lord and Master, for its first motor, promoter, centre and circumference. Thou art my all, both by what Thou art, and by what I am, by condition of nature, by election of understanding, and by choice of determinate will. Accept then the total oblation of this which I am about to undertake, for I protest that I expect and intend nothing in it but the performance of Thy Glory, the performance of my duty, and the carrying out of Thy most blessed will.

Orate Dominum Jesum, ut mihi ignoscat, quia implere non potui quod volebam.

3rd December.—Finished reading Pater's *Marius the*

Epicurean ; curious book, original and not original, some faint re-echo all through of the author's early life and schooling at Canterbury.

15th December.—Drove to Bishopsbourne. . . . The country as we drove along this afternoon looked wet and wild ; heaps of brown leaves raked together and rotting. Big calves huddled under the trees. The streamlet swelled and running fast. Masses of drifting clouds in a yellow west sky. We are going down into the darkest caves of winter—there lies our road, where, two years ago, my Luce fainted by the way, chilled to death in that long six months' winter of 1886. We had to leave her as Jacob left his darling wife. She died in the way and we had to journey on, as we do.

17th December.—I thought to-day about the influence of the Cathedral on people living, as we do, close to it, and often in it. It is the influence of the actual building itself, quite apart from services, and *more* than services ; Lucy soon felt this. I remember her saying, " Mamma, it holds me, it is like a spell."

> And some there are whom God hath set to dwell
> In such old places.

This I find written in her little Apocrypha. They are dear John Starr's words.

St. Stephen's Day.—Lisa to dinner. She ran back across the deep snow at 10 P.M. looking like a phantom. There is a peculiar effect about old buildings in snow. The silence, the muffled hurrying figures, the white mass half-disguising the buildings, the dim uncertain lights, all seem to obliterate the marks of the present time. The bell strikes eleven as I write, and I hear the watchman crying " Past eleven o'clock, and a moonlight snowy night. All's well." Deo gratias, I reply in my heart of hearts, and still and always I think of my sweet Luce, so passionately loved and lamented.

St. John's Day.—Deep dazzling snow lying thick on earth and old buildings and bare trees. . . . Pretty ragged girl came to the door after breakfast with little pup in her arms. She made a pretty picture in the door with the winter background. Bernard will remember this. He looked at the child and spoke kindly, and Agnes brought her tea. The girl's look and manner, as simple as an Italian peasant, and yet only *old* civilisation can produce the type.

New Year's Eve.—It has just struck twelve on the last night of the year. . . . I had a pretty letter from Mrs. Harrison to-night. She always strikes the right chord with me. We and they understood each other and felt alike about a thousand things. The year is gone that took the Archdeacon, and young Loosemore, and young Edward Blore—all familiar faces in and about these old buildings where God hath set us to dwell. He only knows who will be here and who gone when this year also ends. Lord have mercy.

9th January.—E. M. to London. This is her last visit to our house before her voyage to Japan. May God bless her and reward her for all her service and long kindness to me and mine. I can truly say that I have no more faithful friend in the world than she is, nor is there any family where she is so loved and understood.

25th January.—Cette petite figure pâle comme la mort, avec ses gros yeux noirs et cette voix tremblante qui disait d'un accent navrant, "c'est vous, vous seule que je ne sais pas quitter." How much love, tenderness, and service have I and mine received from the faithful friend. If we never meet again here we shall meet elsewhere. May God bless and reward and keep her, and bring her home again.

26th January.—West wind rose in the night. I have heard the wind and waves all day, as Luce and I did in the autumn of 1883, after Agnes sailed for India. The wind used to make me restless all day and night, tossing the branches of the little wild wood with a sound like the waves dashing. How long it seems since that autumn, and yet it is only four and a half years. I have felt low in soul all day.

1st February.—At 2.30 to Cathedral. No one in Crypt. All the floor filled in again, except stone coffin. Beautiful S.-W. light across the west portion of Crypt. I stayed for an Ave Mary in the Lady Chapel—all forlorn and deserted. Saw Canon Routledge taking people up to transept. Went into St. Anselm's Chapel, and sat a little at the end of nave. All was perfectly empty and silent and beautiful, till a verger came clattering in at south door.

Candlemas, 2nd February.—Early celebration with Agnes and Sophy. The altar beautiful with great arums and pampas grass. Such splendid tender lights behind the screen from the south-west rising sun and the stained windows. All that we need is more dignity, reverence and unity in the celebration of the mysteries.

As it is, the place and the manner contradict each other.

8th February.— ... Afterwards I went to the Cathedral, and into Trinity Chapel while the choir sang " Lord ; Thou hast searched me out." I spent the time there till the light faded outside and every one had left the church, and then went to the Crypt, and stayed a while in the beautiful desolate places. Then prayed for Michael at the gate of the Angels' Chapel, and went home.

29th February.—Snowstorms all afternoon. Agnes got out of the box my brother James' old letters, and some of mine in 1858-61. Oh, the freshness of that time ! Some of my mother's letters also, one describing Alfred's first return from India. My father's emotion at meeting him in Paris. He was their darling son. Letters of my mother also about ———. How quiet she sleeps now ; all that at an end. Eternal rest grant them, O Lord ; and let perpetual light shine on them.

1st March.— ... Went into St. Peter's for quarter of an hour's private prayer ; considered the great question. Thought of my dream of the golden net. ...
 ... At 7.15 to St. Peter's. Subwarden was very good on the pure in heart, following truth wherever it may lead. What he said struck in with my vein of thought.

15th March.—Very fine day. With Agnes and Frances to Matins. Heard the Psalms very dimly. Thought much of my darling Luce while we sang the Psalm. I remember at this very time of the year holding her dear hand in mine while the Psalm was singing, on the morning we heard of little Edith Selfe's death. We let our tears fall together. Now hers are wiped away, and mine still flow.

27th March.—Cold and damp. Fall of snow at nightfall. Mr. Reid to see me. Deafness better somewhat, but full of aches and pains in my poor ruinous body. This has been an idle day for me. Miss —— called. *Voilà tout.* Tried to write letters but did not. Tired am I of all mortal things. When shall we flee as a bird unto the hill?

VIII

LETTERS OF 1888

To Francis Holland

CANTERBURY, 3rd *February.*

IT is bitterly cold here, colder than ever. Little ——— creeps close to the fire but cannot keep warm. She is always scribbling, and her poetry runs upon *la grande passion.* Not that I believe love to be *la grande passion.* Other passions take a far more lasting hold of the human heart. Science, once she seizes, never lets go her slave, and ambition " that last infirmity of noble minds." Go to St. Paul's Cathedral on Sunday and tell me what you think of the new Reredos. You will also get an excellent sermon if Liddon or Holland's " learned sock be on." You ought to arrive before 3 P.M. a little.

To the Same

CANTERBURY, 4th *February.*

I believe that if I were talking of you instead of to you I should say that you can produce stanzas, because you have the poetic temperament and are well trained mentally in that direction, and that some day, under press of true deep feeling you might produce something very good in its kind—like Lockhart's little poem liked by Carlyle, or Stanley's one or two lovely things—and really that sort of *jet* of pure deep feeling, taking expression in a classically cultivated mind, is a great contribution to the general stock. But there is no doubt that composition in all the arts, *as* composition, injures the critical faculty. This is clearly seen even in great poets. They do not know when the fire is out. . . . I set the critical faculty higher than the power of writing even very pretty verses. . . . God bless you, my dearest boy, and prosper you and preserve your going out and coming in, now and ever.

To the Same

CANTERBURY, 23rd *February*.

You were quite right to go to Lady S———'s reception. If you are going to lead a London life, you had better go everywhere and see everyone that is worth seeing. The best London society is the best in the world, and it is something to see it. And besides one can always get out of society, but one cannot always get into it. I am quite happy about you now that you are out of the gloomy little No. 10.

To Bernard Holland

CANTERBURY, 25*th March*.

What are you doing this evening, my Bernard? I have been reading your "Sir Justinian" with pleasure and some admixture of pain. It strikes a chord in *my* heart, at least, and past voices reverberate, and sweet shapes and scenes flit by.

I am still deaf and ill, and will not pretend to do

more than send thee a salutation. To-morrow we enter into Holy Week, and into the nearer contemplation of suffering willingly borne.

What a noble army certainly has followed the way of the Cross!

To Francis Holland

CANTERBURY, *27th March.*

I send you Mr. Scoones' letter. I think that you will win—anyhow you have worked well, and if you do not get this I shall say, "It is plainly the will of God," and shall know that you are destined for something else. You will go to a service on Good Friday, I am sure, in remembrance of the death and passion of our sweet Saviour, Christ, and will, with the whole of believing Christendom, make your communion on Easter morning in trust of our Resurrection to Life immortal. If my son does this, then is he close at my side though half the world lie between. You and Lionel are children of one font. I kissed the bright baptismal drops on his tender brow as well as on yours. Carry this note in your bag, or better still, carry my word in your mind to Porlock by the Sea.

To the Same

ST. LEONARDS, *7th April.*

It is very cold here but I feel somewhat braced. Aunt C. and I have just come back from Holmhurst, where we have been taking tea with Mr. Augustus Hare. I really enjoyed this very much indeed. It is a house about the size and shape of Poynter's, and stuffed full of pretty and interesting things. We rambled about it and saw a great many pictures, and heard a great many stories. He was very kind and agreeable, and I should like to spend a week there among his books and sketches.

Extracts from Journal

HASTINGS, *Sunday, 8th April.*—To Christ Church for High Celebration and Matins and Sermon. Certainly this is a great development of the Anglican Liturgy. (If this rite and the doctrine it presents is really ours, it is enough.) But if it is not! I can find or hear no answer to one or two questions that are continually before me. I have just read in Miss Hare's letters the following, which strikes me: "The mistake of my life has been to take God's gifts instead of himself."

Monday, 9th April.—

> Ecce sub vite
> Amoenâ Christi
> Ludit in pace
> Omnis Ecclesia tuta in horto ;
> Resurgens, Christe,
> Hortum florentis
> Paradisi tui
> Obstructum
> Diu reseras,
> Domine,
> Rex regum!

"Creatures were created by God for man, in order that they may aid him to attain his proper end. Thus, then, creatures are for us but *means*, as we have already said. What other consequence can be drawn from this truth except that we must accept all which leads us to our proper end, and reject all that keeps us from it ; we must take that which carries us to God, and leave that which separates us from Him.

"Thus in all which takes place, in all that happens to me, I reflect before God. Yes, this trouble, this sickness, this act of obedience, this cross, it comes to me from the hand of God, it leads me to God.

"Then I take it. On the contrary, this self-seeking, these memories, these affections, keep me from God. I leave, let go.

"Désirer, là est la vie.

"Dieu doit être désiré, car désirer c'est cette tendence de l'âme qui attend, qui appelle, qui prie, et, comprenons le bien, *prier c'est vouloir*. Désirer, vouloir, prier —c'est donc la même chose."

Tuesday, 10*th April*.—La messe, 7 A.M. Breakfasted alone in great parlour. Talk with M. M. Anastasie. Went round the schools at 11 A.M. with her. Dined alone. Went into Church "Notre Dame du bon Conseil." Long talk with Mother Aloysius about her family history. Reception of her sister Bertha, etc. Prayed long in chapel. Benediction. Bed, 9.30.

Wednesday.—La messe, 7 A.M. Breakfasted alone. At 8.15 took my leave of the kind mothers.

To Bernard Holland

THE PRECINCTS, 10*th April*.

Last night I dreamed of you so vividly that I awoke and struck a light, and looked at my watch, and found that 'twas but 11.30 P.M. This was at the convent at St. Leonards, where I went on Monday, and was most hospitably entertained till this morning.

Among other rules, all lights are extinguished at 9.30, and this caused me to be dreaming of you before midnight. I dreamed only that you came and sat on the floor and leaned your head on my knee (this you do not out of dreamland) and told me in a trembling voice that you were ill and tired. What you said and what I replied was so vivid that when I awoke I got up and prayed for you, and not only to the Lord of life, but to His Mother and all the Saints, whose altars stand in the pretty adjoining church. Then I slept again, and this time I dreamed that Lucy, Agnes, and I were in our usual places in the Cathedral, and the office going forward, when the choir began to sing false, and the organ gave a wrong chord, and the music was ending in a harsh confusion, when Luce took up the strain in a note of thrilling sweetness, and sustained the melody till the choir recovered its footing, and the congregation clapped and made loud applause, and I thought—who has ever been applauded here beside Luce? and awoke very cheerful.

On Saturday Aunt Caroline and I drove over to see Augustus Hare, and had tea, and saw his house and all its interesting contents. Here he is really seen to advantage. It is a pretty, low-built house with a broad ivied verandah running all round it. His sketches of Rome and Italy generally are exquisite.

Rye and Winchelsea looked very pretty rising out of their campagna, as we steamed across it under a brilliant blue sky. Thousands of lambs, shining white, with their dowdy woolly mothers, and flights of seagulls gleaming like silver. Nothing else but the sluggish little river taking its time to the sea, and a sulky old fort in the distance.

Extract from Journal

Sunday, 15th April.— Beautiful day. . . . This evening Lisa told Agnes of her great project.[1] She has simply made the sacrifice while others stand considering. This determination on the part of Lisa in the midst of a year of marrying and giving in marriage touches and lifts one like a pure death, the thought I mean of a pure death, i.e. *another life.*

To Mrs. Deacon

CANTERBURY, 16th April.

My dearest Mary—What terrible, overwhelming news Emily Buxton sends us this morning. I cannot believe it. It seems impossible that Mr. Arnold[2] is gone, gone in the moment of meeting, as he was hurrying back to meet, his little gay Lucy.

All his kindness and goodness and genius, his general love and good-will, and his faithful and particular friendship rises up before me. I weep for him, and for his darlings left without him. The thought of their pain is almost intolerable. God alone knows what they must suffer, and that He *does know* is the one comfort and stand-by. What a journey for Nellie through the long night, and what an arrival.

I wish that I could see you. I have not felt anything so much since I closed Lucy's sweet eyes. You

---

[1] Of entering the Kilburn Sisterhood.
[2] Matthew Arnold.

will be one with them in this great grief, and I do not like to imagine that you also are suffering. It is a great thing, however, to accompany a friend step by step through these dark places. It is the work of Christ and of His angels, weeping, strengthening, ministering.

> From pain to pain, from woe to woe,
> With bleeding heart and footsteps slow.
> To Calvary with Christ we go.

These old words, from the Stations of the Cross, used to go drumming through my head, as I went down step by step with Lucy in my arms, to the very gate of death. These events are our Calvarys, our Crucifixions. How well Mrs. Arnold knows it. Her sweet, suffering, pale face is before me. Write me a word to say how all is with them, and with you. I feel much love to them all, but I can do nothing but pray for them, and that I will do as long as I live.—Your ever loving   SIBYL HOLLAND.

To Bernard Holland

17th April.

I daresay you have heard more by now. Mr. Arnold fell as he was walking towards the tramcar with his poor wife. She raised his dear head and cried out for brandy, but there was none, and none in the doctor's house into which they carried him.

Yes, the emperor is dying. All these things cast the soul on God alone. We accept His gifts instead of Himself; hence our despairing tears.

To Francis Holland

CANTERBURY, 20*th April.*

I think you had much better shut up all your books and take Sunday and Monday in the country. I feel sure that it cannot be a good thing to go on working up to the last minute. Do take my advice and come down and have a good ride or a walk by the sea-shore—you will get a spring in your mind which will make you do everything better. . . . You are twenty-three to-morrow. It seems to me a wonderful thing. Twenty-three springs have your eyes looked upon. It seems to me, however, much longer than that since you were born. Everything now seems to me so long ago. I do not know exactly why this is so. I will say nothing more, my darling boy. You know all my love for you. I turn away my thoughts from the Exam., because I feel as if my anxiety would add to yours. I wish that you were not anxious.

To Miss Arnold-Forster

CANTERBURY, 20*th April.*

. . . Mr. Holland desires me to return to you with his love and thanks these stanzas on Arthur Stanley.[1] How well the four last lines of stanza eight suit your dear uncle himself. I thought so when I first read them. . . . My dear Frances, how people suffer! What a crucifixion this life is! I have been reading Gordon's letters to his sister; his clear faith, and insight, and light touch on life are very helpful and animating.

[1] Matthew Arnold's poem.

To Francis Holland

CANTERBURY, 9*th May.*

You may think how pleased we are. Agnes flew out into the clear dusk of the Precincts ten minutes ago where I was walking with a party of High School girls and little ———, and gave me your telegram.[1] I lifted up my heart and opened it, and there was just light enough to read your two words. Is not success a strange *quiet* feeling. Things seem to fall into another perspective as soon as one has what one wants.

To Bernard Holland

CAVENDISH, SUFFOLK, 1*st June.*

I wonder if you are meditating any serious measure while you are yachting, or whether you are wholly given to the winds and waves. . . .

. . . I came here on Wednesday, and yesterday made a long excursion with Aunt Cathy to see churches —Bures, Nayland, Wissington, Stowe, Kersey, Gifford's Hall (which still belongs to the Mannock's, who held it 400 years ago), Bosford, and Assington. The country is rich and well-watered, and the villages all look prosperous. The children all well shod and plump. The smell of the bean-fields delicious—" the smell of a field which the Lord hath blessed," the pastures all gold and silver, the copse woods crimson and blue with blue bells and sweet campion, immense tufts of laylocks peeping over all old walls and out of all old gateways. Gifford's Hall is a wonderful old house lying buried in tall pastures and beech, a long

---

[1] As to winning a clerkship in the House of Commons.

old small avenue of elms running to it and out of it. The laylocks in full bloom blowing about the fine old red gateway of the little quadrangle.

These are just the sort of places mentioned in John Gerard's Life and Edward Campion's. I wish that you had come down here instead of yachting.

To Francis Holland

CAVENDISH, *4th June.*

I should so much like you to see a beautiful old house called Gifford's Hall near here. Aunt Cathy and I went by train last week to Bures, and drove thence to see a number of churches. At Stoke, by Nayland, there is a splendid church, and in a side chapel the fair alabaster monument of Sir Gilbert Mannock. Further on, at the bottom of a green chase, and standing knee-deep in waving pastures and lilacs blowing about the old doors and windows, we came upon the ancient Hall—a red brick gateway, and within a small old quadrangle. All was perfectly silent, but, as we looked through the tall arch, we saw the figure of a young girl flying past the long low window in the upper storey. The place still belongs to the Mannocks, but is let to the Arnolds.

Extracts from Journals

Wednesday, 6th June.—Canterbury is a beautiful place to return to, but oh! for a little more leisure. " Que rien ne te trouble. Que rien ne t'effraie! Tout passe. Dieu ne change jamais. Tout réussit à la patience. Rien ne manque à qui possède Dieu. Dieu seul suffit." St. Theresa.

29th June.[1]—Bishop of Minnesota staying with us; also Bishop of Grahamstown and Bishop Bickersteth of Japan. The first of these three is one of the most striking persons I have ever seen.

30th June.—Fine morning. Large luncheon party from 12.30 to 2 P.M. Knutsfords by special train with the mass of Messeigneurs. Reception of Bishops by the Primate in the Cathedral a very fine sight.

To the Lady Knutsford

CANTERBURY, *July*.

... It was so good of you to come here, and I was so sorry to see you go. I am sure that, if you are right and that the measure of affection is to be taken in the absence of friends—I am sure, then, that I must adore you, such a charming and interesting figure of you shapes itself ever in my mind.

All the things I left unsaid seem so much more important than anything I said to you. What a large part of oneself are the things unsaid and undone.—Ever, *in sæcula sæculorum*, affectionately yours,

SIBYL HOLLAND.

To Bernard Holland

THE LODGE, *9th July*.

I am always so sorry to see you go. Everything that you like I like, and my pleasure is always doubled by your presence. It was in this part of the world that we began to be friends, and hereabouts we shall

[1] The Bishops of the Lambeth Conference were at Canterbury.

probably end, only, I hope, to begin elsewhere. What
I write to you about at this moment is merely to say
how pretty it is to sit at my window and watch the two
mowers who began at eleven o'clock on the other side
of the terrace fence, and are now just finishing their
seventh swathe. At twelve they stopped, ate and drank
just this side of the Bigareaus,[1] and then lay in the sun
by the old orchard gate on their faces like dead men
for an hour. Then they rose and silently resumed their
scythes, bowing their strong backs to the rhythmical
toil. They are good bearded creatures, and *keep on*.
The seventh swathe is just in a line with the Bigareaus.
Now the short mower is beginning the eighth, and I
see his straw hat and red handkerchief at his belt
moving under the low boughs. Chancy, with a foolish
expression of authority, is advancing with more beer.
The wind has gone to the south-west and is blowing
the elms about. All the hop-oasts are testifying to the
truth of this statement. There is something fascinating
in watching the ridges of grass fall. Do you remember
the wonderful chapter in Tolstoi where Levine mows
with the mowers?

To the Same

THE LODGE, 13*th July*.

We have such a splendid morning after the cold
whirling storms of yesterday and the day before. The
dashing rain, and waving elm branches, and scattered
roses, and sodden earth made a most melancholy
picture. Now the sun is come rejoicing out of his
chamber, and is running his course like a giant, and

---

[1] Cherry trees so called.

all is warm and tranquil and fragrant. The haymakers, who will presently be reinforced by the maids, are raking the long swathes into lines at right angles with the garden fence. The mowers are bending to their work at the top of the hill by the firs, and the air is full of humming and singing. All the storm is over and forgotten. . . . I have read but little as yet of sweet Dorothy Osborne. What an odd thing it is that there should not be more letters like those. I suspect that thousands of collections of family letters have been burnt in past times, exactly as Mrs. Harrison burnt the mass of the Archdeacon's correspondence to save herself the trouble of looking through and sorting out. It is a pity, but one sees how it comes about.

To the Same

THE LODGE, 17th July.

We have just come to the end of a long fine summer day. Yesterday the rain kept off, and, towards midday, the wind rose, so that the hay dried fairly well, and the afternoon was very fine. This morning I woke at 4.30 to the diabolic cries and clapper of the child whom we have hired to drive the birds from the cherries. You never heard such a child. We have fed him twice from our own table to-day in order to keep him quiet, but he begins again more than ever. We can hardly hear ourselves speak. The birds make angry retorting whistles and squeakings from the elms. Agnes and I have been gathering black currants; they are as big as grapes, nearly. At 12.30 Ida Field and her mother appeared to lunch, and early in the afternoon Lisa drove up with a friend, then Canon Routledge, and then B. Battye. So the yard was full of vehicles;

quite a garden party. We gathered cherries and strawberries, and carried our tea into the hayfield, near the old Bigareaus; every one seemed to enjoy it. After the company was gone, we resumed our currant gathering, and old Hearn made himself neat, and came up to converse, and to propose a bargain for our "surplus fruit." Three half-pence a pound is the market price of cherries. The French people say that fruit is much cheaper here than in France. Hearn's outline against the sky, as he stood on the highest point of the garden path, was very finely curved. There was a glow in the west which set it off.

To the Same

THE LODGE, 20*th July*.

I am glad that Gordon had his wish, but then he goes as close up to the line that lies between life and death as a soul can live. The clause in the Litany really means "sudden" in the sense of "unprepared" death, or unfortified by the Sacraments, but I think that in the Latin it runs "à morte perpetuâ libera nos, Domine." The thought of Gordon is so sweet to my mind; and still I think his desertion the worst stain on that Government, and the endeavour to lessen in the eyes of the people the brightness of his glory the worst thing the Liberals allowed themselves to do. It was all so *false*. Gordon with his pure eyes saw it all, and disdained it, but forgave it.

On Tuesday Agnes drove me to Goodnestone and Graveney. We came back through the hamlets and superb orchards that cluster at the foot of the hill between the sea marsh and the London road. It is all really beautiful, and unlike, both in its wildness and in its cultivation, the ordinary English rural scenery. Troops of sturdy children were making their way from school to the old doors of their old homes, calling to one another, and scattering over the bye-paths that run everywhere through the gardens and orchards as they do in Italy.

To Francis Holland

THE LODGE, 26*th July.*

I have ended Margaret, Duchess of Newcastle, and think that I understand Charles Lamb's feeling about the book and its author. Her description of herself and her own bringing up at the end of the book is very good. It is a pleasure to read of a singular person, who felt herself to be singular, and singularly blessed, and who watched her own life and its adventures and developments. There is more than enough of such introspection nowadays, but in former times it was rare. The charm of Montaigne chiefly consists in his account of himself—what he did, thought, read and wrote, and in his way of tracing back to the fountain head all that he observed in himself. And there is much of this in Charles Lamb also, don't you think so?

Now I am entirely engrossed in Shelley's charming letters. The force of language can no farther go than in some of his descriptions. I read slowly and savour every page, as the French say. Will you get for me from the London library Parkman's *Montcalm and Wolfe*, or if that is "out" any one of Parkman's books except *Frontenac*, which I read at Milford?

To Miss Arnold-Forster

HARBLEDOWN, 30*th July.*

... The story of the doll does please me. It came like a fresh little voice out of the past, and though, as I write, tears blind my eyes, yet I am pleased. How happy we all were in your pretty house. I seem to remember every flower in the border round the house, and the fair mountains all about, and the Rotha brimming to his banks and flying and gleaming like a swift silver smoke. How all these things must speak to your mother and your aunt!

To E. M. (in Japan)

THE LODGE, 15*th August.*

... I send you a note of ———, which will make you see where I am as to a subject of the deepest importance. I don't want to write about it, and, if you were at home, darling E. M., my dearest and most faithful friend, I should not speak to you of it. I *have* nothing to say, but if things are made clear to me I shall act, be the cost what it may. And it is no light thing to take one's life and all that one has, and cast it, as it were, into the deep, and to turn, old and solitary, into a life which makes the greatest demands upon the human soul. Do not make a trouble of my trouble; the time is short and the only thing to live for is the will of God. You once said to me in reply to a question of mine, " I should never speak to you again," and so has said another person, or as good as said it. But I shall not mind if you never speak to me—you would not refuse to embrace your poor friend, and that would be enough. . . . How often August has found me thus alone—the warm summer wind filling the quiet house, and bringing in all manner of rich scents and soft country sounds. The children have set up doves and guinea-pigs again. This is Bernard, who for ever recurs to the pleasures of his childhood. It is just about this time two years ago, my E. M., that you were with us at Canterbury, and for the last time your Lucy threw her arms about your neck, and you kissed her pale cheeks and brow. Often and often I think that were you and Agnes and Lucy with me in Paradise the joy would be too great—it *is* too great to imagine. There are other dear, dear souls of yours and mine, but somehow my dream is of just this.—Ever, my own dear loved friend, yours till death and after,

SIBYL HOLLAND.

Extracts from Journal

HARBLEDOWN, *Saturday,* 1*st September.*—I looked out of my window about 3 A.M. this morning, and saw the wondrous brightness of the moon waned to a crescent boat, and riding high in the south. Orion brilliant, and the Great Bear wheeled about and plunging towards the fringe of the dark northern woods. This has been a lovely autumn day, a fine light mist hanging about and a warm sun.

Sunday, 2*nd September.*—We all drove over to Godmersham for morning service. All looked so lovely and unchanged.

Green swell the hills, the woods wave fresh as ever.[1]

---

[1] A line from some verses written about Godmersham by her father.

Godmersham, as one comes down the slope from the Temple woods towards the post-office, making always the same effect. It is a sort of peculiar untouched soft beauty. Something in itself entire and perfect, like a pearl; and there lies my pearl, my lost pearl; and, away south-west of London, against the south side of another chancel wall, lies my sweet Alfred. The thought of St. Lawrence, his martyrdom, his bliss, his possible power of intercession came overpoweringly into my mind as I knelt at the end of the Communion office.[1]

Monday, 3rd September.—This is the second anniversary of Lucy's death. Day of grief and mourning for us—for her, sweet soul, the beginning of everlasting joy.

Monday, 10th September.—Fine day. At 7 A.M. in the hop-gardens with Bernard. Everything so fresh and lovely, and such a soft multitudinous sound of women's voices coming up from the steep sloping grounds.

To Francis Holland

HARBLEDOWN, 18*th September.*

I remember my one flying sight of Isola Bella, with the mountains beyond. I felt a passionate desire to remain on the lake and to visit those isles, but we pushed on over the pretty low hills and down upon Milan. The beauty and prosperity of Milan, Florence, and (perhaps) Turin, take one by surprise. Bernard says that the Swiss hotels are generally the cheapest and civilest. We were horribly fleeced at Turin. . . .

---

[1] Godmersham church is dedicated to St. Lawrence.

The Italians are not at all honest and truthful, which I suppose the Romans were; at least I think that Gibbon says that in the matter of truth the English more resembled them than any other nation does.

To the Same

THE LODGE, *19th September.*

Your description of Sirmione made my tears flow. I don't quite know what touches me so much unless it be the thought of my young son looking upon that ancient beauty, as so many young and ardent souls have looked before, gazing and gazing, but unable to grasp the whole of its perfection. What a priceless gift it is, my Frank, to be able to feel the deep living loveliness of nature and art. I do so rejoice in your joy, and I am glad that you can travel alone; some people can't. Everything in Italy attracted me. The scenery, people, art and religion, for that religion, with all that can be said against it, is the one religion to me—and I shall go a stranger all the days of my life *in hac lacrymarum valle* unless I find my way into it. . . . Besides all the pleasure to me and others, letters are far the best form of journal, particularly when they are written to the mother who bare you, who nursed you, and taught you, and loved you and loves you with passionate tenderness.

To Rev. W. H. Bolton

HARBLEDOWN LODGE, *25th September.*

I have read the paper[1] through several times and

---

[1] A paper on the Athanasian Creed, written in reply to a Latitudinarian clergyman.

with much profit and pleasure. I think that it is the reverse of "poor." It is full, solid, and clear. I should like to talk with you about it, or rather to hear you talk. Some parts of the paper I particularly appreciate.

With regard to Mr. ⸺ I am sure that you would find that, if you brought your controversy with him to a plain issue, it would be brought to a speedy end. You and he do not agree in first principles, and therefore really have no common ground. You will find that you differ from him in the belief in the existence of God. So from what can you start? Newman says something to this effect—We need not dispute ; we need not prove ; we need but *define*. At all events let us if possible do this first of all ; and then see who are left for us to dispute with, what is left for us to prove.

Controversy in this age does not lie between the angels of heaven on the one side and the powers of evil on the other ; but it is a sort of night battle, where each fights for himself, and friend and foe stand together. I think that is so true about going on defining instead of disputing.

I like all that you say in the beginning of your paper about the first business of the Christian being to hold the Catholic Faith. Certainly the *ordinary* difficulty felt about the Athanasian Creed is that people don't understand that it applies simply to Christians whose first business it is to hold the Catholic Faith ; and then I think they imagine that the whole creed is a sort of call upon their *Reason* and not their *Faith* and that it fails of its object.

To Bernard Holland

THE LODGE, HARBLEDOWN, 3rd October.

We have had bitter cold weather since you left, and have begun morning fires. Yesterday was excessively cold and gloomy. Agnes and I gathered all the scarlet and white dahlias in Mount's piece and took them into Canterbury for the churches. This was in anticipation of the frost, and we were right. This morning all the plants are drooping under the icy touch laid on them last night. At 6 A.M. I looked out of my window and saw the sun rising well south of west; in a lovely barred and flecked sky, but the whole earth white with hoar frost, and a pale blue mist floating behind the hop-oast and all across the valley. The horizon clear against a clear whiteness. A blue mist was also rolling up the hill behind the park elms. Chaney is exercised by a delay in putting up the greenhouses. Mount has not worked for two days, and all Chaney's plants are unhoused. Old Potts has cut down, and bound together for burning, the two apple-trees, and pruned the third. When I went out to speak to him after you had gone on Monday, he was recovering the wounded roots and said: "I humbly beg your pardon, ma'am; I thought I was doing right in having of her down. I'll take and cover her up and comfort her a bit, and, by the blessings, let's hope she'll take no harm." I do not look upon these people as rude. I gave the old man a jug of Irish stew at night, with which he made his way home through the dim woods to Rough Common, where he has an old wife with a bad leg. He is now engaged in planting the young trees. He remembers your grandfather and grandmother very well, but has nothing at all to remark about them, except that he "can see Muster Lyall coming along the road plain enough." Yesterday I lunched in the Precincts and had a long talk with Uncle Alfred.[1] He is a person from whom one can differ without a shade of bitterness. He does so like the study, and particularly my room, and says that he shall be so sorry to go. He wants to write about Warren Hastings. Mr. Reeve has asked him for an article, and he means to write it; but meanwhile "can't help reading about the gnosticism of the third century." This comes from the repugnance to decisive action that lies in the Lyall disposition.

To the Same

THE LODGE. *October.*

—— is here, nice and clever but rather dry, advocating cremation and prayer-book reform, etc., etc., not at all "retrogressive." She has missed something which would have made her perfect. Perhaps she has never drunk of the fair fountain of religious truth—Catholic truth, the only true "waters of Jouvence," and which lie away behind suffering and isolation of spirit; and so straight and narrow is that path that few there be (comparatively) that find it. But she is a dear person, and dutiful and generous.

We had a piercing cold wind yesterday and to-day also. It abated towards evening, and I walked up the park to superintend my path. Old Potts is a good workman, and reached the rise of the hill before sunset. It shall be called "Pott's path."

---

[1] Sir Alfred Lyall, then occupying for a space our house at Canterbury.

Then we walked round the meadows and entered your walk, and went by the way that we went with Margaret and Dorothy, through the dim tranquillity of the woods, and by the moist cart track, and out upon the right of way; when we saw all the little valley alight with the bine and bush burning, the blue smoke hanging in the air, the red glow of the after-sunset, and a lovely crescent moon.

To Francis Holland

FOX WARREN, *24th October.*

This country is looking at its best. When the white morning mists roll away, the colour, the dryness, and the warmth of the whole district make themselves felt. Yesterday at 3 P.M. I was set down at the gate of the little Hatchford Park. I went to the churchyard and then into the church, which is always open. Then I went to Poynters, and finding the house empty I sat a long time in the sunny verandah reading Mr. Arnold's poems and waiting for my friend to return. This she did, but only in time to give me a cup of tea and a quarter hour's talk. Then I walked home down the lane, and across Chattley, and in again under the dry warm woods—all was dark, and soft, and silent, and I thought of many things—of my own young days in those places, and of your sweet childhood. I looked back upon the long road I had travelled, and forward to the short way that yet remains, and to the narrow door through which we must pass alone, one by one. What a mystery it all is!

To the Same

CAVENDISH RECTORY, 29*th October.*

You cannot think what pleasure your last letter gave me. There is someting very delightful in a true correspondence. I take the greatest care of all that you write—and some day you will have your letters back—and will recall vividly what you and I were thinking and feeling in the mild autumn days of the year 1888. Here the country still looks pretty. The elms are the purest pale gold, and the pear and cherry trees burning red. Something in the air and look of things reminds me of Cambridge. I wish you were there under the clock and opposite the plashing fountain, and then I could go and see you and walk with you down that avenue, and see the yellow leaves flying across the gray buildings, and hear the soft chimes. But your image is gone from those old courts like the leaves of a past autumn. "Dies mei sicut umbra declinaverunt, tu autem idem ipse es et anni tui non deficient," says King David. . . . How dear you all are to me God alone knows, and there is Lucy, who died here, and who lives to God, and with her I think that some of us died to some things, and with her we more live to God than had she been still with us. What an unspeakable hope I carry in my heart that some day—no, not some day, but when all days are gone—I may be able to say, Here am I and the children Thou gavest me. Montaigne is right, but there is more behind.

To Bernard Holland

THE LODGE, *All Souls' Day.*

... Yes, Sir James Stephen strikes as hard for a friend as he would against a foe. There is no one like him, and if ever I live to hear of his death I shall feel the pain while I breathe. And I believe that so just and true a man cannot but be pleasing in the sight of the God of strength and justice; in short, just as he is, I am very much attached to him, or to my idea of him.

To Miss Mason

PRECINCTS, *Advent Sunday.*

... I am so glad to get into Advent. Far off down the darkening ways we can see the lights of Bethlehem shine. We are deep in snow here. Roofs, and trees, and bells, and old ivied walls, from which the fluffy half-starved birds noiselessly alight on the frozen ground. The clock has just stuck fast, likewise the weathercocks.

To the Same

THE PRECINCTS, *7th November.*

My dear Agnes—Your Sunday letter caught me on the wing, and yesterday I was too busy to reply. We are plunged into all the horrors of a double bazaar, and, until this is over, neither our time, or our house, or our hands are our own. Coming back into Canterbury is incomparably more arduous than our old return to London used to be. There is a sort of luxury in the first few weeks in London, a tacit agreement on the part of one's friends to ignore your return, and to conceal their own. But here every one rushes at you at once presenting threads, and requiring you to take them up and to fall to work. But there the threads may lie; if I drop my Epiphany Guild-thread, I will take up none other. I wrote to Canon Furse a week ago and asked him to decide for me, and he writes back clearly and without the smallest hesitation that I had better give up the headship of the Guild.[1] So that is done, and with all my heart I beg that you will forgive me for going against your opinion, and that you will continue to regard me friendly, for I must always love you. Never in all my pilgrimage have I found in any one more generous affection and ready and intelligent service to a cause in hand than I have in you, and now I will stand aside and see what you do, and everything that you can tell me will be of the greatest interest to me.

Canon Furse wrote most kindly. He says that he does not in the least wish to give up the Guild Wardenship (I sounded him as to this) but that he would always "without the smallest jealousy give up in favour of dear Scott Holland whom I love."—Ever am I, dear Agnes, your affectionate and grateful friend,

SIBYL HOLLAND.

To Francis Holland

PRECINCTS, 10*th* *November*.

I am glad you are at Wherstead; write me word thence. We have sun this morning after a week of piercing wind blowing under a gray sky. I hope you will have a fine Sunday, and will see the sun shining

---

[1] On account of her doubts as to Anglicanism.

on the Orwell, and the last yellow leaves of the elms in the park ; for I imagine a park with elms. . . . There is really much more in the ordinary person than meets the eye. I have often been surprised at what very commonplace (seeming) persons can receive and give out if any one gives them the lead, and the " fine gentleman " or fine lady is often at bottom a very simple person, who is really rather dejected for the want of other gifts.

To the Same

ST. LEONARDS-ON-SEA, 18*th November.*

G. C. P. is in a sarcastic vein, but is completely established here, *au premier*, with plenty of books, and all the sun that shines, and a fine sea rolling up just across the road. The only persons I know within reach are —— and my friends at the old convent, but I shall not go to look for any of them. This large gay place, with its broad white pavement and bright shops, and plenty of good-looking people about, is very pleasant after the dark, sticky little Canterbury streets, but I shall go back to-morrow night. I am going to read Montaigne. I like reading after you ; and perhaps his *esprit positif* will be bracing.

To the Same

CANTERBURY, 23*rd November.*

I think that in reading the classic authors it must repay you from every point of view to read slowly and to master the whole idea. I wish that I had had a classical education. It really would not have been thrown away. I should have taken delight in Greek and Latin. . . . I went down with Mr. ——, and we talked over his sermon. 'Twas Browning's *Ben Ezra* that he read at the end. He owned to having felt a little discomfited by an elderly gentleman walking out half-way through the poem. " Didn't go to church to hear Browning," I am sure he will have said.

Extract from Journal

PRECINCTS, 26*th November.*—On the whole the summer and autumn have been wet and cold, but I think that I am less sensitive than I was to the influence of the weather. Partly it is my constant preoccupation of mind that shelters me. . . . I have given up the Institute, the Middle Schools, and the teaching of the Blues. Also I have given up the Epiphany Guild. This has been very painful in many ways . . . but it is done. I continue to go to the Warden's lectures, and the daily service at the Cathedral is dearer to me than ever. I feel an extreme tenderness to all my friends ; every common person seems so dear to me. E. M. has written twice since she knew my intentions. Once very severe, once passionately tender. . . . On Friday evening in last week poor Meredith died after sixty-seven hours of incessant convulsion. I was a long time in the room on Thursday morning. His poor sick wife sat rocking and moaning at the foot of the bed, and Mrs. M—— stood by his head watching him with that intent, firm, experienced look one sees only on the faces of those women who are always assisting at death-beds. No *man* ever has that particular expression. It is the look of the mother, and yet is almost stern, a look such as I imagine the Fates wore, such an intense and *certain* expectation of what must come.

To Miss Mason

CANTERBURY, 29*th November.*

I think the *Flying Leaf* is so good. It begins to fulfil my ideal of a magazine full of what one wants to know and nothing besides. I wish I could embrace you for all you are doing. I have so many things in my mind to say to you. I do say them in my mind, for you are dear to me, and always will be, whatever befalls.

Mr. —— always rather tries one by that way he has of talking all round; he wheels round so many subjects, then he draws his circles closer and closer, and settles down upon himself, and then, if there is time, from that point he may come to you and your affairs, and is very much indeed all there. He is one of those quite truthful and really artless *strong* men who can assume nothing, and can only work just in their own way.

How different from the strong-winged eagle, who dwells on the top of the high rocks, whence he can descry all the dwellers upon earth, and, taking a direct course, tears your soul out of your body before you know where you are. . . .

To Mrs. Deacon

PRECINCTS, 30*th November.*

My dear Mary— . . . Yes. I am busy and ever busier, "as the rapids of life shoot to the fall," but I intend this winter to draw out of it all. There are things I want to do at home. I begin to detest the sight of my bonnet and cloak except as a means of appearing in the Cathedral. Our music is very good, and the sweet music of the Psalms and solemn canticles and anthems hold me more and more. No one else goes but a few cracky persons. I was rather touched to read in Fleury that there was always room in the early churches for *les possédés*, only they were walked out before the Eucharist proper. I often think that I am one of them.—Ever, my dearest Mary, your affectionate   SIBYL HOLLAND.

To Bernard Holland

CANTUAR, *5th December.*

... I am very busy with all sorts of things, chiefly friends, who run after me for one thing or another. As I came out of the Cathedral after evensong this afternoon into the clear twilight, the lovely crescent moon was sinking in the due south, where the sunset still lingered. The crescent looked largely curved, and one could perfectly see the whole disc of the moon "in its arms." To the left the evening star was throbbing quite brilliantly.

Last night they gave Spohr's *Last Judgment* in the Cathedral. I had gone across to the rehearsal, and, sitting at the far end of the unlit nave, listened to the storm of music which represented the multitudinous cries of the souls bidden to depart. Then, after a pause, came the song of the blessed. It is an exquisite piece of music.

To Francis Holland

CANTERBURY, *December.*

I suppose that in all *action* there is that which goes beyond reason, which is *faith*. I doubt whether reason ever forces a man to *action*, however convinced he may be that he has arrived at his conclusion without a flaw in his chain of reasoning. No doubt but that Napoleon had *faith* in his star, and Carlyle in his own power. I wish you would get from the London Library Newman's *Grammar of Assent.* It is not a controversial, hardly a religious book, but it is very explanatory of those questions. . . . I delight in your letters, and shall answer your important one when I can call home my thoughts, which go wheeling and whirling like flights of birds. I think one's imaginations are very like flights of birds.

To the Same

CANTERBURY, 14*th December*

Of one thing I am quite sure, which is, that the more you believe the less you can *argue* for your belief, and that the most complete argument sometimes leaves one without belief. Belief is a venture, and a venture always means action. But belief must be supported by reason, or it degenerates into mere credulity. There comes in the whole question of authority. I always intended to read Sir George Cornwall's book on *Authority.* It is one volume, and is very masterly I have heard. All this is very interesting to me. . . . Why should you put the word *delusion* as interchangable with belief in your letter? Why not say "the man who would produce an effect in the world must first *believe in something,*" instead of "must *find a delusion.*" To suppose that there is nothing to believe in is of all delusions the fatalest. The fool hath said in his heart, "There is no God," and setting aside the eternal question, the fact remains that a man without faith is a man without action. His life-blood, that by which he lives and moves, is sapped. 'Twas unbelief that brought sin and death into the world. 'Tis the enemy's old game. *Hath* God said? Doth *he not know?* Eat and satisfy that which you *do know*—all the lower part of our nature. But it was not for this that *you* were born, nor your fair childhood nourished.

To Rosamond Stephen

CANTERBURY, *Xmas Eve.*

On Saturday night I posted to you a solid sort of bottle to stand on your dressing-table and to hold perfumes, which perhaps you dislike and despise.

But I do not think that the particular lavender water made at Canterbury will displease you, and, if you like it, I will presently send you some more. I wonder what like was the perfume contained in that alabaster box of ointment very precious. One of the Fathers comments upon the passage—says that the fragrance of the ointment has ever since filled the church.

I hope, my dear Rosamond, that in the course of this coming year you will pay us a visit here. It is a very long time since I saw you face to face. If you have any new photographs of yourself or of Dorothea I should like so much to have them. The one that your mother gave me of you many summers ago in a little letterweight is always on my table, but it is fading quite away, and hardly more than a pair of bright eyes looks out of it, and one that I had since has been mislaid. I have looked for it in vain.

Give my love to your mother and to the judge, and believe me, my dearest Rosamond, your affectionate god-mother, SIBYL HOLLAND.

Extracts from Journal

SATURDAY, 8*th December.*—This day dear John Starr died five years ago. Fast in Paradise he is. "O that I once past changing were, fast in thy Paradise where no flower can wither." There he certainly is, the innocent, ingenious mystic soul.

14*th December.*— ... So ends my day, but how little does what I write represent to me the events of the day. The real events are those that go on in my mind and soul. Mr. Field, in his Wednesday sermon, spoke of the dull routine of our lives. This I *never feel*. I am more sensible of movement, change, new and surprising ideas, and a world of possibilities. I am tired often of the effort of keeping pace with myself. I think of a thousand things to say when I only say half a dozen.

Saturday, 15*th December.*—Slight thaw, white fog, very cold. After matins with flowers to Agnes in vestry. Within the Cathedral is another climate, another world—everything so much larger, clearer, and quieter than in the town outside. In spite of three or four days of very hard frost, Chaney has sent down little red roses, large daisies, chrysanthemums, plenty of laurestinus, and, from the greenhouse, carnations, sweet geranium and scarlet, so that there are plenty of flowers about the house. A bunch of pale mauve chrysanthemum and laurestinus and Christmas roses in Lisa's little vase below my pale crucifix. O Jesus, love of heaven and earth! detach me from myself, attach me to Thyself. I will bear the cross, and the cross will bear me, if only, my sweet Jesus, Thou dost sustain both the one and the other.

18*th December.*— . . . To Cathedral. The fog so thick that at a dozen yards' distance one could not perceive anything of the building, only a thick white blurr. Inside all clear and heavenly. The tender lights in Trinity Chapel very beautiful. . . . Fog lifted late at night and the moon shone like silver, streaming over Bell Harry and the great church from end to end, while the white masses of mist lifted themselves and floated over the city wall at the breath of the south-west wind.

Thursday, 20*th December.*— . . . Then to evensong. Anthem, " Thou shalt keep him in perfect peace whose mind is stayed on Thee. The dead men shall live— with my dead shall they arise. Thy dew is as the dew of hills." The lovely sounds flowed round the lofty roofs, and empty sanctuaries, and broken tombs of the princes and great prelates of old time ; but we are still in the dust we made when we tore down the altars and broke the shrines. We have no dew.

The lessons of Isaiah and St. John's Revelations are wonderful. These we have and the ever-blooming Psalms.

Tuesday, 22*nd January.*— . . . Letter from Bernard apropos of our conversation on Sunday night. He advises delay, and says, " It is not as if it were a question of religion or no religion." But it is almost that with me, though I do not like to say so because of casting a reflection on the religion of my family. No one but myself can estimate what it will be to me, at what a conscious risk I shall relinquish the idea, and, as I write, I know that I would rather relinquish my life. If I *were* to die to-night I should die in the Faith but not in the Church.   I shall starve to death where I am.

Tuesday 19*th February.*—All these are the days in which my darling Luce began to be ill three years ago. As long as I breathe this mortal air these sad yearnings must recur. Her beautiful little head, and oval face, and sweet rounded chin, and clear large eyes and splendidly shaped throat are often, always, before me. And her voice so rich, and full, and varied in tone. Oh! my Luce!

IX

LETTERS OF 1889

To Bernard Holland

THE PRECINCTS, 23rd January.

THANK you for letter of Monday evening. I cannot well reply, for I am in the lowest depths of a most violent cold, such as has not seized me for years. I believe that one's declining strength, while it makes one less subject or offers less material to these ravaging disorders, yet, if one once succumbs, makes it much more difficult to eject them, and I have quite gone under this time, but "*on est heureux quand on sort de la santé pour entrer dans la sagesse.*"

All that you say is good and sound, but of course no one but myself can estimate the loss and pain of such a move as that we were speaking of. I have waited a long time, and I shall wait again, but I have not so very much time left.

I do not at all think that every religious emotion or attraction comes from God. There is a great deal of self mixed up in all these human determinations. But this is the one subject about which I have really thought and read and prayed, and it is difficult for me to turn back upon myself and undo what is done. But I cannot write about it, though I am glad to have heard from you, and you are always kind and generous to me. The path to the Church of Rome is an old, well-worn way, and my case is that of many others. I am under no delusion. I don't expect to be made more good *malgré moi*, or to be enchanted with the services or with the persons I should meet over there. They are the reverse of attractive to me. I should go on in a dry way, but I should find what I sought.

To the Same

THE PRECINCTS, *13th February.*

Yesterday Agnes and I drove to Godmersham ; it was beautiful and lonely as ever, a few white snowdrops here and there on the three graves, and a cluster of deep purple violets at the foot of the old rose tree. The cistus green and vigorous against the wall. The hill and park were white with the withered, bent grass, but the river, brimming and flowing rapidly against the due east wind, was sapphire blue in the westering sun. The secular yews were covered with their little powdery blossom. The place is perfect in itself and whole like a pearl ; and so was the child we laid in its earth.

To Miss Mason

CANTUAR, *20th February.*

I have signed my unworthy name with the sense that those that are first shall be last. But there it is. . . . It is all the plotting and planning for other people that makes your busy head ache.

When you get an interval let me know that you are

coming down to Canterbury to laugh and sigh a little with me. Mild March days, such as sometimes are given, are pleasant enough in these quiet old places. I wish that I were a quiet old lady to watch them. I *am* to all appearances. Well, good-bye for the moment, *chère rachetée de mon Dieu.*

To the Same

THE PRECINCTS, CANTERBURY, 12*th March.*

. . . I think that in the end Mrs. —— will be left supreme, will reign for a moment, and then will come home, and the whole project, with all the aims and hopes and fears and prayers of the human souls concerned in it, will go into the great waste-paper basket of our day.

I wish that the father, who lives only for Christ, and who has nothing, and clings to nothing, nor fears to lose anything, but possesses his soul in patience, would write a word of warning to the one and of comfort to the other. Mrs. —— will be left to settle down upon her lees, while the other woman will be emptied from vessel to vessel till she becomes the pure wine of God. I cannot write to him, because I have displeased him, and there it is.

Whenever you can come here you will be welcome.

To the Same

THE PRECINCTS, CANTERBURY, 20*th March.*

. . . But what I want to say to you is this. You must not suppose that because I managed to talk cheerfully to you the state of things in which I find myself is not always very painful and often almost unbearably so. To think otherwise would be misleading from several points of view. I assure you that it is hardly possible to imagine the sort of death that it is, and one of the peculiar anguishes that one cannot say a word *naturally* about it even to those with whom one is intimate, or whom one loves (as I love you) without being intimate. The question so naturally arises, If it is so painful why do you do it? and one has no answer that one can give without putting into words the very inmost feelings of one's heart, that belong indeed to God only. I do not want you to reply to this. I feel that it is hard on you that I should write it. Perhaps *really* I ought never to have cherished your friendship under the circumstances. However, there it is. I intended no malice. God bless you, my dear, and order all your days in His peace.

To Miss Arnold-Forster

CANTERBURY, 21*st March*.

... Your letter has been too long unanswered. It has been every day since going about with me in my little letter and key bag, and I have a hundred times been reminded of you by it. All that you say about marriage is gospel truth. Marriage is ordained of God, and is so natural, and the family life which it brings about is so complete and beautiful, that to those who renounce it, or miss it, Christ had to make the splendid promises which the Evangelists record. . . . You sound such a nice little party of all ages and one heart and mind. I wish I could fly along the coast and look in upon you. I am rather rheumatic

too, and rather tired of creeping in and out round
about these old stones. The rooks and jackdaws do
the same thing over my head, but they fly in the blue
while I must creep in the damp below.

To Bernard Holland

THE PRECINCTS, 23rd *March*.

Yesterday I went to Harbledown. The March air
blew very sweet round the high ground and purpling
woods. The young trees look well, the old ones ill and
mossy. I think we should have cleared more of these
elderly creatures away. Old Potts was cutting and
building and had been planting. These are actions
which a human being can wage however old and trembling he may be.

. . . Yesterday was the anniversary of my mother's
death. How well I remember passing you as we went
up the long hill that clear windy March day. You are
not to feel grief when you see me laid in the earth—
but gladness that all is well over.

To the Same

PRECINCTS, 25th *March*.

It was singular that you should have met Mr. ——
there, for the first time after a long interval. By devious
roads God calls whom he will. Lord L.'s idea was to
bring up his beloved daughter as a philosopher, but he
rough-hewed his end. Yes, both yesterday and to-day
have been the spring in the kingdom,[1] and I have felt
almost a horror of the old stones and bones which
survive so many springs both in the actual world and

---
[1] Kingdom of Kent.

in the souls of men. We have primroses and violets from the Lodge, and there will be plenty by the time you return.

Extracts from Journal

5th March.— . . . The bells to-night seemed to ring in my heart, and I could hardly bear the wind-borne melody.

Sunday, 24th March.—A lovely day, but such a storm in my soul, of remembrance and grief and longing for the one and only consolation. Little Kathleen's baptism in St. George's Church. She is baptized into nothing less than the great Catholic Church of the West.

Thursday, 4th April.— After matins with the Sheppards in library. Helped to look out the Dirige Psalm, etc. Said to Mrs. Sheppard that I meant to die in *that* Church. Dr. Sheppard said, " Well, that is a continuous Church, and the mediæval religion has much against it." She said nothing.

Monday, 9th April.—Talked with Dr. Sheppard in the library till nearly 1 P.M. He is very kind, and has a large tender heart, full of the very dew of kindness, under his rough old body and face. But his religion has no symbols, no system, nothing but the sense of the power and love of the Father. This is the religion of the scientific man. But I feel that the man is dear to Jesus.

To Miss Mason

THE PRECINCTS, CANTERBURY, 5*th April.*

. . . Edith's letter is too pretty to burn. I have not the heart to do it. I read to the end twice through and send it back to you; it breathes of youth and spring, and of the pretty country where it was written, and which I know so well. I know the firwoods and the deep paths and whortleberry-covered hill, and the wide aerial plain, but not St. Martin's, unless that is the Christian name of my cousin John Shearm's church at Holmbury. Do you know those places? Albury, with its terraced yew-hedged garden and long bowling-green and stone fountain at the top, and the "silent pool" full of great blue carp, and Wotton, John Evelyn's home, with its little gray church and hanging beechwoods. I should like to go there with you.

To Francis Holland

CANTERBURY, 15*th April.*

I sent off your garments this morning, my darling boy. Fair fall your dear feet in the "sweet green fields of Wales," as Matthew Arnold calls them somewhere. —— is gone to-day to ——'s funeral. Certainly her sweet soul is in Paradise.

To the Same

CANTERBURY, *Easter Eve,* 20*th April.*

I am writing before breakfast, the mild south wind blowing across the oaks, and all the vanes of Bell Harry pointing to Godmersham. I am sure that you are enjoying Wales. I am still disappointed that you don't go to St. David's, and so is the Savant. He says that we shall make an expedition there when Parliament is up—an antiquarian expedition. Here, we had yesterday a most perfect day. . . . I have been reading again Hook's account of the settlement of the English Church under Parker and Elizabeth, and I laugh aloud at the notion that I am at all bound by the arrangements made by Parker, Leicester, Bacon, and Elizabeth. The clergy are, but the laity are not. The case for me remains as I have ever put it to myself, that I doubt whether a wife has a moral right to do as I proposed. Yet, if she has not, if in things spiritual also she is one with her husband, it would be difficult to disprove what has been in some places alleged, *i.e.* that the woman is but the complement of the man, and has not, properly speaking, a soul of her own to save, and one or two expressions of the Apostle somewhat fall in with this. But I am not writing very seriously—do not suppose it.

To the Same

CANTERBURY, 2nd *May*.

Prince Kugo has sailed back to Japan, by doctor's order. What a misguided expedition for him it has been! and what a mercy that the poor child did not die in London. Where and how are the bodies buried of these gentle Pagans who die in our great roaring mill? Did you read about Father Joseph Damien and the lepers? Another priest and two or three sisters of charity have gone to supply his place and carry on his work. This sort of thing is the glory of the Church of Christ. It is the standard held up and handed from one to another down the ages.

To Mrs. Deacon

THE PRECINCTS, *2nd May.*

My dearest Mary—Your note made me weep. I wish to Heaven that I were on your lawn, and could see that flush of blue under the great trees on the rising ground opposite the verandah. I always did so love your house and everything in and about it. We were always at Fox Holm in May, "in the sweet spring days, with whitening hedges and uncrumpling fern, and bluebells trembling in the forest ways," as your own dear poet sang.[1] He is gone, but what a joy and gift it is to have had him, and to remember him in all the pleasant places.

Agnes is away at this moment. If you are so good as to give her a teapot it will be a most good present —nothing could be better—a plain prosaic pot. I believe that William Bolton has accepted, or is on the point of accepting, a small benefice at the Land's End. As far as the east is from the west, so far will be set my girl from me. The Bishop of Truro wants him to come into that diocese, and this wish, several times reiterated, seems to constitute a sort of "call," so that one has little to say, and perhaps for a few years they may have a pleasant scrambling life in that remote place, contending with the Wesleyans, and within sound of the thundering Atlantic. If he accepts St. Sythney they will marry latish in June.

Michael goes to Canada in August with Gerald Spring Rice. I should like you to know Michael. There is a sort of charm about him. He is the most active, simple, humorous, and altogether engaging

[1] Matthew Arnold.

creature of eighteen. It is almost intolerable to me to think of parting with him, but I suppose it will come, as sure as sunset. . . . Give my best love to dear Mr. Deacon, and believe me, my dearest Mary, for ever your most affectionate friend, SIBYL HOLLAND.

To Miss Mason

THE PRECINCTS, 6*th May.*

I can think of nothing but Scott Holland's lectures, and three times this blessed day I have read them through, twice to myself and now again out loud to Mr. Holland and Agnes, and this has taken so long that now it is post time. I like them better than anything of his that I have ever heard or read. I think them quite extraordinary. He goes to the very root of the matter; no wonder that as he spoke he sighed.

Are you vexed about——? The thought that perhaps you are a little downcast makes me long to have you in my arms.

To the Same

CANTERBURY, 7*th May.*

Stupid of me not to have sent back Mrs. N. Here she is, a feeble drop of apology in a whole sea of misunderstandings and misrepresentations. But, as you say, it don't signify at all; it has no meaning whatever. Yet Mrs. N. is a dear sort of woman. However, I can think of nothing but first principles with Scott Holland. I cannot cease reading those lectures. I got up this morning and read them through again. They are a great deal to me. I wonder what they are to other people. Scott is all on fire and can penetrate. To teach like this is certainly to please the Master.

To the Same

THE PRECINCTS, 10th May.

Dear me, or dio mi, which it is and means, is a very sufficient expression with which to close a conversation on things in general. What can you say more, or less? The Grahamstown letter is very pretty and interesting, but I am glad that you are not abroad. There are so many things that are against our missionary work that I hope you will not go to Persia. I hope that you will go nowhere where Father Black does not himself send you.

I am still under the influence of Scott's lectures. I observed the added fulness of the fourth lecture. I suppose that what makes the form in which a thing is put so important is that in no other way can that which underlies be expressed; it is the essential for us, the soul of the matter, Dio mi!!

We have had visitors all the week and begin again to-morrow with five young men in the house till Monday. But young men are never the least trouble. I don't mind how many mothers' sons I have about. Apropos of young men, will you carefully for me thank Father Black for his kindness about Michael, who is the youngest of young men; and also, if you think of it, will you say that Lingard, the R. C. historian, wrote a treatise in which he quite passionately defended Matt. Parker's ordination? Also Charles Butler and Canon Tierney, who are distinguished R. C. writers. Have you ever read Stubbs' letter to a Russian "On the Apostolical Succession in the Church of England?" I wish it were published separately.

But only say this if conversation flags. Break off no good talk for this purpose.

I wish to Heaven, Agnes mi, that you were settled. Your projects make my blood run warm, as an old French friend said to me yesterday.

My Agnes marries on the 29th June.

To Bernard Holland

THE PRECINCTS, *21st May.*

We are having very good May weather on the whole. On Saturday afternoon Aunt Cathy and I drove over to Godmersham, rolling swiftly along the road in the Nackington carriage, lent me in the owner's absence. Aunt Cathy had not been there since 1886. She is very much pleased with everything, and indeed nothing could look more restful and lovely than the place. The three little graves so trim and smooth, the roses in bloom, the cistus in bud, and the thick grass in the rest of the churchyard full of flowers. Margaret had twisted up for me the loveliest wreath imaginable of lilies, large and small, with tender long sprays of copper beech. She is a dear, faithful girl, and I really love her.

I like your figure of the barbarian brilliant tide slowly flowing in. Our arrangement for the London season is very good. How lapped in luxury and prosperity many of them are, and how much in danger of what dear Gordon calls " settling down upon one's lees! " How some souls, on the other hand, are, by inward and outward events, emptied from vessel to vessel until they become the pure wine of God! The former rear a fine race for their country—the latter bring forth the ideas by which men live.

Yesterday we entertained eighteen pilgrims from Beckenham. They arrived at twelve and went away at six. Aunt Cathy and Uncle Robert stay till Thursday. Their visit is a great pleasure for me. The Warden preached last Sunday evening in the Cathedral and celebrated Father Joseph Damien of the lepers.

To Francis Holland

CANTERBURY, 1st June.

It is such a lovely morning, Francesco mi. On such a day years and years ago, my father would walk about on the lawn of Godmersham murmuring, " This morn is merry June I trow, the rose is budding fain," etc. I remember hearing him then and often on after June mornings and thinking the words very pretty. In October also, he would mutter from Coleridge, " The grapes upon the Vicar's wall were ripe as ripe could be." He was a great quoter, as I am disposed to be, but I always feel that to make quotations is not the part of a woman. A quotation has a tendency to stop conversation, whereas it is the woman's part by subtle means to promote it. ―――― is here till Monday—a most innocent intelligence and gentle generous heart under a somewhat awkward though pleasing exterior. She is quite a wild-flower blooming in the long rows of the south-west.

To Bernard Holland

HARBLEDOWN, 17th June.

I was so pleased with your charming letter describing Cobham.[1] Edward Bouverie writes that it is "a divinely beautiful place," and he hopes that you

---

[1] Lord Darnley's house, near Rochester.

enjoyed it as he did. I am sure that you did, for you have the faculty of seeing, which is also a divine faculty. We have a cold east wind this evening, and a clear sunset, and a bright wood fire. We have plenty of roses; let me hear if you would like some; and our first dish of strawberries this evening. . . . Sophy and Frank went to Hales Place yesterday, Sunday afternoon, to see the French play acted by the boys for their parents and friends. One boy sang beautifully and Père du Lac kissed him on both cheeks after the play was over. It was all very pretty and graceful. I am reading Von Sybel[1] and find it of absorbing interest.

To Francis Holland

THE LODGE, 20th June.

Agnes is in London. Papa also; and I am, as I shall often be, alone in the midst of the house and garden. I look into your little room, into Bernard's, into Agnes's — all is orderly arranged, and the "summer wind fills the silent house." Two men are mowing in the apple orchard and among the young cherry trees. I should feel as still as everything around me were not my heart and ears filled with the coming sounds of next week. But "come what may, Time and the hour run through the roughest day," and will run me through Saturday, June 29th.[2]

To the Same

THE LODGE, 12th July.

. . . I do not, however, think so much of Hamlet's scepticism, because it was that of a very young man

---

[1] *History of the French Revolution.*
[2] The day of her daughter's marriage.

whose intellect rather overbalanced his character. Besides, Hamlet is so lacking in the cheerful present moment and practical turn which is natural to the real sceptic. I don't believe that Shakespeare himself was a sceptic, but he lived in a time when it must have been very difficult to belong heartily to any outward form of religion. But now, Frank, why should you hate to go to a ball at that princely and hospitable house? You *must* go, and tell me all about it afterwards. I shall be very vexed if you do not. As you love Shakespeare so much you ought, like him, to be cheerful and to like to see and observe all sorts and conditions of men.

To Bernard Holland

THE LODGE, *12th July.*

The weather *is* trying. The south wind, a little moist with rain, blows against our slope which seems to send back the heat into the house. There is a languor like that of Rome in September. Yesterday the sun was excessively hot, and yet there was now and then a little misty rain. Last night it rained for some hours. The morning is all glorious again. The hops are in ecstasy at the weather, and the little rich hollow of our high valley is overflowing with the dark stream of trellised leaves. The yaffells also highly approve of the warm moistening of their hunting-grounds, and I see their strong squat gaily painted shapes at early dawn, digging with a sort of fury in the garden banks, while the blackbirds and starlings work gaily in the Bigareau, that forlorn hope of the orchards towards the north. What years the birds of God have pillaged that old tree! I have spent some quiet evenings gathering currants with the maids in the Potager till the brilliant light faded on the elms, and the moon shone high in the south, and the colours of berries and leaves become one. There is all night a belt of light in the north-west, which remains till the wide spaces of the east pale and brighten. I do not mind being alone. When I am alone you all seem to be with me again. When you are all here I look in vain for two sweet faces. Besides, I am well accustomed to it. What innumerable summer nights, when you were little or at school, have I wandered about the fields and woods at Fox Holm; what early mornings and what quiet late afternoons!

On Wednesday evening I took a walk in the woods. The silence of the open high common was immense; not a note or a rustle, nor did a leaf stir of the strong growing copse. I came back by the path that turns down to the brooklet, and up through the dark "tonnelle" to the cart track and right-of-way.

To the Same

THE LODGE, 16th July.

What charming letters you send me, my dearest Ber! I am so glad that you always go on preferring Kent to Surrey; but I am not sorry that you were reared in Surrey. Yesterday I provoked St. Swithin by forgetting his day and attempting a *fête champêtre* of Middle School girls and mistresses. The rain fell hard on the large tables spread on the lawn, and all was hurry and confusion, wet umbrellas and piles of mackintoshes. In the midst —— arrived and roamed about gloomily seeing no prospect of dinner, until Michael conveyed provisions to the greenhouse, where I presently saw ——'s old back bowed over plate and bottle. He worries me in my present mood, and so does the stream of Canterbury people who make their way up to ask how Agnes is, and if I do not feel dull without her.[1] If I could only be out of sight and out of mind for a little while I should think myself happy ; as it is I feel worn interiorly. . . . I wish I were a man for six months, both for my sake and for yours. The worst of being a woman is that one must always act in character, or one makes oneself ridiculous.

To Francis Holland

THE LODGE, 21*st July.*

Friday was a lovely day here and I drove with Mick after an early cup to call on Mrs. D——, who lives in a pretty house just off the lane that runs round to the right when one gets to the bottom of Herne Hill. He was not at home, nor she either, but there was a homely civility in the manner of the waggoner who opened the gate for us, and the butler who answered the bell, which betokens well for the character of their master and mistress. The view of the Faversham flats, all bathed in a haze of western sunshine, was beautiful as we came down the hill, and so was the Canterbury side as we faced it on our return—Bell Harry eyeing us sternly over the woods, and the noble old road with its steep descents making straight for it. We had hardly been back at the Lodge a quarter of an hour when Micky brought round Barnes caparisoned with a pack-saddle, on which he persuaded me to mount, and we took our way across the parklet, through "Frank's Gate," over the common and into the

---

[1] Her daughter Agnes had married and departed from Kent at the end of June.

darker woods where the heather is so high, across the cut down spaces where the lily buds are, sharp down to the little runlet, and up through the very dark arched " tonnelle " to the main cart road, and so to the right-of-way stile, where I got off, and Michael rode Barnes down Love Shaws and by the road home.

To Bernard Holland

THE LODGE, 25*th July*.

Dorothy and Margaret came to breakfast on Tuesday and stayed till 1 P.M. Many messages to you from the former of an involved and dubious meaning, but I have forgot 'em all.

There is a perpetual roaring in the elms—'tis the south-west wind at play. He is tossing many a league of green branches, all that is left of the little wild wood of Fox Holm included. How often in the long summer days there I have shut my eyes and wished it were the sea rushing up. I am glad that Agnes can see the Atlantic when she will. That is a great thing in one's everyday life. One wants something great and continuous. The Sea, the Mountains, or the Catholic Church.

To Francis Holland

THE LODGE, 1*st August*.

It is really hot this week. As Shelley says, writing on a summer afternoon many years ago, " The warm wind fills the silent house." So it does to-day. The great elms do not cease to wave and rustle sleepily, and the perfume of the stocks and heliotrope comes in great puffs across the lawn.

To Bernard Holland

THE LODGE, *1st August*.

Thanks for your charming letter. I *will* go to Bruges some day if I live much longer. I expect Mr. Raleigh with you on Saturday. Bring me Fitzgerald.

We are having a fine sun. The hops spread themselves splendidly in it from end to end of the summer day. . . . I like the leisure of my life here, and if I did not often feel so unwell I could make some use of it. J'ai trop avalé de larmes ; it is better to shed them. Agnes is extremely happy and this makes me very happy. I must read you her letters when you come here.

Lisa Rawlinson is come out of her convent to take care of her father for a month while her mother is abroad. She is robed in black with poke bonnet and black veil, but cheerful as ever. Nor did I see, in 1885, when she and Luce and Agnes were so much together, what would be their separate destinies. One in heaven ; one in earth ; one 'twixt heaven and earth.

To the Same

HARBLEDOWN, *9th August*.

Your father is enjoying himself moderately in *la belle France*, and much admires the Eiffel Tower and the audacity of its conception. He says that it is both graceful and stupendous. "Stupendious" Evelyn would have said, which is indeed a more expressive word.

Yesterday, an hour before sunset, Michael and I

drove to Bigbury Camp. There is a fine new cherry orchard west of Denstead, in that sandy rough meadow that makes the approach to the fish ponds, and the double staking and straw wisping of the young trees seems a very good plan. The wheat is all in shock under the wood, and the hops in sheltered places in full bloom. The currant bushes are all stripped and tied neatly up. The plums ripening to the full. Stout brown women with sturdy babes in waggons were making their way home to the old doors through all the bye-paths. Beer had lately been transported to the Hatch as we could see by the traces of Finn.

From the camp, where our appearance disturbed 200 rabbits feeding under the sky, the prospect was enough to make a Kentish breast burst with exultation. When I could raise my eyes from the contemplation of the tracts of fruit, wheat, hops, and clover, there was the line of the Ramsgate cliffs, the mill beyond Adisham, the wide circling woods almost touching us at the camp foot, and Michael, young and alert, his slight figure and charming curled head against the pure evening sky. I find myself always looking at him, knowing how soon the Atlantic will lie between him and his home.

To Francis Holland

THE LODGE, *15th August.*

Mick's last two days were dull and wet, but he was sunshiny enough and went off in good spirits. We shall all miss him—I most of all. All yesterday, after he was gone, I kept expecting to see Agnes or Lucy come in. It was quite an illusion. I was alone and wept alone, but that is best. If any one had been here

I could not have wept. I have swallowed too many tears—it is much better to shed them—and I am quite content with everything and every one but myself.

To Bernard Holland

THE LODGE, *27th August.*

Last night I dreamed of you and of Lucy very vividly.

We have a lovely still morning to-day, but yesterday storms of rain assaulted the hop-pickers, driving them here and there. This morning they have cheerfully resumed the attack on the poles, which are garlanded with the finest hops imaginable. Mr. and Mrs. Stickles spent the day here on Saturday. To-day Pugh and his sons come, and to-morrow Charlie Goulden and his mamma. Such are my humble but worthy guests. . . . Things go on here precisely in due season. Adams is making large quantities of plum jam. Chaney is on a ladder getting the keeping apples; the squirrel scampers across the lawn and scratches up the wooden posts of the steps; a flight of young martens sits along the garden rail, learning to fly and fed incessantly by anxious swift-darting parents. A stoat has just lept from one flower bed to another and galloped up into the meadow, and the yaffels are tapping in the elms and laughing at their own jokes. The village row is silent as the desert, nor does Harry Hearn stir within the Plough. All these things Luce saw and noted three years ago in these very days, and drew in the strong air laden with the sharp fragrance of the hop-oasts.

To Francis Holland

THE LODGE, 27th August.

On Sunday, when we were walking through the fruit and hop gardens, talking of one thing and another, I ought perhaps to have told you that I had a day or two before, with your father's knowledge, taken the irrevocable step and separated myself from the Anglican communion. But I trembled—and do tremble lest any shadow should come between me and the child who is so unspeakably dear to me. It is a strange thing to fear one's children, but I do. If you can write to me that you shall always love me as well as ever, pray do —any way write me something kind. I have suffered *much* and there is plenty more to suffer. The hardest thing of all to bear is the thought of your father. No words can express how kind and generous he has been to me. Certainly God will bless him for his mercy and forbearance in my regard, and all the rest of my life shall be devoted to show my gratitude.

To Agnes Bolton

THE LODGE, 9th September.

I will not say much more about the end of your letter, my darling girl, but that I think what you feel is natural. My share is not all "joy" by any means. There is a great and irreparable loss on all sides but one, and I do not look upon you as you look on the dissenters. This may be illogical, but it remains a fact. I am not conscious of much difference in feeling towards the Anglican Church from that which I have always had ; that is to say, a feeling of doubt and uncertainty.

You forget that all I hold dear remain in her communion. Take this trouble about me, and wrap it up in a neat little parcel, and lay it down at the feet of our Lord, and leave it there. His Mother will smile if she sees you. There is no *sin*, it is only a tangle; don't try to unravel it, pack it up. The will of God for you, and for His poor at St. Sithney, is as clear as the light of this lovely harvest day. If He wills anything else, He will show you. I have the most perfect and quiet trust in this. I always see, in my mind's eye, you and Luce walking towards the light.

I believe the (Burgate) music is simply awful. Oh that you and I were together listening to the smooth rise and fall of the Cathedral Psalms, as in the days that were. Well, we have *had* them. Tout passe. Dieu ne change point.

To the Lady Knutsford

BATH, *17th September.*

It was very kind of you to write to me. . . . My own feeling with regard to my friends is one of immense tenderness, and this is natural enough when I reflect that I have given them a right to withdraw their trust and kindness, while, if I lose them, I have nothing to put in their stead, but must go bare and poor all my days. So your note brought me great balm and comfort, and, while I read it, tears of love and gratitude flowed. . . . We have heard nothing of dear Meta's illness. She was looking so sweet and well in June, but that seems a long while ago now. . . . Farewell, my dear, kindest Margaret. I *am* grateful to you. I will be your bedeswoman from this time forward, and will pray for you and yours by every thread and channel that the old religion affords, and they are many.

To Bernard Holland

BATH, 18*th September.*

I quite see why old Landor was so fond of Bath. It *is* like Florence, seen from the high ground. Yesterday I took a drive, selecting from the stand an aged driver, who looked as if he was an ancient old Bathonian, and garrulous. So we set off, I telling him that I wanted to see all the fine views. " Oo ay, I'm your man for that job"; and so he was. I was most of all pleased with the beautiful view behind Prior Park (a great Benedictine house which stands above the city, well backed with woods) over towards the Wiltshire Downs, about twenty miles of beautiful country ; then the bare hills, and the afternoon sun shining on the great white horse cut out on the steep slope of Westbury Down. "As nigh like a horse as nigh can be, and a man can stand in the eye of him," said my driver. . . .

. . . I am beginning to have a number of letters on the subject of my step—*all* very affectionate, but in various stages of dismay. Aunt Margaret, however, has written most sweetly and kindly, and I shall ever be grateful to her. . . . G. C. P., as I expected, is the severe friend ; however, he sent me his love, but he says that it is every way "a serious wrong," and I feel this condemnation very much, because I am so long accustomed to take his standard of things.

To the Same

BATH, 26*th September.*

Frank and I have been all day at Bristol, and I find your charming letter on my return. Bristol is a horrid place, but Bath is beautiful, and I shall be so glad to see you here on Saturday. I can imagine that you were sorry to leave the yacht. Cette vie intime, nursed on the breast of the wild waters, and under the wide sky, has a charm. You and ——— will always remember it with pleasure. I was so happy in that way one year at Freshwater, when H. C. spent five or six weeks with us, and devoted himself to my amusement. I think that a real friend is a perfect treasure in family life. Anything, a place, a person that a whole family agree to love, extends at once and doubles and trebles that by which men live.

To the Same

ST. SITHNEY, HELSTON, 8*th October.*

I came here on Thursday *via* Exeter, where I slept one night. Evensong was beginning as Frank and I entered the Cathedral, and I was well pleased to hear again the sweet, solemn chaunts resounding. It is a noble church, and seemed particularly rich in interest, both ancient and modern. Afterwards I went to look for the Roman Catholic church, which was not far to seek. It is large and coldish and brand new, compared with the Cathedral nothing of interest having, yet, compared again, possessing all things. Next day Frank and I parted company, and I came on here—a pretty journey of six hours, the line running for some distance between the red cliffs and the shining sea. Villas scattered about, and plenty of ilex, arbutus, myrtles, and fuchsias, like, in a humble degree, the growth of lovely Sestri. For the last two hours and a half the country is barren enough. I changed at Gwinear Road, and perceived the fineness and delicacy of the air. I alighted at Helston, and drove up here. . . . From the churchyard the country rolls in all directions but one towards the sea, the fine glittering line of which one perceives from all the hills. We took a charming drive on Saturday, and walked for a mile or so along the green edge of the cliff, and watched the Atlantic dash on the rocks below, and run up into the hollow murmuring passages. The little fields, with banks and walls and hedges, deep lanes and good wide roads, remind me of Guernsey, but the immediate coast is nothing so fine. Will seems to be preaching in all directions. I heard him on Sunday night. He is quite remarkably good; and this greatly because he founds and grounds himself upon the Fathers. I gave him the Oxford translation two years ago, and he is always reading therein for his sermon. Then he has advantages of voice, and quiet yet rather moved and moving manner.

To Francis Holland

ST. SITHNEY VICARAGE, 11*th October*.

My dear Hobbist—What a silence since we parted at Exeter, the Lady of the West! You will be vexed to hear that I have not resumed the philosopher of Malmesbury; but I have not lost time, for I have well digested what we read together, and it has never been long out of my thoughts. . . . Agnes seems very content in her little house up on this wind-swept hill. From the churchyard one looks upon a country rolling in three directions towards the sea, the fine glimmering line of which marks the horizon. Yesterday she and I made our way to a charming sheltered bay, where we sat in a summer sun and watched the great clear waves break upon the rocks, and run up into the hollow murmuring passages. The hedges are loaded with blackberries, the air fine and mild as milk; stone cottages, narrow lanes with stone banks, and abundant growth and small divided pastures make a country not unlike Guernsey.

To Bernard Holland

CHELTENHAM, *16th October.*

I came here yesterday *via* Plymouth and Bristol. The first ten miles along the pretty coloured lanes and rocky slopes, as far as Camborne, in the country diligence. In all, it took me eleven hours and a half from Agnes's door to this. I left her and Will standing in the road by Jordan's cottage; the old woman watching the little parting from her old door. Good, tall Trevithen, the gardening man, with his barrow emptied of my box and bag, and all wrapt in the light, the blessed light, of the clinging October mist. A mist in my eyes too, and in Agnes's, but none in Will Bolton's, as he caught her hand from mine, and bid me a cheery farewell.

To-morrow I sleep, if I still wake, at 18 Queen's Gate; next day I hope to return to Canterbury. You are quite right in supposing that I do not wish anything but good to the Church of England, bless her! I shall never enter into any plot to her disadvantage. I was very much struck by Charles Gore's speech.

All you say on the subject interests me much, but I cannot put what I should like to say in a letter.

Coming back by road from Penzance one Monday, a violent demagogue entered the vehicle in the shape of the postmaster of Marazion. He went on furiously haranguing the universe from the moment the omnibus moved. I felt much interested, and presently struck in, upon which he darted to my side, and we talked incessantly, till I clambered out at the stone stile nearest St. Sithney vicarage, when we shook hands, congratulated one another, and parted.

He was a Devonshire man, with a private grievance; this was the low lying original fire to which he added all the other fuel; and in revenge for which he would pull down Church, and Crown, and Aristocracy.

To Miss Mason

HARBLEDOWN LODGE, *23rd October.*

Pleased am I to see your handwriting again, and to have your word for it that you are not too much scandalised to love me.

I am very glad that you wrote first. You see I must leave it to my friends to decide whether or no they go on or leave off. I have made a sort of ending, and I have no right also to make a beginning, but I shall correspond exactly to what their behaviour announces. If you had never written to me again, I should have perfectly justified you in the depths of my mind. As you have written again I take you as a new and perfect gift, and shall ever treasure you. Perhaps you will come some day to see me. If you do not, will not, I shall look for you in Red Lion Square when I go to London; but that may be months and months to come. I have got yet to settle *down*, and go *through*, and tide *over*, and put *up* with, and be put up *with* ; in short, to use up all the prepositions, with all the uncomfortable verbs in the language (or are they adverbs?)

And it is all more solid and serious and close to me than I can express.

I feel the greatest possible interest in the Guild affairs, and anything of any kind that you can tell me I shall be always glad to know, or about yourself, or Father Black, only it seems an impertinence to ask.

To Mrs. Deacon

HARBLEDOWN LODGE, 24*th October.*

My dearest Mary—Will you for the sake of past Octobers send me a bundle of plants of the St. John's wort that grows in and under your hedge? I cannot get it about here. Any scrappy pieces will do, pulled up anyhow. It is sure to grow.

Mary! what have I not gone through, and made other people go through! What a war and enterprise at my age, with no strength left in me! What a risk of both worlds, and loss of one! And what thorny, solitary paths ahead! It does not bear thinking of, much less writing about.

It is such a comfort to know that *church* matters were never the platform on which I sat with you, but love, joy, peace, and all the other heavenly and healing gifts of God ; blessed for ever be His holy name— and love of children, and birds, and bluebells, and purple commons, and dim autumn woods, and cheerful fires, and dear poor good people, and hymns in Hatchford Church, and the Poet with all that belonged to him. These things were where we sat, and sit, together. Bernard was at Fox Warren Sunday week and wrote that the woods and lanes were lovely to see. I am often there in spirit, and see you in all the old places. Do not exorcise me. I am a harmless ghost.—Your ever affectionate SIBYL HOLLAND.

To Miss Mason

CANTERBURY, 10*th November*.

... Your affectionate note pleased me, because it was so affectionate. I am happy in having a few good extravagant friends, and really it does me good at this moment to be a little cosseted, because of the painful weaning from the breasts of the Anglican Church. I hear as I write the deep hum of the organ beginning the Magnificat. After a gray morning a splendid broad sunshine bathes the great church from the west tower to Beckett's Crown. Miss D. is walking with the Canon, Fanny Macrae is lying on a small portion of the great sofa with eyes closed, and I am writing to you, dear Agnes Mason, dear servant of Christ, chère rachetée de mon Dieu. You who really spend yourself and are spent for the souls of others.

I am glad that we went out together into that good sunshine on Thursday; 'twas better than creeping about these ancient enclosed places with their past and thrice buried past, and melancholy and confusing shadows and sounds. What a phantom has the Dean often seemed to me! and yet how dear he is as part of things which have gone to make up my life. Well, farewell, and God preserve you.

To Francis Holland

CANTERBURY, 10*th November.*

From Canterbury to Rome is a far cry, but what a traffic of pilgrims used to go between this Metropolitical city and the "limina apostolorum S. Petri et Pauli." I was reading yesterday the adventures of William of Moreton on his way to Rome (the chronicler calls him romer Duboricam). He went over the Alps by Barzi, and was robbed at Placentia. His business was to see about the canonisation of Thomas à Becket in the name of the brethren of Canterbury—they being ignorant that the Pope had already settled it. I wish I were with you. Canterbury is something of a purgatorio just now, but that is as it should be, because through purgatory I may emerge into light and refreshment and rest. Old Mrs. McQueen has come to an end— a quiet end, full of years and full of charity. . . . The house is full of roses and chrysanthemums from the Lodge—a third bloom of roses. The air is mild as milk, so that fires seem too much and I long to be somewhere on the top of a hill.

To Miss Arnold-Forster

CANTERBURY, 11*th November.*

. . Please do not think of coming on Thursday, if you can only come to lunch. It will make me very uneasy and may make you very unwell. It is not worth while, dear, kind and faithful little friend. We shall meet again some time in *hac valle lachrymarum*. If you cannot come to me next time you are in the south I will come up to London to you. . . . Let go the Canterbury plan and, if you can weave another, throw one end of the thread to me by means of a post-card.

To Francis Hollana

CANTERBURY, 12*th November*.

... I have often in Memoirs met with the nuns of Trinità de Monte, and they are always as you describe them. I daresay if you went every day to call on them they would be quite pleased. That is their *way*. Every order has its own peculiar way of behaving—just as an individual has. An Order is like a person who does not die but goes on. The first duty of a novice is to imbue himself with the spirit of the founder. The more thoroughly he does this the better a religious he is. ... Please remark the statue of Sophocles in the Lateran Museum—I thought it so wonderful. So is the head of the young Augustus in the Vatican and, among the pictures, that room which contains the Transfiguration of Raphael and Domenicho's last Communion of St. Jerome. But the Sistine Chapel pleased me beyond all things. Everything of Michael Angelo's is beyond all others in power of conception. ... It is such a pleasure to have your letters—almost as sweet as if I were with you in Rome, but the bare thought of what that would be brings tears into my eyes.

To Miss Mason

CANTERBURY, 13*th November*.

... The daily mass *is* everything in heaven and earth to me. You are right there. Earth-born clouds may sometimes veil Him from His servants' eyes, but

He comes, He comes certain as sunrise. No doubt, Agnese mia, but that my talk must often have seemed to you a mass of contradictions but, however it may be with other people, it is always the case with me, that, if I speak truly, I speak all sort of contrary things. The truth itself perhaps lies too deep for words. It is true, but overlaid with other and mixed stuff, which has to be shovelled away by Agneses and other, if any, industrious friends.

What you say of St. Paul's is true, perhaps, and I think that St. Augustine would lay hold of that living Church and bring it again into communion with the Chair of the Apostles. He would not be satisfied short of that ; do you think he would ?

The little Imitation will be a treasure for me, not too large for a pocket, and nearly 300 years of age. I will leave it back again to you in my will, and be sure that you come to my burial. This I shall count upon, that you attend if you are anywhere in England. I will look at those places in the Imitation that you mention ; only one book is really familiar to me.

I do mind what you say very much in the sense of giving heed to it, but if I thought you did not deal fairly by me, giving me truth for truth without let or hindrance, I should first be seized with regret of having spoken openly, then with melancholy at the *déception,* then our intercourse would pale, sicken and die out. So pray continue the prophet-like strain.

The piano is tuning in the adjoining room, and a barrel-organ is vexing the very bowels of Burgate, making a hellish discord in my ears, and goading my pen ; so enough. *Thank* you for the spectacles ; I am consoled for your trouble by considering the prophet-like rebuke you administered to the attendant. I see

you are a prophet, though this only occurred to me at the third line from the top of this page.—Ever yours,
SIBYL HOLLAND.

To Bernard Holland

CANTERBURY, *19th November.*

I so perfectly remember that summer evening, and see Arnald de Grey cross the lawn with a great faggot of tall river flowers, and a quiet look on his face. I have always thought of him since just as I saw him then. This was God's will for him; this was to be the end of the short stay of his quiet harmless life. A dim vision, far less distinct probably than that left on my mind by his two days' visit, will be all that will remain for his little small sons.

Your verses are charming, the first you have written for some time, are they not? I am very fond of that *sort* of poetry; *it pleases*, which is a great thing. Sometimes when I read George Herbert I am extraordinarily pleased—all seems so dainty sweet.

To the Lady Knutsford

CANTERBURY, *21st November.*

Thank you very much indeed for the mother o' pearl Cross, which came safe to hand yesterday. I have hung it again in my room with a sigh. . . . X. was here for a few days in the beginning of the month. I was very glad to have her, she is always so kind and content. Yet 'twas a torment, because of the impossible questions with which she plied me, and the deductions she made from my false and fleeting replies. Who can truly say in a dozen words how or why he began to love his friend, or how he has arrived at his political belief or his determination as to beauty and perfection, or what a place is to him, or a poem, and why? Belief is another thing from opinion.

A great many singular things happen here, more, I suspect, than you meet in your great world; but this is happy for you.—Ever, dearest Margaret, your affectionate
SIBYL HOLLAND.

To Bernard Holland

THE PRECINCTS, 23rd November.

I am going to post this at 3 P.M., and perhaps it will reach you to-morrow in the ancient demesne of Ashburnham. Your good letter came in at twelve, and I was so pleased to get it that I gave old Maxted[1] a handful of the pale chrysanthemums that I was sorting in the hall by the open door. For the air to-day is so mild that even in these low and shadowed places all doors and windows stand open, and the rooks have come over to look at their nests. They seem a good deal irritated by the apparatus on the pinnacle on Bell Harry—the ladders and ropes—and no doubt look upon it as some deep-laid human plot directed against their skiey haunts.

To the Same

THE PRECINCTS, 28th November.

I hasten to say that whatever I wrote to you must not be read as though I repented me of what I have done. I know that to-morrow if things were as they were I should make the same move, and also I know

---

[1] The postman.

that in my soul I have a point of abiding peace and joy which spreads, and will spread, till all else is submerged and swallowed up. But apart from myself, and you cannot think how difficult it is to me to see questions *not* apart from myself, I think that there is much in all G. C. P. urges. Perhaps the thing that interests him most in all that his eye surveys from his niche in St. Margaret's Street is the Established Church, with all her claims, temporal and spiritual, holding her own in the battlefield of the world ; and it *is* a singular and wonderful thing to behold. Dollinger thinks that she is an instrument in God's hand, and is reserved as a meeting-place for the older churches. He wrote a little book called the Church and the Churches, or some such name, putting forth this view, after he broke with the Vatican.

G. C. P. did depress me because I could not speak openly to him, and he got very angry and severe, and scolded me for not speaking. He tried to make me give my reasons in order to confound them ; in short, it was perhaps as painful an hour of the sort as ever I have spent in my life. At last he said : "Well, it's a mystery," and told a story of his churchwarden who had stolen the church money, and every one knew clearly what he had done, but he could not be got to say more than " It's a mystery seemingly," and this he said over and over again.

At 9.30 A.M. yesterday morning we were overtaken by a violent storm of snow with a due westerly wind, and in half an hour Bell Harry's long roof was white from end to end, so were the red roofs of the opposite houses, so was every leaf of ivy on the old walls, and your father's trencher crossing the Oaks to matins, and the newspaper boy's jacket advancing with the *Times*.

Snow levels like death, shrouding all alike. In the mystic interpretation of colours, white is the earth or death, blue is the air or aspiration, gold is splendour or knowledge, purple the sea or endurance, scarlet the fire or charity.

Canon Mason is talked of as the probable successor of Bishop Parry. I *wish* this may be so. Mrs. ——— says: " Well, of course, we all like old friends, and we *wish* for Canon Holland," adding, " Canterbury is a city that does not desire anything new. We like to know *what* we have got." I believe that the idea of the middle class is that the Church should take the *lead everywhere*, and should be on friendly terms, but wholly patronising terms, with all other denominations. This is what they are themselves with their numerous dissenting relations and friends. Mrs. ——— wouldn't dream of entering a chapel. Church people *won't* do that, but she likes to bring her friends to the Cathedral. The Church to them is like the big old family of a neighbourhood. Affable, largely hospitable, knowing everybody, and doing as it chooses without consulting the public.

To ———

THE PRECINCTS, *Sunday Night*, 2*nd December*.

You have taken what I said in too strong a sense. I cannot bear myself for having written anything at all. By "masculine" I only meant the entire absence of that part of a woman's character which, on certain matters, holds other women aloof; that which makes the rule of a priest or doctor, or household master, more easy to many women than that of a mistress, or woman doctor, or Red Mother. You have no littlenesses at all in you, and an immense indulgence, and the quick acknowledgment of every sort of merit wherever you find it, which is the very essence of generosity. This is all that I meant, and how in the world could this hurry you down any slope? It might hinder you somewhat in the educating of these dear souls, and that is all I meant. But here, I now believe I did you wrong. When I come to consider it, I believe that I was partly judging myself (which is, after all, all that one really has to judge by).

What you said about girlish beauty rather hit me, because I often feel a sort of *mad benignity* towards quite young people and children. It is far as the poles asunder from what I did and felt in bringing up my own children, and it is not the best side of me. I mean that I could not *work* with it, and to get a letter like the one you sent me would pull me up very short. But then you see that you have never talked to me about that child, and I ought not to have expressed any opinion formed merely on the sight of two little letters without asking you what you said in reply, or making any inquiry at all. I have sinned a little against friendship in this, but I know you have forgiven, because really my mind and heart were full of love and wonder. I cannot think how you can keep all these souls in hand. You have more than a woman's strength, that is the fact, and I come back to it. They feel it and cling on.

. . . We have a house full of people, and I am tied to strings upon which everything seems playing. And the first Advent out of the old church tries me much and unreasonably. I ought to keep silence outwardly and inwardly.

To Miss Mason

CAVENDISH RECTORY, SUFFOLK, *9th December.*

Agnese mia—I am going straight through London on Saturday, so don't expect me that evening. It is too near Christmas Day to linger among the millions. I only regret the loss of another talk with you, but we shall have it elsewhere in times to come, either in *hac valle lachrymarum*, or in the place of light, refreshment, and peace. This sounds solemn, but is a commonplace that is ever in my mind on all occasions of loss and gain.—Your affectionate and faithful

SIBYL HOLLAND.

To the Same

WAITING ROOM, CHARING CROSS, *12th December.*

Here have I been already for some little time, and the train does not go till 3.30. I might have sat with you for half an hour more at least. Isn't it like one of your girls to sit and write to you half an hour after leaving you. There are things that I have left unsaid. One is to wish you a good Christmas and New Year; another is to ask you, if you do see S. C. to tell her about your work, not to mind telling her. She will be so interested if you do. She is not in the least bit clever, rather the contrary, and has hardly any power of expression among ordinary people. She goes trembling and discouraged to all her undertakings; her own family thinks nothing of her. Yet she can keep a whole roomful of rough, poor men quietly waiting for her words, every separate soul being of extraordinary importance to her. She is very nervous, but does the boldest things. What you and she are doing is almost the same work, and almost in the same manner, only you are such absolutely different people. I bless God that He leaves me your friendship, which I might well have lost, and that I still know S. C.; but she is not my friend. I think it will be good for her to know you. She does not know any one like you, but very likely you would get on together.

Now farewell till we meet again, chère rachetée de mon Dieu. Remember me at the altar, that great meeting-place of all faithful hearts.—Your ever affectionate
SIBYL HOLLAND.

There is such a crowd and bustle all around. I say a Pater, and an Ave, and a Memorare for them all.

To Bernard Holland

CANTERBURY, 23rd December.

You are hard at work on your birthday instead of at leisure here in this mild pale flower of December sunshine. Yesterday's continuous rain has washed the roofs and lanes of the old city, and I pray St. Thomas to keep us clean till over Xmas week. The Kentish bells are chiming as they chimed when you were born three-and-thirty years ago. You are now the same age as I was when the first tremendous misfortune of my life overtook me, and I hope for some blow of *good* fortune for you. Men do, and women suffer.

To Rosamond Stephen

THE PRECINCTS, 29th December.

My dear Rosamond—Rosamond, my dear! your kind little letter came like a reproach, for I had suffered the days to slip by till Xmas Eve without writing to you, as I had fully proposed to you, and then, finding that the posts would all be a confusion from Xmas Day and Sunday falling together, I again put off, but you will forgive and forget if you have a letter within the Octave of Xmas.

Bernard says that James will presently bring you to Canterbury, and this will give us all very great pleasure, for I have never seen you since you have become a grown-up young lady with regular evening dresses, and most likely a beautiful crest of hair twisted up upon the top of your head. We are deep in snow here; it lies glittering two feet deep all round the Cathedral. On Christmas morning the sun rose in a clear, pale blue sky, against which the great Bell Harry Tower shone rosy red. All the old houses and ruined arches were muffled up in shining white, and every branch and twig and ivy leaf carried lines of snow three times its own thickness. In an old city like Canterbury this has a strange effect; towards evening, when the light fades, everything looks disguised. The dumb streets, the muffled-up hurrying figures, the dim burning lights, the bells and clocks in the sharp air above, all this seems to blot out modern life. Yesterday in the Cathedral at morning service I heard every now and then a low thunderous noise. This was the heavy masses of snow, a little loosened in the midday sun, slipping from the lofty steep roof of the nave.

To-day is the day of the famous murder of St. Thomas à Becket, who was done to death by the four Norman knights in the north transept of the nave. I am sure you have read Dean Stanley's account of that, and of how, when it was all over, and the body of Thomas left alone in the dark church, the people of

Canterbury all came pouring in making a dreadful noise and lamentation. Kentish people have always been noisy and rough. I daresay you have read how they hustled and snowballed Mr. Gladstone at Dover, and played unfeeling tunes outside the town hall while he was talking inside. And at the last election, when the people of the parish of Northgate, Canterbury, understood that the Liberal candidate was coming to make a speech in their part of the city, they made preparations to throw him into a pond. He heard of it just in time and kept away. But all this violent and rude behaviour need not make you fear to come to Canterbury, and I hope to see you when the weather is mild and the days draw out a little.—Ever your very affectionate godmother, SIBYL HOLLAND.

X

LETTERS OF 1890

To Francis Holland

CANTERBURY, *6th January*.

THE midday post has just brought me a letter from Aunt Mary, with news of your illness. She wrote on the 3rd. I have been expecting to see you walk in any time these last three days—and I have not imagined any other delay than picture-galleries and churches at Florence. This is what I say—there is *no* intimation of the pain or peril of those whose life is so infinitely precious and unspeakably dear. Mary says you have been well doctored and nursed, and that I am not to feel alarmed. But it gave me a shock, and though I reason with myself yet I am anxious. Leo XIII. must have given you *a frisson* that morning. Dress clothes are too light, and I daresay you had no overcoat. I have begged Aunt Mary to advance you some money for nurse and doctor and journey, and you ought to give something over and above to the kind people at the hotel. I wish that I knew Major and Mrs. Ross. I wish that I could thank them. I hope that some day I may meet them. I will write again to-night, this is to catch post. I was enormously interested in your account of the Pope.

To the Same

CANTERBURY, *7th January.*

I thought of you the last thing last night and the first thing this morning, and I shall think of you every hour of every day till you come home. I hope that you will have this heavenly mild weather for your journey back. The air cannot be much milder in Rome itself, or herself, and the nights are beautiful. We have not had one hour's darkness in the twenty-four. This morning at 6.40 I saw Bell Harry flash in the dawn, while the long shadows still fell from west to east cast by the full and sinking moon; and this evening, before the sun touches the horizon, the moon will silver the whole eastern sky and glitter upon Becket's crown and all the eastern heights and depths and steep slopes of the great Gothic church. She shines too upon the wide Campagna and the dome of St. Peter's and on Trajan's column, and glitters on the plashing fountains of the Eternal City, where my darling boy's head lies sleeping, I hope, and free from feverish dreams. I have got a book from G. C. P. which I know you will like because it is your period —Charles I. and James I. You shall have it when you come home. Mrs. —— with her daughter and niece are here till Thursday, and I am hoping you will not arive till they are gone. But they are quiet, intelligent *old* friends. There is nothing in this note. "Hic canit errantem lunam solisque labores"—is not that a Virgilian line?

To Lady Egerton

PRECINCTS, CANTERBURY, *17th February.*

My dear Lady Egerton—I cannot say how much pleasure your letter has given me. My old love for you has lain in my heart all these years, and when I read your kind, sweet, faithful words it sprang up into a flame. The frost of the heart is silence, some old writer says—this cry of the heart is fire, is charity. It is of no use for me to enter upon the subject of your letters. I took this step at the risk of losing all that makes earth dear. I risked everything, and, besides, I risked the possibility of being mistaken, of losing one world without gaining the other. But God is good. Our family union has not been injured, and many friendships have held firm in spite of the severe and singular strain put upon them. Still, looking back I cannot conceive how I had the courage to do it.

There are a thousand things that I should like to say and to hear, and if I thought that when you came to London we might perhaps meet, it would be a very great pleasure. Naturally I have lost a certain number of interests and friends, and I have made no new ones— nor is it probable that I shall ever do so, as I shall never enter the great Catholic coterie. So you may imagine how three and four times dear are faithful and indulgent friends like yourself.

Neither of my boys were able to be at the dance at 32 De Vere Gardens last week. I have therefore no news of the dear people there—nor have I liked to write to Mary, not knowing how she might feel about my retrograde movement.—Your very affectionate
SIBYL HOLLAND.

No I do not feel in the least separated from other people, nor do I think that they feel divided from me. I feel an infinite affection for my friends, and a sort of *slavish* desire to serve them.

To Bernard Holland

PRECINCTS, *9th February.*

I quite fall in with your remark on the Lincoln case. The larger High Church party, who are the successors of the old religious minds, will never be satisfied short of the Mass, and the Reformers' one great object was to do away with the Mass, and they would have swept it away altogether had it not been for great Eliza's instincts and poor old Parker's principles.

. . . The bell is chiming for 4 p.m. evensong, and the Cathedral is glittering from Clock Tower to Corona in the south-west sunshine and due east wind. The rooks are holding a parliament. Huggins is rolling the grass in the Oaks, and your father, in trencher, is making his way across to the great church. So it has been (not from the beginning but) for 300 years, is now, but whether it shall ever be or for how long—who knows? It will last my time in any case.

To the Same

PRECINCTS, *19th February.*

. . . I was amused this morning after 8 A.M. mass to see the little school children patter up the church and crowd round the altar rails to receive a little dab of ashes on their innocent foreheads. They swarmed up, and knelt one behind the other, making treble rows and smiling with delight while the immense P. P.[1] passed quickly along saying ancient Latin words and making a black mark on each. The grown ups all went up also. The delight of the children amused me: the babies squeezed forwards and came triumphantly back. The bigger ones looked at one another with laughing eyes, and made joyful gestures. One would have thought that some great pleasure had befallen them. It is not easy to explain the intense pleasure children take in customs.

To Miss Mason

PRECINCTS, 25*th February.*

I should not have allowed so much water to have run under the bridge, but that I have had to put all my letter-writing aside for other things. First, Agnes has been at home, and, after five pleasant days, fell ill of influenza, and has gone back to Cornwall to-day still unwell, after a fortnight in the house. Then the sick people outside have been innumerable, and now the Warden's wife at St. Augustine's is lying at the point of death. She was seized with influenza on the ninth day after the birth of her child, and has inflammation of the lungs and other things—all the terrors of the Pale King. Nurses, doctors, appliances of all sorts are in full array, and I am absorbed in the *contest of life and death.* You know what it is—how one's mind beats about in vain. We know not what is the will of God as to the issue. We cry to Him, and He answers by deeds, not words. He speaks to us by what He does, and our only true answer is contained in what we do

---

[1] Parish priest.

in return. Words are nothing more than groans and cries.

Well, Agnese mia, can you come down? I have seven empty rooms and a warm welcome. Do come, and change back into a human being, any day, and any hour, and for as long as you can. For the rest of Lent? Do. And do send some nice girl into that *pays d'or*.

To Francis Holland

CANTERBURY, 4*th March.*

Last night was the coldest registered in these parts for many years, and this morning there were 10 inches of snow in the Precincts. Poor Fox,[1] plunging about in the drifts at midnight, did not cry "All's well." I looked out and saw his retreating solitary figure, and the dark holes left as he drew his feet out of the snow. At midday the wind changed and all the vanes stood to the south, the sun came out and the waters flowed everywhere. But at sunset it froze again, and I could hardly keep my footing as I walked back with the old seneschal.

To the Same

CANTERBURY, 14*th March.*

I have been more or less unwell all the week, or would have written. The weather has been lovely, but this has made me restless. I cannot get away from these old Stones and Bones, and I long for

---

[1] The watchman of the Precincts, whose duty it is to announce the hour, the weather, and to say that "all's well."

something quite different. I should like to carry you and Ber with me far out of London, but I don't know *where*. . . . The antiquarian excitement has gone on all the week, but with all the discussion no sort of certainty has been arrived at as to *who* the Archbishop is, nor will it ever be discovered. I have finished *Unto this Last* and handed it on to Mrs. —— as a change from Tolstoi's *What shall we do, then*, which is goading her to desperate deeds. . . .

To the Same

CANTERBURY, *20th March*.

I have congratulated our savant, who came in this morning early and stayed two hours discussing Tolstoi's *What shall we do, then*, instead of going on to pursue his researches in the Cathedral. Tolstoi is a very goading writer. I suppose that it is because so much of what he says is true, and he has a steady purpose before him in every line he writes. . . . According to Tolstoi, Michael is the only one among us who is leading the true life. This is a considerable comfort to me in considering Mick—that Tolstoi approves. . . . I wonder if Henry Holland of Staffordshire, educated at Eton and Oxford, and one of the Jesuits who were thrown into England in Charles I.'s time, were any relation of ours. He sounds just like one of us. I daresay that he was, and that after the troubles the Jesuit took to business and Nonconformity as a safer line on the whole. I have just come back from reading to an old bedridden Irish papist. It is very easy to visit poor Catholics, because they delight in devotions, and are more grateful to you if you say a Litany with them or the Way of the Cross, than for any other thing you can bring them. I do not know whether they are really more religious than our poor people, but if they don't practise their religion they are nothing, whereas among Protestants the actual religious practice is somewhat stunted. Were you not affected at hearing of that wave which swept Sir Howard Elphinstone into his vast and wandering grave? Such a fate in the heydey of active life! If Bismarck lives to see Europe in another great war, and the socialists getting the upper hand, he won't sing Nunc Dimittis very cheerfully. I suppose the Revolution is going on over the world, but when the masses are at the top they will become the classes, and it will not be much forwarder.

To Bernard Holland

20*th March.*

I did see the strange fate that overtook Sir Howard Elphinstone. The Queen will have wept for her good soldier.

Yesterday we had snow and rain all day, and to-day the same. Tuesday was fine and dry, and I took the Warden's three little boys to tea at the Lodge. They were very happy careering about. We found anemones and primroses, and came home about six o'clock. The house smelt very sweet and I wished to remain. Yesterday in the library I opened a little memoir of Sumner,[1] and found him described in pleasing terms as of that civility which Cæsar himself had observed in the inhabitants of this part of the island, and of that same courage and determination

---

[1] Sumner, the antiquary and local historian.

which had caused the men of Kent to come forward with branches in their hands to make a bargain with the Conqueror. I like this patriotic way of writing, and I think that for the future I will not go beyond the kingdom in seeking for comparisons, figures, and tropes. "There's plenty ready enough to want to come into Kent, but I never heard of nobody who'd no call to go out of it."[1]

Your father and I walked down to St. Peter's on Sunday afternoon to be present at the baptism of the Warden's motherless babe. There was old B—— there, who sat against the wall at right angles with his old parson, and never took his eye off him till the end of the service, when he asked him to step across to "look at his old gal, who is wore completely to skin and bone and deafer than ten postes." So we did, and during our visit papa asked B—— if he had ever been to London. "No," says he, "but I have been pretty well everywhere else. I was wonst beyond Chatham, and felt lost. Why! I thought I should never have got back to Old England no more." This is very confirmatory of your view.[2]

I said to B——, "How is it that your son-in-law is always out of work; he is a good engineer blacksmith?" "Well," says B——, very cautious and solemn, "I suppose he done wrong. He had a very good place under Mr. D—— at Hales Place—the college,[3] you understand. But he done wrong. In the course of his work he came across the place where they kep the sacrament wine, and I do suppose he

---

[1] A remark by some one at Harbledown.
[2] That when East Kent people speak of Old England they mean East Kent.
[3] The Jesuit College.

drinked it, made an end o' the whole lot, kep' going back upon it like, so he was forced to leave." You can't think what a singular expression B—— had in telling me this.

To Francis Holland

CANTERBURY, 26*th March*.

Mrs. T.[1] is in the hall partaking of sherry and biscuit and waiting to see papa on quarter-day matters, while he, unconscious, is lingering in the Cathedral. I am struck by the piety and solemnity with which she prefaces her glass of sherry. Her health-drinking is like a sincere prayer. She ends with "poor Mrs. Machins and God bless us all." Mrs. Machins has gone quite blind, which *is* a double calamity. This custom of health-drinking is really something of a religious act, and 'tis a pity that it has gone out. Did the Romans and Greeks drink healths? . . .

To Bernard Holland

PRECINCTS, 26*th March*.

Mr. and Mrs. Lewis of Cambridge come here tomorrow and stay over Sunday. He is an authority on gems, and came to discuss the unknown Archbishop's emerald gem. When first that Archbishop was laid in that stone coffin he must have looked himself like a jewel in a case. His head mitred, his shining ring and jewelled staff, and broidered and jewelled shoes, and gold silk vestments from head to foot, and cold-pinned pall, and chalice parcel-gilt. He who wore these things was stately and delicately made.

---

[1] An old nurse, retired.

Lying at the bottom of that stone coffin he must have shone wondrously. The antiquaries are cross and quarrelling.[1]

To Miss Arnold-Forster

CANTERBURY, *1st April.*

... We are deep in snow here; all the old roofs and towers and ivied walls wrapped in a sheet of dazzling white. A perpetual draught is kept up in our very cold house by people making short cuts through it. I shiver all day. I have a good many sick people also, and a great many things to do and to listen to, and often I am very tired. It *is* tiring, my Frances, to come and go, and listen, and run about, and fetch and carry for people, and all the time to be sure of their disapprobation, but after all I don't make myself a slave for them, but for Him, blessed above all, whose name I cannot take on my lips, or even think of in my heart, without smiling for joy. You must just lie in the hollow of His hand, and trust Him, and trust *Him.* You want a long rest. ... Let yourself go a little more; do not try to find words or to think consecutively. Let your heart and mind empty itself, and keep yourself very still, so that if Jesus speaks, you may hear Him. Don't try to hold anything fast. If you must have words, take some very simple prayer, and keep entirely to this and the Lord's Prayer.

[1] The tomb of an Archbishop of the early thirteenth century was opened in order to endeavour to satisfy some antiquarian curiosity as to which Archbishop he was.

To the Same

CANTERBURY, 9*th April.*

... For this, and for innumerable other blessings, I praise His holy name. I do, and will remember you, dearest Frances, in the proper place and hour, in the ancient words which have sounded and resounded through Christendom so many years, and which will go on while the world lasts. Yes, that is a wonderful text, St. John xii. 24, especially if we take it with the two following verses. The corn grain of the Incarnation cast into the field of the world, the seed of the elect and the Church.

As some old Father says, if we would be of the harvest, we must also be of the sowing ; whosoever will be of the heavenly bread must first have lain in the earth of humiliation, and have been buried in forgetfulness of the world, threshed on the floor, crushed under the mill-stones, passed through the water and the fire of troubles, affliction, and repentance. Yet God does lead souls by an easier and fairer path, and may He so ever lead yours. His government is infinitely varied in method, answering to the infinity in creation.

To Agnes Bolton

CANTERBURY, 10*th April.*

... Bernard persuaded me to go to Bruges with him for Easter Day, so we set out. Our expenses there and back and our bill came to £2. It was tiring, but I enjoyed seeing the old city, with its belfry and steeples, and the vast mixed multitude that came crowding up hour after hour to the altars to be fed by the pale patient priests. The whole city seemed to communicate easily, devoutly, and thankfully. At 6.30 I formed one of a dense crowd of persons in a side aisle, and it was the same at three other altars in the cathedral, and at all the other churches. Old crippled people, young children, big boys and girls innumerable, rich and poor of all ages pressing steadily forward, and streaming back with clasped hands and downcast eyes. A loud continuous noise of chairs moving and feet treading, but not a word, look, or smile.

To Francis Holland

CANTERBURY, 10*th April*.

Thank you very much for your charming letter from the "green fields of Wales." I am glad that you have seen old Sam with your bodily eyes. He is the last of the old set except George, and he had much more to do with Knutsford than ever George had. I remember him coming there in my early married days, and all the jokes between him and Aunts Mary and Lucy, and his first pretty little wife Annie, of whom they were very fond; and I stayed with him for a night during the tour in Wales I took with Aunt Lucy and Bernard, and we saw an otter hunt. I think that Wales has a great charm. We will go to St. David's together some day. . . . I went over with Ber to Bruges on Easter Eve and returned Monday. It was rather tiring, but I liked seeing the old city and fine churches. I should rather like to have a room in the old English convent there and to go over sometimes, but lor,' as Tomlin says, I shall never do nothing of the sort.

To the Same

CANTERBURY, 15*th April*, 4.30 P.M.

All day long Canterbury has been burying the good Bishop of Dover. There has been a very great stir. Military, volunteers, fire brigade, schools, colleges, parochial clergy, all the shops shut, and every living creature but me in the streets and cathedral yard and cathedral. It is all over now—bells and organ and music and trampling feet, and he is left quiet at the top of S. Martin's Churchyard, where a "thousand suns will stream on him, a thousand moons will quiver." I am grieved for Mrs. Parry, but she has dear sons, and who knows better than I do all the hope and consolation that lies in that thought.

To Miss Mason

THE LODGE, 28*th May*.

Thank you for the two kindest notes. I am glad of your friendship and grateful for it, and it does not matter (except to myself) that you think me more of a person than I am. I have been reading such beautiful things this morning, some in dear George Herbert. I wish you were here to share the feast. On so many matters we feel alike; that is clear, and to me very delightful.

Before you leave England let me know whether I can do anything for the Guild on the 21st of June. Don't leave me in a sea of doubt as to that. . . . I often think of that little church to which you guided me yesterday week. I liked it better than any Catholic Church I have been into in London.

I forget when you are going. Write me two words to say that you are gone, and come to see me when you return.—Ever and aye your affectionate friend,

SIBYL HOLLAND.

To Francis Holland

CANTERBURY, 4*th June*.

I trimmed my long dinner-table last night with pinks and roses, and it looked pretty, but this flagging south wind makes me feel very tired. How it will rustle to-day in the great elms at Eton, and how quiet the moonlight will lie upon the castle and river at midnight when the pretty play is over and the company dispersed. How we fly forgotten—a dream, a spark, an arrow, a bird, such is our course. The delight of books is the continuity they make. I am reading St. Theresa's life of herself. I perfectly understand her. Her mind lives and touches mine. As she found people and things, in the main, 300 years ago, so I find them now. *Loss and Gain* is a very clever book. There is something so incisive and clear as crystal in Newman's way of putting things, and it is, no doubt, a perfect picture of one side of English life so many years ago. We had a houseful of ordination candidates —good young men—not of a high stamp mentally or otherwise, and not at all trained in ecclesiology, very natural and not at all supernatural. Not at all like Willis, nor even Bateman, nor with White's æsthetical proclivities. Don't you love Bateman?[1]

---

[1] Characters in Newman's *Loss and Gain*.

To the Same

CANTERBURY, 11*th June.*

Yesterday Père du Lac wrote to me to say that in August he and his whole house give up Hales Place and return to France for good. He says, "Je n'ai pas voulu vous laisser apprendre ces nouvelles par bruit public."

I am very curious to know under what circumstances they return. He says, "Notre maison de Slough, qui n'est pas un Collège, prendra notre place ici." But what can any one *but* a college want with a great house like Hales Place? I am sorry they are going, for they were an interesting feature at Canterbury—more interesting and less formidable than a set of English Jesuits would be.

Do you think it a good thing to read such contradictory authors at the same time? It would worry me dreadfully. I like to abandon myself to an author. I think that natural religion is little more than the worship of nature, and fails one entirely at the great moments of life.

To Bernard Holland

CANTUAR, *Sunday,* 15*th June.*

I wonder where you have been to-day, which is just drawing to a close by means of the curfew, though the sun is hardly set and the twilight will last till dawn. Mrs. Loosemore, who has been long ill, died at three o'clock. The boom of the bell startled me sitting alone in the garden. I went over and found the poor girls in tears, and the old sister saying that there had never been a happier marriage, and that her brother and his wife had had the happiest life in spite of many troubles. Such is family affection.

A very old Jesuit father (English) staying at Hales Place preached at St. Thomas's this morning. It was a great pleasure to look at his bent head covered with snowy hair, and to listen to his low but clear voice. He spoke like a man of vast experience, who knew all that there was to be known, and had been conversant with men all over the world.

Père du Lac called here on Friday and sat for a long time. He says that the reason the college is to be broken up in July is that it draws boys too much from the Society's colleges in France, and that his own time is over, and that it is not thought worth while to begin again with a new rector. He is very sorry to go and spoke very warmly of England. I am sorry, though I never see him; it is the loss of something that might have been. The *tradesmen* are quite brokenhearted and write him "the most beautiful letters." The house is taken by the French Jesuits of Slough. This is a noviciate. There will be about 120 of them, but they will not circulate either in purse or person.

To the Same

PRECINCTS, 26*th June.*

I am very rheumatic. This warm rain works me in woe. Roses and strawberries abound. June is certainly the prime of the year, and we have had this week the still, warm, fragrant nights proper to the season. The sun is quite hot at 4.30 A.M. Last night papa was dining out, and I was so tired that I went to bed at nine with all my windows open, worn out with arranging and distributing a mass of roses. No sooner was I stretched flat and comfortable, with a book and shaded lamp, than the Warden was announced on business. So I got up and threw on a dressing-gown and white shawl, and went and sat with him for an hour, very pleasantly, in the twilight drawing-room. He had got a case of conscience, and wanted a woman's uncalculating opinion upon it.

Our dinner went on and off on Tuesday. . . . We have dined about 100 people since Easter, besides our big excursion parties, so I think we have done our part.

To the Same

THE LODGE, 1st July.

It is so delicious here, though the roses have suffered from the heavy rain and boisterous south wind. But all is still and sunny and fresh as Paradise. I came up this morning bringing little Douglas Reid with me. He is a lively wandering elf of a child, and except for twenty minutes' dinner, has been on his feet the whole day. Up the hill where the five mowers are bending in rhythm to their work, and across to the wood for foxgloves, and into the kitchen garden for strawberries. He wants nothing of one but an ear for his adventures. " I believe I have been here quite a month, and yet I have a thought that we came this very morning," he observed just now. Mrs. Tomlin is here, and Adams and an Industrial Blue for change of air, and a younger servant, all glad to "transmigrare sicut passer ad montem." So am I. Every June my heart bleeds in the Precincts ; it is a *via dolorosa* for me. While I live, and live in these places, I go the round of the seasons with my sick child. The only time I am free of it is from the 3rd September to the 16th February, and then she seems to be about with me in Canterbury. I don't fancy these things, but they are always with me. If only people knew what Lucy was to me, and what it is to me that she is gone, they would forgive me and excuse me. It is a folly so to love. If she had married and left me I should not have known a day's easiness, missing her from my side. I ought not to write these things to you, reviving perhaps your pain, you who most shared my grief, my dearest Bernard; and you must not think me melancholy. I have had a very happy afternoon, arranging my pretty rooms, and cutting my storm-blown roses, and I feel the better for the air already. I have plenty of books, and I mean to-morrow to call on Mrs. Hilton.

I enjoyed my afternoon at Margate; the air is quite delightful, and so is little Lucy and her mamma.

To the Same

THE LODGE, 15*th July*.

The weather has turned with the "translation of Swithin, B.C." Yesterday was very warm, and towards night the wind fell, and after sunset there was a balmy stillness, which prevails also this morning. I spent most of the day in the Potager culling fruit, aided by an orphan girl from Canterbury, to whom the place is Paradise. At six o'clock, as I was writing in the drawing-room, Père du Lac drove up. He came to ask me to call upon a young couple who have taken a house in Summer Hill for six weeks. "Ce jeune homme n'est pas de notre côté, c'est plûtot un ennemi, mais enfin il est venu me demander quelques renseignements, j'ai connu son père, et je veux bien lui montrer toute la charité catholique possible, ainsi, Madame, etc., etc." All this he said, and more, with a most sweet and bright expression of countenance. He much admired the Perugino, and stood looking at it. Indeed, all our religion is in that picture. As his carriage turned out of the gate, he turned also and took off his hat. I bowed from the window, and he was gone. I never see him without emotion.

After this Amy came in to say that Miss Skipps and all her girls[1] were in the yard. They had come up in spite of all the prohibitions of . . . etc. "Well," said Miss Skipps, "we couldn't hold out any longer." So a ladder was set against the Bigarreau cherry, and with cries of joy the girls flew to contest the spoil with the starlings. Delia looked charming high up on the ladder, throwing down the cherries to the little girls, knowing, as a maid of Kent should do, how to plant a ladder, run up it, and reach the fruit.

Then the swing, and the summer-house, and the willow-tree occupied them till it was nearly dark, when they sang a hymn, and clattered off down the drive, and I betook myself with my rosary to the clump, always my walk when the house grows quite dark. It was light on the top of the hill, a clear zenith, and great violet clouds with orange streaks to the west and north, where the sun had gone down. All the hay cut and sending forth an immense fragrance. The night jars wheeled round and round me as I sat motionless, and presently one settled on the wire fence close behind the clump, and gave forth a sound that seemed to fill the world. His mate continued to wheel, uttering clear

[1] A training home.

whistling notes at intervals. These things I did, saw, and heard yesterday, but the thought of you unceasingly filled my heart. My darling boy, it always seems to me that God would have something of you that you have not yet given Him, and that then all would be well.

To the Same

THE LODGE, 16*th July*.

Yesterday was a deep summer day. I wrote till eleven, then gathered fruit with my orphan, under a burning sun till one, when Mrs. Reid arrived to deposit little Douglas again. The currants are large and hang in great clusters, the black ones each throwing off a jet of light, under the heavy green leaves. Adams stirs her great copper pan all day and the house is filled with the fragrance of the fruit. " The silent house," Shelley once wrote in a past summer,—"the silent house is filled with the warm summer wind." How often have I felt that!

After lunch, I turned all hands but those of Adams, the confectioner, into the orchards, and, while I went to spend the rest of the day at Oakwell, the maids, Chaney and Mark, worked with a will, and on my return at 7.30, all was combed and swept and a neat little stack built up. As I came slowly along the high terrace road towards Tyler Hill, I observed with delight the cobalt blue of the atmosphere in which everything was bathed. The cathedral, the city, the ridge beyond, the Thanet valley, all was pale bright blue, against which the immediate foreground, the massed summer woods of Hales Place stood out with a peculiar clearness. To the left, that is to the north, the little houses and stacks and orchards of Blean were sharp and bright as possible against a white horizon. It was one of those transparent days when one is so aware of the sea. It is that waste of waters all around which gives us that blue, and that pale brilliant horizon. Only Florence and the children were at Oakwell in the Blee. They accompanied me, walking, on our return as far as the Clergy Orphan School. I ate two eggs and salad and coffee, at 8 P.M. put Douglas to bed and went up to the Clump, where the air blew cool over the darkening landscape, and my friendly night-jars wheeled round again, but were silent. Now, I am going again to gather fruit.

You are not a minute out of my mind and heart.

To the Same

THE LODGE, *17th July.*

We are clearly to have full summer weather now, the blessed sun disperses all sorts of mists and earth-born clouds. Yesterday, again, I picked fruit, but this time alone, the orphan having been summoned home by her aunt. She went, bathed in tears, at mid-day, but in the evening re-appeared with a sort of desperate expression of countenance. We have asked no particulars, but I shall send her back again to-night. I fancy that at all risks she has seized this one more day, and I don't blame her. Her poor little childhood has been so moped away amid privations of all sorts, and she is not yet sixteen. Père du Lac appeared again yesterday to tell me about some poor woman I had asked him to recommend to his successors. He apologised, "mais c'est toujours plus facile pour moi de venir ici que de vous voir en ville et puisque je pars—enfin."

Miss Ward drove up at four, and stayed till after supper. After tea, as she and I sat at the Clump watching the hay-carrying on the breast of the hill, and admiring the active figures of the men pitching, and the men receiving, a whole party of people, Powells, etc., who had been calling at the Hiltons, climbed up and joined us. The hay is superb after all.

Mr. Powell says that an old Selling farmer of his acquaintance, as soon as the year's almanack is out, *i.e.* in December, and as soon as he has thereby ascertained the course of the moon in the coming year, sits down and makes out the weather beforehand, and is always right within a little. He says that he finds from long experience that the weather depends upon the time of night or day in which the moon's changes occur. Some weeks ago he showed Mr. Powell that we should have a period of fine weather from 16th July when the moon changed at 12.50 in the night— and we have it. Such it is to be a farmer of Selling, Kent.

To

THE LODGE, 23*rd July*.

What I meant by a full surrender is just perhaps what would have prevented you from making a false step in all this business. I mean a full and entire reference to God in every step of your life. "I will bear the cross and the cross will bear me provided, O my sweet Jesus, that Thou dost maintain both the one and the other."

But now, all my hope for you and my consolation

lies *there ;* nor can I believe but that the Commander-in-Chief looks with eyes of tenderest love on His soldier and servant and His child. Sacrificium dei spiritus contribulatus est, cor contritum et humiliatum Deus non despicies. You are as He would have you ; you see plain. He has let you take your way.

Keep your heart close to Him, as the noble and solitary soldier said, of whom this generation was not worthy,[1] and He will bring you out of the mire and clay and set your feet upon a rock and order your goings.

I don't for an instant mean that by a mere emotion of the soul you should throw yourself upon God and do nothing, but my profound belief is that in so doing you will see clearer and gain courage and tranquillity of soul ; your imagination will be ruled and your judgment strengthened.

To Bernard Holland

LOGGIA, *24th July.*

... We have a fine blowing day after a still, warm, and starlight night. I looked late out of my window. The sky was light in the north, and in the south one great planet shone and throbbed far above the rest. The great elms made a great darkness opposite the windows, and bats and moths, with their hoods and woolly capes and beaded eyes, were on the wing.

If you had been next door to me you would have been looking out too. I often think of you standing on the top of the little outside staircase at Fox Holm, in moonlight and starlight, or early morning.

[1] Gordon.

To Miss Mason

THE LODGE, HARBLEDOWN, *8th August.*

I might really be able to look in *en route* from York. I will write thence on the chance.

But I cannot fix anything because I am at the mercy of the winds and waves, that is, of the unruly wills and affections of my darling family, and may have to scurry straight back here from York.

Then again I shall be all redolent of the York convent, and perhaps ought to go into quarantine before introducing myself and box into a healthy Anglican household.

Agnes and her husband are here from Cornwall, full of the pleasure of your brother's company. All he said and did and looked was perfection. I can well believe it.

To Bernard Holland

THE LODGE, *11th August.*

After you and Will were gone yesterday, Agnes and I avoided successfully two sets of callers by rather ignobly hiding in the nut copse while Amy conscientiously searched the premises, and the horses uneasily pawed the slope, and then we went to walk in the breathless woods. The copse is all grown too high, and the common is almost impassable, and while the wind sits in the west there is no air. We were glad to emerge again at the right-of-way stile, and to trend homewards to the teapot. I ought to fulfil my word to-day, and go to pace the alleys and walled gardens of Hales Place with the gentle and accomplished Père du Lac, but I cannot make up my mind to it. Something cries in my heart in all the Augusts of the years of my life, and makes me turn from offered pleasures. So I shall go on till the night is done and in the morn those angel faces smile. I am not unhappy, but I want nothing. The only source of unhappiness to me at this moment is that my dearest son is not happy, but still I am persuaded that, if he takes this from God he will be guided into peace.

Agnes's visit gives me great satisfaction. She is perfectly well and quite content. She has excellent sense and a firm hold on her religion, and she will, I think, increase in strength of purpose. Will is a fortunate man to have her for his friend and faithful companion. She has all the best qualities for her calling.

To Francis Holland

THE CONVENT, MICKLEGATE BAR, YORK, 18*th August.*

York is much more of a capital than Canterbury. A much prouder city, but there is no charm or mystery in the huge minster. The most beautiful thing in it is the lovely Chapter-house—circular, perfect, and delicate, as the bell of a flower, larger than the chapter-house at Westminster, and the beautifully poised roof unsupported by any pillar. I think that one is sensible of a different climate from that of Kent. The sky is dun—and the meadow grass coarse—perhaps because of the huge smoky cities not many miles away. There is nothing of the violet horizons of Surrey, or the pale bright blue of our own kingdom. This is the oldest convent in England and derives from Mary Ward, an interesting person in the days of Charles I. She was of noble family and allied to the best blood in Yorkshire, and had many strange adventures, and a lovely countenance. She was not successful in her own lifetime—being before her age—but all modern convents are carrying out her ideas of increased liberty and higher education for women. Farewell till we meet, my dearest boy. I shall have time and much inclination to pray for all graces and blessings for you—and do you think of me as you walk about the fields and see the sunset over the woods and the divine pallor of my tea-roses in the waning light.

To Bernard Holland

THE LODGE, 3rd September.

Agnes and I intend to drive over to Godmersham this afternoon and sit awhile by St. Lawrence's low church wall. But Lucy is not dead, sunk though she be beneath the " flowery " floor. We shall see her again after we ourselves have fought through the shadows and phantoms of this lower world ; and long before that day comes, I think that you will be free from difficulties, and be found serving God with a quiet mind, pliable in all things to His will. But I am often frightened to perceive how earnestly I desire for you, not, perhaps, so much what God wills, but what you will.

To E. M. (in Japan)

THE LODGE, 5th September.

My darling E. M.—Your letter of 6th August has just come to hand, and its words burn themselves into my heart while my tears drop upon them. Your poor Jugero, Christ's poor Jugero! What does it matter whether an angel or a hand of flesh and blood threw the "pice," the miracle is the same, if it came direct from God, to His poor child tramping the lonely hills. I will pray for Jugero, and I wish he would pray for me.

Why not your Quaker friend, my E. M., why not combine? He is doing Christ's work: he is not smiling in scorn, and setting limits to the Gospel. But oh! my E. M., if you and he did but belong to the old faith that rejoices in just such things as those that have happened to Jugero? I don't want to persuade or to disturb, but if you only knew or could imagine! There are plenty of things as regards discipline, and perhaps some of doctrine difficult to arrange with, but when one has made but half a dozen steps within the vast precincts of the ancient, first, and last Church, all the noise of commonplace dies away and is infinitely removed and remote. You *cannot*, my E. M. imagine it, and it is of no use to tell to you, though I feel as if I would almost give my soul for yours. There is no delusion on my part; it is all true and the only truth —a thousand times you have acknowledged it in our old readings, you must have done so. Well, don't answer me in this, you will only say something that might hurt, and all I want is to have you back, and to hold you in my arms. That is all my immediate aim, chère rachetée de mon Dieu! You know that it is.

You will remember, my E. M., that everything I have in the world is yours, and that I have always now too much house-room, and too many servants, and that if you will make us your headquarters for life there is nothing would please us better, and you will never imagine that I should worry you on questions. No one feels that who lives with us or visits us. I have not a shadow of anxiety about any of Christ's servants, and only bless Him with my whole soul that He has permitted them still to love me.

With love from all here, I am ever your true and faithful friend, SIBYL HOLLAND.

To Bernard Holland

THE LODGE, 12th September.

Our superb weather continues. One day certifies another. The hoppers rejoice, and all the roses are out again.

There is nothing to relate; no news except that at 4.30 A.M. the silver crescent of the moon rides in the east just above the dark elms, while the rosy dawn flushes the sky to the south and south-east, and the Great Bear wheels round on his head, preparatory to plunging below the northern fringe of wood.

And, of an evening, as we sit talking by Frank's fire on the hill under the fir clump, the evening star hangs in the sunset, exceeding fair, and the hop oasts give out a piercing odour, and the young men standing on the waggons sling up the great round sacks.

Are such things to be seen at Brome, in heaven and earth? Have the tea-roses, the September roses, the divine pallor in the twilight that mine have? Can any curfew be heard when the winds are still? Have troops of pilgrims ever tramped the road to Scole?

Is there any place like Kent?

To Francis Holland

THE LODGE, 20th September.

Our weather has broken, and the gales of the Equinox are all abroad, roaring in the tossing elms and sending the delicate rose-petals flying. But the sun is out, and the country shines like a clear mirror.

Papa will be tossed on the ocean. He sails the 24th. I will send you his last letter when I know where you are. He says Vancouver is a paradise. Bernard and I have much talk.

To Francis Holland

THE LODGE, *22nd September.*

The Judge [1] *is* very like Dr. Johnson in many ways—exterior and interior. I have always thought so. There is a particular kindness about him, almost a tenderness—don't you think so? He was ever most kind to me, and I hope he has not put away the kindness in spite of my aberrations. . . . I hope that you will never give way to the demon of melancholy. Nothing so hinders and paralyses all the best part of the mind. A passion of grief is another thing. That even restores occasionally, but a settled melancholy is to be abhorred even for only an hour. My head is full of rheumatism, and I cannot write.

[I left England for India on the morning of Monday, 29th September 1890. My mother drove with me from Harbledown to the station at Canterbury, where I was to take the Dover train. I parted with her at the door of the station, and last saw her as she still sat in the carriage which had brought us, never to see her again in this world.]

To Bernard Holland

THE LODGE, *1st October.*

I drove away from the station on Monday feeling very ill, nor have I yet lost the physical sensation. It

---

[1] Sir James Fitzjames Stephen.

is, however, of no use to say more as to this. You know, or at least can partly guess, all that you are to me. I hope that as you move along courage will return. . . . I spent some hours in the Precincts, sitting talking with Mrs. Rawlinson in the bowling-green, and then got a telegram to say that Uncle A. would not be home till the late boat train, and so drove up here and read some old letters, and wrote some new ones, and said the Itinerary for you, which you will find in the *Garden of the Soul*, and then talked to Anne Frossel, who suddenly appeared and was very nice and affectionate.

I don't know what is portended by the arrival of all these old servants. Sarah on Sunday, Anne on Monday. Anne slept for a night, and went off shedding tears next morning. I have hung up your straw hat in my room, and put all your room in order. I miss hearing you shut your window at night, after your evening meditation, and there is no one to want an early cup of tea. When all the children go, besides the actual pain of losing them, the mother loses her occupation.

To Francis Holland

THE LODGE, 9*th October*.

I so very much value all your expressions of affection. My children give me far more pleasure than anxiety; but I am not precisely anxious, but, as it were, bereft, missing their sweet company. Yet I like them to move about. Your sojourn in the Lakes has given me pleasure, because I can imagine and be sure of yours. I fell in love with that country, and that you love it also gives us another thing to love in common. Hobbes says quite truly, All pain is prospective. It is the idea of the long time that Ber will be away, and that he may not during that time be happy, that grieves me, not the fact that he is at this instant away.

To her Niece, the Hon. Mrs. Charles Cropper

22 HALF-MOON STREET, 21st October.

My dearest Edith—I have put in here for the afternoon on my way home from Surrey to Kent, and Frank has just told me that you have a fourth little daughter, and that her name is Sibylla. It only shows how much communication has lessened in my direction that I should neither have known that this sweet soul was on her way to our world of varied good and ill, or that she already breathed this mortal air, *for mortal air it is.*

I do not for a moment imagine that you gave her my name because it is mine, but that you did not avoid giving it for that reason; and that you did give it makes me feel an interest in the child, and I shall always remember her in my prayers, and be her bedeswoman at shrines not approached by any other of the dear family.

I think with pleasure of your little visit to me about two years ago, and I shall always hope that you may come again, and that you will believe that I am ever your affectionate aunt, SIBYLLA.

To Miss Mason

LODGE, HARBLEDOWN, 22nd October.

I have been away. We fed a hundred clergy and teachers last Wednesday; as I live we did so feed them, and next day I fled before the face of bishops and archbishops, but crept back here last night, and am now engaged in reducing a pile of letters, among which yours meets my eye only and my heart. I have remembered your brother every day in psalms and hymns and spiritual songs. I do pray that all may be laid out for him, and that he will see his way clear as a shining track of light.

I am in a sort of demi-high spirits at the idea of your arrival on Wednesday. Half of me rises like an ill-kneaded loaf.—Your ever affectionate

SIBYL HOLLAND.

To Bernard Holland (in India)

PRECINCTS, *7th November.*

We came down here on All Saints Day, and the Lodge already seems to be fifty miles off. Our weather is mild, a blustering south-west wind whirling the lime leaves into space, and carrying the rooks and jackdaws round Bell-Harry in joyous circles. Now and then a pale sun illuminates the too familiar scene. Papa and I drove to Godmersham with some white flowers for our lost white flower. The church from the road below the bridge was set in every tint of gold and amber, behind which rose the Down white with the bent grass ; the stream ran clear, swift, and strong below. Our little graves were all clipt close and neat, all was quiet, in order, and full of bright transitory colour. Tell Uncle James I thought of him at Godmersham ; I always think of him there. Afterwards we called at the Vicarage, then at the great House where no one was at home, but the butler was so glad of some one to talk to that he made us quite a long speech. Then we called at Chilham Castle where all were out. Then we took tea with Mrs. ———, very solemn, kind, and pious, with a lurking spite of her neighbours. Then to the Cockerells where all was youth, good humour, and wild spirits. Did I tell you that I went for a Sunday and Monday last month to Cambridge? In the morning I went to mass in the new church, not very interesting somehow, and in the afternoon to King's where I met Katherine Stephen, and next day went with her over Newnham which pleased me much on account of the great attention to detail, and the general thoroughly feminine air of all the arrangements.

I am very busy with my sick people, etc. Castle's daughter's husband dying of consumption touches me very much. So simple and tender and hard-working; so sorry to lay down his tools and leave his good little wife and boys whom he has overworked himself for, such a natural dread of the awful change, and such a humble dependence upon God.

To Miss Mason

CANTERBURY, *Sunday Evening, 9th November.*

Somehow I always take a long week to settle down in the Precincts, which must be my excuse for not having written to you. I have thought of you very often, and of your brother, wondering a little about what God has in store for him, whether to call him to high office or to leave him in the ranks,—far happier so in my opinion, for dignities mean so many bonds.

After you were gone a sadness settled down in my mind, because of you, and it is still there. I suppose that it is that each time we meet and *talk* a difference is accentuated. You can speak freely to me, but not I to you. I understand you but you cannot by any possibility understand me. I can talk your language but not you mine.

However this enforced darkness does not and cannot diminish my love for you, perhaps it increases it, just as I used to be much pleased to hear my young sons talk of matters which they had no experience of, nor I wit enough to show them the truth about. Their honesty, candour, and ingenuity pleased me, and I knew that the experience would come, and then that they would go a hundred times more surely and intelligently than ever their poor mamma could do. With you the experience will not come, *voilà tout!* but you must never, my Agnes, persuade yourself that you can perfectly judge the matter without it.

I have been reading all day Mr. Mackonochie's life. It is very interesting, and shows him so good, and so great and simple in his work and character, and there are many such men in the English Church. I am pleased too with a blue cloth book called *Our Lady's Dower* by Father Bridgett. It is not controversial but of research, and contains many pretty and pious things. Ever my dear Agnes—Your affectionate poor friend,
SIBYL HOLLAND.

To Francis Holland

PRECINCTS, 24*th November.*

Our weather continues to blow warm from the south. I have a large bunch of roses from the Lodge. The watchman cried all the hours last night. I lay awake and responded. I could not sleep for having talked to ———, old friends have a right to ask questions, and it is a sort of relief to talk openly—at the same time it raises ghosts by the thousand, nor are they laid without exorcism.

To the Same

1st December.

... I am wholly swallowed up by the papers all the morning, and by the *Egoist* of an afternoon and evening. But I am longing to get to the last chapter and my freedom of mind again. It is too much. He makes me feel myself an egoist. As for Parnell he is like Milton's hero in council. I agree with every word he says (for the Irish), and admire his wondrous tactics. The whole question of the Irish party lies in Parnell's words *If you sell me*, etc. etc. Meantime how good, kind, and wise does Balfour radiate, with his well-cast schemes and courageous responsibility!

To Bernard Holland (in India)

PRECINCTS, *4th December.*

Take all my greetings for your birthday, and for Christmas. You will at least, I think, have a cheery Christmas in India and I like to think of you making one with the party there. Ever since I was a little child of three or four years old I have had to think of India. At Godmersham your grandmother used to end the Christmas toasts with, "and Cousin John in India!" a Cousin John who never came home. We have been deep in snow and ice. All the towers and roofs and ivied walls wrapped in white silence. It has been cold in Cornwall too. Agnes writes that as she sat alone in her little drawing-room writing to me, at nine in the evening, a little wren, scarcely larger than a bumble-bee and noiseless as the down before the wind, lighted down on her paper. It must have been in the room for hours. It spent the evening with her, playing about on the table and carpet and replying to her whistle with a cheerful chirp. If nothing comes of your hawk and her wren I shall think that our mysterious relationship with birds is over, and that they have settled down upon ordinary good fellowship. . . .

. . . I am absorbed by the Irish debates among themselves, but as events will have moved by the time you receive this letter I will only remark that on his side of the question I am inclined to think Parnell in the right. He knows that morality has nothing to do with the matter, and if he leaves the saddle to please Nonconformists how is he to know that he can ever mount again? Those words of his, "Don't sell me unless you can get fair value for me," seems to contain the whole question for the Irish party. I don't see that they will get much value for him.

E. M. (*in Japan*)

CANTERBURY, 3*rd December*.

. . . Did I tell you that I had a long sit with the Canon of Westminster last month? He looked very well and was full of nothing but Newman, got out letters to show me, and went back upon things, and talked with all the enthusiasm imaginable of the great man. I sat silent enough, for somehow the Cardinal's personality is nothing to me. I think, E. M., that it is a fault in

me to care not enough about *persons*, at least the
persons of writers. If you have their writings you have
the very best of them. I would much rather *see* and
observe C. W. F., for example, who isn't a writer but a
man of action. But you know it is rather a silly position for me when I sit to hear eulogies on a Cardinal
by an Anglo-Catholic. I havn't got anything to say in
reply, and I came away full of affection, but empty
otherwise. And I am getting a sad habit of silence.
You must come home and break it for me. You must
determine beforehand, my E. M., that you will say and
let me say. Do not let there be any blocks of silence
between you and me. I shall not wish to try to convert
you, but I shall love to talk openly.

We are full of snow and ice here, a silent city.
Bell Harry rears himself with all his fretwork picked
out with snow and his long gray back clad in a white
mantle. The red roofs of the houses and the old ivied
walls are all covered up. The fluffy birds alight noiselessly as feathers on the frozen ground. Mysterious
humped-up figures flit round the great church; they
may be Deans and Archdeacons, or they may be
butchers and bakers, so levelling of outward distinction
is the heaped up dazzling snow. I went across to the
Cathedral at 4 P.M. and sat down in the lovely half-
light of the north transept, and said my rosary to the
sweet whirling music of the psalms. Over the purple-
drawn curtains the choir lights struck up into the high
vaulting of the roof. I thought of many things and
of many persons. How often have I seen Lucy cross
that transept to and fro with her sweet face set as
though she were hurrying on a way. Do you know
the expression? You cannot imagine, my E. M., how
I cry out for Lucy. In this empty house I cannot

help sometimes listening for her step overhead—folly it is.

Bernard writes happily from India. As he sailed the Indian Ocean and was quietly playing chess on the upper deck, a hawk flew in from the sea and settled on his head. And two days ago as Agnes was writing to me alone in her little vicarage in Cornwall at nine in the evening, a tiny wren alighted on her paper and spent the evening with her. No bigger than a thimble, she says, and light and noiseless as down before the wind. But I have suffered too much to be any longer superstitious.

I remember catching your eye, your dark eye, the last summer at Fox Holm when we were sitting on the lawn and a robin flew in at Lucy's window.[1]—Ever your loving SIBYL.

To Francis Holland

CANTERBURY, 10*th December.*

I am fascinated by the *Egoist*.[2] The scene in which, while his mother's death is imminent, he pictures his own, and wants to make Clara *swear*, is extraordinarily good, and that word of hers, " I can only be of value to you, Willoughby, by *being myself,*" contains the very gospel of marriage. So many marriages are more or less spoilt by the man wanting the woman to be his echo—not his friend.

I think that Mr. Dicey's letter in the *Times* is very good. I suppose that the only principle in admiring Parnell consists in the sort of admiration one feels to

---

[1] There is an old country idea that wild birds entering a house predict a coming death.
[2] Meredith's novel.

any super-eminent quality, by whomsoever exercised. *Beauty* strongly calls it out—so why not *courage?* David could not help forgiving Absalom, because of the personal beauty in which he had delighted.

To Miss Trueman

Thursday Evening, 8.30.

My dearest Florence—I wish that . . . had not been here to cut off a few parting words. Not that I have anything especial to say. That silent kneeling side by side, in the most sacred part of our dear Cathedral was far more than any words. As I write the sacring bell of St. Thomas' strikes the three strokes for the end of Benediction. I pray our dear Lord and His blessed Mother to have you in their holy keeping while you are away, and to bring you back in peace to your dear ones, among whom please reckon me who loves you truly and tenderly.—Ever your affectionate friend,

SIBYL HOLLAND.

To Bernard Holland

CHRISTMAS DAY, CANTERBURY.

I was much interested by your account of the discourse of the Cambridge Mission preacher at Delhi. Möhler's famous book on Symbolism is written to show that the central point of difference between Catholic and Protestant lies in the way in which the doctrine of the fall of man is held. The Calvinistic view (originally derived perhaps from St. Augustine's writing) is that no good was left in man. The Catholic view is that the image of God, in which he was created, is ineffaceable, though distorted and defaced. He was created in it, and it is an integral part of his nature.

I went to the Cathedral this afternoon with Frank and Uncle Alfred. We had the Pastoral Symphony, the Handel Chorus, and " Hark the Herald Angels." As we came out of the little south door at 4.35 the light had faded eastwards, but the west was like a great curtain of orange and rose, where the sun had just gone down. Uncle Alfred and I walked across the oaks, and round by St. Martin's Hill and Barton Fields before tea. The ground is hard as ice, one could skate along the roads ; everywhere is ice and silence, and a biting air. All the children look like red apples, and everybody treads in the middle of the road, and no one stands still for a moment. I have sent out numberless plum puddings, bottles of wine, and Churchwood rabbits to all my old friends ; and, notwithstanding the pinch of cold, a cheerful feeling seems to prevail.

XI

LETTERS OF 1891

To a Lady expecting a Child

CANTERBURY, *10th January.*

... OF course, for general purposes, I hope for a boy, but a little " fair maid of February," coming among the snowdrops, would be very pretty too. Still, " Father and Son," " Son and Mother," are great names in heaven and earth. But all is as God wills ; and from my heart I say His will be done ! His will be mine ; His will be thine ; blessed for ever be His holy Name !

To Miss Mason

LONDON, *13th January.*

I return the nice letters ; good material for the flying leaf. I do hope that you will make quite a new booklet for the Guild. That Guild paper with the two squat rule and prayer papers danced before my eyes in the night, and assumed proportions of such size in regard of commonplace and stupidity that I caught myself imagining that it was enough to prevent people joining the Guild, and really, by *daylight*, I think that a wholly new paper is a pressing need.

It was good of you to come up through the fog; you are just the friend to appear in a fog of any kind, and to hand one out of it. Now I come to think of it, it is your very calling. I am off at 1.50; every vein in my body streaming towards Canterbury, and my own room, and household, and husband.—Ever am I your grateful and affectionate,   SIBYL HOLLAND.

To the Same

PRECINCTS, 14*th January.*

It is the hand of God, my darling girl; it is the will of God. It is His design from all eternity that thus, just thus, and at exactly such a time this should come to pass. So He willed it when your father's soul first left His hand, so He fulfils it now when He calls it back to His hand. But oh! the pain for you, and for those dear to you; and oh! your father might answer, *the rest for me*—the sleep in Christ, the place of refreshment and light and peace, the morning instead of the evening, the renewal and increase of life. There are a thousand consolations, but nothing that touches upon or lessens the parting.

I shall think of you every moment, my dearest Agnes; and I know how all your many friends, whom you love and serve so faithfully, will feel for you. Your name will be in all our hearts, and on all our lips.

It is of no use for me to write more till I know more; write when you are able.—Your faithful sorrowing friend,   SIBYL HOLLAND.

To the Same

CANTERBURY, *Sunday, January.*

My dearest Agnes—I am so glad and thankful to know about your blessed father. What a quiet and beautiful death: and how beautiful his face must have looked these days! White on his pillow, and the world all white without. I am so glad to have seen him in his house among you all. I always think of him in two places—one, walking lightly along that broad walk along from the house; and the other, sitting easily on the gate by the roadside waiting for us. He was not in the least like an old man. There was something so graceful in both mind and body.

Your mother is wonderful, but don't count upon it too much. There is a sort of *throw off* of the mind under a great shock, and this must be a great shock. You must take infinite care of her dear body. And you yourself, my dear Agnes, who have lost so much. It is easy, comparatively, to draw deep draughts for other people, as long as one can oneself draw from the living spring of unalterable home affections. You have suffered an immense loss, but it came so suddenly, and with so much of sweetness and mercy, that your heart has been full of love and thankfulness. It is all beautiful, but the pain must be there.—Your loving,

SIBYL HOLLAND.

To the Same

CANTERBURY, *January.*

Oh no, my dearest Agnes, I would not discourage you. I think that all is right with you, and it is not

possible but that our Lord looks with the tenderest love
and approval upon all that you do, and say, and feel
in respect of your blessed father, of whom really one
may say he was not, for God took him; and it is a
great thing to have been spared that hopeless struggle
for life, and that dread of parting which, as Möhler
says, testifies to the unnaturalness of death. Man was
not so *created*.

I daresay that your father looked beautiful in death,
with that mystery of both worlds on his placid brow.
It will be very good for your mother to be with the
son who was not there, and to have to tell him quietly
all about it.

To Francis Holland

20th January.

You are at work again to-day in the centre of
things. I am glad that you were admitted to the
M.A. degree in such a solemn manner and with the
greatest imaginable words. I wish that I could for
twenty-four hours have been a young man and your
best college friend, and come also to take my M.A.
and to sit up into the small hours with you. How
fond I should have been of you, and I daresay you
would have liked the company of your little brown
friend. In the other world (and may the Father, the
Son, and the Holy Ghost bring us there), where there
will be no age, I shall renew my youth and you will
know me young as you have known me old. . . . I
have some very sick people on hand, and visiting them
keeps my spirits piano piano. They are poor, but
young and reluctant to die. I said to a young man,
" The weather is milder and the men will be out to dig

the hop grounds." "Yes," said he, and burst into passionate weeping, "and there is nothing for me but the cold grave, and I have so loved to work."

To E. M. (in Japan)

CANTERBURY, 23rd January.

... The difficulty of mission work seems so great now. What made the natives catch fire in former days and come in to the fold of Christ, never to return to their old gods? Why does not the Spirit blow as He did then? The missionaries are as believing and devoted in many places. Something has grown cold in the world, as St. Francis said. I think that at home here there is a fast increasing indifference among the working people to all religion. The Catholic religion has no more hold on them than anything else. They are neither in the parish churches nor chapels, and, as far as I can see, they are quite indifferent to the Salvation Army. They all, more or less, believe in God; but they live their own life.

In many respects Christians are now far inferior to their mediæval forefathers. The more I read the more this strikes me. . . .

. . . I think that I shall never see my children's children, but that is as it pleases God, blessed for ever be His holy Name, for all that He gives and all that He withholds. He gave me your friendship, which was a great good gift to me and mine. I don't fret for my scattered children. There is alway much to do here, even though I am out of all committees, etc.; but the sick-visiting tries me rather, because I cannot say my whole mind to my sick. I cannot think why they so like me to come, except they think that I too have known trouble.

To Bernard Holland (*in India*)

CANTERBURY, 23rd *January.*

Old M—— has been ill all the winter and has just paid me a visit. He sat sipping a glass of wine and pronouncing upon things. He has got a great many phrases, such as, "We are not all made alike, nor is it fit we should," a familiar Canterbury saying. He observed that "Our Lord went through the world with a great amount of goodness and no interest whatsoever in worldly affairs, and this enabled Him to see clear and to speak plain." He says that he finds there is a great deal of truth in the gospel, and ended by saying that of all things he was fond of "ruralising," and had been since a boy, by which he meant moralising. His own father had made away with himself in the Stour, and was found near Sandwich twenty-six days afterwards, whereas the Duke of —— "had gone off with firearms." "'Tis mostly fire or water," says M——, "sometimes they are cast into the fire and sometimes into the water, by which we may plainly know who sets the temptation agoing."

Not much happens externally. In myself I am much at peace, and were you happily settled in life I should cease to desire anything ardently, except to live in charity with all men, and to make a good end of my careless life. I should like to know whether any one who comes after me will ever be a Catholic, as I am, for to him or to her would I leave the few things that I hold most dear among my small goods and chattels.

To Francis Holland

CANTERBURY, 30*th January*.

I am so sorry that I missed Frank Newman's letter. It is very odd of the old man to break out now against his brother. I think that perhaps he has been for many years devoured with jealousy. He was thought his brother's equal in intellect as a young man. But a man who only pulls down cannot make the same mark in the world as the man who builds up. Nevertheless I have sometimes thought that perhaps Cardinal Newman has been over-estimated. I wonder what he would have done had he remained out in the world instead of withdrawing into a charmed circle at Birmingham. Perhaps this very withdrawal, together with the *Apologia*, and the careful arrangement made with regard to the publishing of his correspondence point to some existence of the *ego* still alive and moving in his noble heart. "A strange creature," G. C. P. says, "J. H. N. always was." But I must try to see his brother's letter.

To Francis Holland

CANTERBURY, 18*th February*.

We have a thick white sea mist this morning. Bell Harry all shrouded, but tolling for the funeral of George Austin. Yesterday I spent chiefly in bed, and amused myself with the Layman's mass book, a thirteenth-century book of devotions in English, and also with Ward's *Ideal*, which entertains me very much because he states so exactly all my old difficulties as to the Anglican Church being identical with that of the

Fathers, and there is something so audacious in the way he goes along, for at that time he was an Aglican. I should like to read Bishop Berkeley, and will "when the May is white with blossom, and the fountain flows again."

To Bernard Holland (*in India*)

CANTERBURY, *26th February.*

I thought that by this time I should be able to give you some news of dear —— but none has reached me. February is, I think, a very good month to be born in; all the year lies ahead with its bloom and fruit and ingathering.

I just see in Newman's letters that his birthday was 21st February 1801. Newman's anxiety and careful arrangements as to the publication of his letters after his death is a singular feature in his character. I sympathise in his immense desire of being understood, and in his idea that to misunderstand him was in a degree to misunderstand his religion, but yet I think it somewhat of a weakness. However, I have only just begun his letters, and I may take a different view presently. I wonder whether, if Newman had been born a Catholic in Catholic days, he would have been a great Churchman. I rather think that polemics quickened his spiritual nature, and that he owed much of his special influence to the fact that he was in opposition. Something in his way of letter-writing reminds me of yours. I am also reading the *Tracts for the Times*, and all the occasional pamphlets straight through—it is very amusing reading.

We are having perfect weather for the special affairs of the kingdom.[1] The ground has been made

[1] Kingdom of Kent.

so friable by the frosts that it hardly wants turning over before putting in the seeds. Bell Harry is wrapt in moonlit sea mists all night, but by 8.30 A.M. casts off this veil, and is clothed in majesty by the clearest sunshine. I am leading a silent and busy life, and find the day too short for what I have to put into it. Two of my sick people are lying dead, and their wasted bodies contrast with the springing year; but the streets are full of children; every girl skips and every boy drives a top. This invariable custom comes into play on Candlemas day. It is cheerful, but impedes traffic. No one ever reproves a child in Canterbury. I have always observed this. Perhaps the children, if scolded, would not go out hopping or fruiting with their mammas. There is probably a solid reason somewhere for this extraordinary indulgence.

To Francis Holland

CANTERBURY, 7th March.

Monday, the London antiquarians will be here again. The director, Mr. Milman, has rummaged up an MS. in which Henry VIII. is made to say that he never give no horders[1] for burning the bones of St. Thomas, but on the contrary that they were buried in a certain round tower. So there will be more explaining and talking, which is a great amusement to me. My teeth are all right again now. Nothing is as bad as it seems in prospect. . . . I might perhaps go to London for Thursday and Good Friday. I should like once to hear the famous Tenebrae. . . . I see that Froude had a notion that there was a strong re-

---

[1] Kentish way of talking.

semblance, body and mind, between Julius Cæsar and Newman. But surely there was *not*. Newman had not governing talent; he would have made a bad bishop, and it is impossible to imagine him a Pope. Whereas one can easily imagine Julius Cæsar in those capacities. Then he says their mouths were the same. But where in Julius Cæsar's face was that underhung lip of J. H. N.'s? Froude always talks so *loosely*.

To Miss Arnold-Forster

CANTERBURY, 10*th March*.

I am surprised to hear of you still in London. I was thinking you were at home again. You will certainly have enjoyed seeing so many dear kind faces, and hearing so many friendly affectionate words. Friends are so dear, so unspeakably dear; I feel this more and more. Love *costs*, but it is the pearl of great price, isn't it?

To Bernard Holland (*in India*)

LONDON, *Good Friday*.

Your letter from Isa Khel enclosing verses gave me the sweetest pleasure. It really is charming, and the verses are beautiful. Your muse has returned, my son.

I am here surreptitiously for Maundy Thursday and Good Friday, just for once, to hear the voice of the Church in the Lamentations and great chanted Antiphons. . . . I am cheered by your last letter and verses. They read happy and strong. I trace Tolstoi. I am reading his book called *Life*. Some passages in it affect me as passages in Gordon affected me, and when he names Christ I kiss the page. He *is* a servant of Christ and a saint, I think, and he speaks from the heart of things.

To the Same

PRECINCTS, 2nd *April.*

I was in London for Easter Eve and went to all the morning services at the Oratory. They brought the new fire into the church; blest the fire, the water, the oil, the salt, the chrism—in short all the great preparatory ceremonies for Easter Day; all carried out finely, great order, promptness and very fine music. I saw things done as St. Gregory I. established them in the days of St. Augustine. The melodious cry of *Lumen Christi*, as they lit the first candle from the fire struck at the entrance of the church with flint and tinder, was very striking. This was repeated again in the centre of the church under the dome, and again in the sanctuary on the lighting of the third candle. So was the ancient "prose" sung by the Deacon on the lighting of the great Pascal candle, and so were the twelve long lections read from the Old Testament and the Holy Saturday mass and the first great Alleluia. I was very much pleased.

To the Hon. Mrs. Duckworth (on the death of a young married daughter).

THE PRECINTS, 12*th April.*

My husband has shown me your letter, and my tears flowed as I read your natural expressions of grief, and renewed my own. Heart-rending it truly is to part with these darling creatures and to survive so much hope and joy and love.

I know what I say, for I too have lost children—a boy whom I loved too passionately, and a charming daughter in the flower of her age. He was suddenly drowned on a summer day, and her I accompanied step by step through a long year to the very brink of the grave. I know how God can strike and I know how He can heal, blessed for ever be His holy name.

In these great sorrows two thoughts sustained me. After the boy's death I one day opened an old book and read these words written to a mother whose only son had been killed in battle: "You must know, madam," the letter said, "that neither did marriage give you this child, nor did death take him away, but the *Will of God.*"

This, I thought, was true, and I went on to consider that this very thing that had happened to us and our sweet springing boy had been the exact Will of God for us and for him through all eternity, and that the whole story of the child's life had lain in the Mind of God, and that when He sent his soul into the world He knew precisely in what hour and on what day and under what circumstances He should recall it; and that my life lay in the same way in the hollow of His hand, and that this deep grief was a part of it, and that all that was left me to do was to enter into His design.

> O dolce lume a cui fidanza i entro!
> . . . . . .
> In la sua volontade è nostra pace
> Ella è quel mare, al qual tutto si muove.

And again, through the long illness of Lucy so loving

and tenderly loved, and so worthy of love, I thought of Calvary, and a thousand times as she lay dying, for there was never any hope, I carried her to the foot of the Cross, and laid her there, where Jesus and His Mother give to us poor mothers and children tear for tear, wound for wound, love for love. It is the only habitable place in all the universe for a mother and her dead or dying child,—there we strike the bottom of the ocean of grief, and thence we draw the power of still living and loving and hoping. Here your heart, though pierced through and through, is yet enlarged and set at liberty, so that you love all tender and young married women in your lost daughter—and she lives; of that we are certain, and, while our tears fall, she is sunning herself in Paradise. She is risen with Christ, and there is no more death for her. I often think of Fénelon's words: " Encore un moment et il n'y aura plus de quoi pleurer, c'est nous qui mourons . . . elle ne moura plus."

You say you have been so happy; how good God is! We must not take His gifts instead of Himself; that is such a great mistake, and leads to so much pain. I know how you must suffer, and that life will be different—this is what God wills, but He will comfort. I pray for you with all my heart.

To Francis Holland

CANTERBURY, *4th May.*

. . . May some good angel speed B.'s business . . . this is a day of Paradise. I wish that you and I were in Normandy, in an old farmhouse buried in blossoming orchards sloping down to the clear waters of the Seine and set thick with primroses.

To the Same

FRESHWATER, *30th May.*

... Christ and His apostles seem to intimate that wealth and poverty will always continue, and that the kingdom will to the end of the world consist of those who resist its influence. It is the essence of Christianity to give up ease and comfort for Christ's sake, to go down and live among the poor, and to help them to bear the inevitable burden. ... He (Tolstoi) says that if no one ordered yachts or pictures or fine buildings the slavery of the world would cease—and certainly, Frank, I believe that the slavery of free England to-day is a thousand and a thousand times more miserable than anything the negroes have ever suffered. It darkens the sunlight to think of it. Yesterday I went a long walk with the old poet (Tennyson), and he talked a great deal. He can walk for *miles*. He attacked me about my religion as we plodded up a long hill. He led up to the subject, but I beat about a little; but at last he was absolutely direct, so that I was obliged to reply and the storm broke. I stood my ground notwithstanding the war of the elements, and when the thunder ceased and the clouds rolled back, we were found discussing *ghosts* with quiet minds. It is delightful to feel the freedom and assurance with which one can talk to a distinguished intellect, no accommodations are necessary, one has only to be quite honest and clear and one is certain to be understood. If I walk again with him, I will see what he thinks of the subject of your paper. The weather is lovely. We have had a cold wind and a few showers, but none of your Epsom weather. I am so glad that this will find you at Fox Warren—all the bluebells will be out on the lawn at dear Fox Holm. I wonder that my astral body (which the poet was talking of yesterday) does not flit about those wood walks in the deepening summer twilight or in the light morning mists. I have often been out on the lawn at 3.30 A.M. and seen the dew lift in clouds of light steam as the June sun rose. Nowadays base thoughts of rheumatism keep me indoors if not in bed.

To E. M. (*in Japan*)

PRECINCTS, 18*th June*.

... All you say about Jugero made me weep. I feel about him exactly as you do. Who is worthy to receive if such a simple believer is turned away. He would have adhered more clearly to Jesus had he been one of those who heard the wondrous and searching words of St. John vi. It is to be remarked that our Lord expected what He there says to be taken as it stood. He seems to have made no attempt to explain them to those who had hitherto followed but now left Him. It would not have made any difficulty to Jugero, mark you, nor to me. ... Jugero's soul is safe with his Master who loves him as a mother may love her babe which has died before it could draw the breast. Happy you who begot him in Christ Jesus. That expression of forming Christ in the soul, and bringing forth and giving birth to children in Christ must be very applicable where you are.

... Early this month I spent a week at Freshwater. Every day I talked and walked with old Tennyson, which interested me very much. He is so absolutely simple and veracious with his rough manner and few words that he attracted me powerfully. Besides, I have all my life been enslaved by his enchanting poems.

I enjoyed my visit to darling Agnes. Saltash is a very pretty and singular place and more cheerful than you can imagine. Agnes's house is all neatness and order, and she and her husband lead an excellent useful life. I have been alone here eight or nine days, while F. is at Saltash. All the rooms empty, nothing but the warm wind filling the silent house. Where are Bernard and Agnes and Lucy and Frank and Michael and E. M. who shared the sunshine and the flowers with us all? *Japan*, and the *Rocky Mountains*, and far *Kashmir*, where Bernard is drifting in a light house-boat, under the flowery forests and in sight of the eternal snows, and *Cornwall*, and *Westminster*, and *the fields of Paradise;* these places hold them; they have passed like shadows from their mother's house. Oh, E. M. come again to see me, before we all go hence one by one.

To Bernard Holland (*in India*)

PRECINCTS, 26*th June*.

The nightingales have sung in the Precincts this year; heart-piercing notes in the silence of the early summer nights. Last night, just as the bell practice began, a sudden storm from the sea, preceded by a thick mist, swept over Canterbury, great claps of thunder and streaming lightning. It was like an assault on Bell Harry, the lightning played all round him. "The bells kep on," as George Castle observed, "and come right through, and when all was said and done there they was, and by the time the curfew begun all was cleared off and you wouldn't know nothing had happened."

To Miss Mason

THE LODGE, 5*th July.*

My dearest Agnes—This letter has been waiting for you since Saturday mid-day. You did not give me the Sandgate address, so I send it to the Metropolis. Our conversations still work in my head, and your sweet manner to me is alive in my heart.—Ever your affectionate   SIBYL HOLLAND.

P.S.—The post has just brought your letter, and the man waits while I write a word and change the cover. What a nice account of Sandgate, but why not bathe on Sunday? (Plenty of reasons for not doing so occur as I write.) You might have bathed in the summer moonlight just before midnight on Saturday. That is a mysteriously delightful thing to do. I knew two brothers, beloved of all, who used to swim out into the shining furrows of the moonlit sea, and come back plashing up the beach.

I haven't time to say anything more than that I am eternally yours,   SIBYL HOLLAND.

To Francis Holland

THE LODGE, 9*th July.*

We have nothing but rain here. The pilgrimage on Tuesday did not go off badly, notwithstanding the weather. I saw the long line of pilgrims and banners coming along the Dane John ramparts, and down High Street. They walked three and three very steadily, the mild-eyed citizens stood at the shop doors and smiled good-humouredly. It was the dinner-hour and Canterbury chiefly occupied in munching. Father

Ephraim sang the Gospel at the pontifical mass very sweetly in the old benedictine "tone." He came in to dine afterwards and said, "Ah, all the time I sang I thought you were hearing me and would be pleased and it gave me courage,"—he is such a simple person.

To Miss Mason

THE LODGE, 12*th July.*

My dearest Agnes—I ought sooner to have returned this very charming letter. "Wild" it is not, rather a steady fragrant flame of love to God and man. You are happy to have such a sweet strong friend working hand in hand with you. Have you got a photograph of her? I should like to see her.

I liked your description of your gardening with Mrs. Mason. I can see your strong hands and brown head and bright weed-searching eyes.

I can't write more. Dear you are to many, to none perhaps more than to me.—Yours ever,

SIBYL HOLLAND.

To Francis Holland

THE LODGE, 13*th July.*

You will be here next Friday, and to that I shall look on with pleasure. Why should I be here alone? The four young "H. Sch. Maams" enjoyed themselves yesterday—such sweet, intelligent, and affectionate creatures. . . . The weather is fine but flagging. The sun hot on this hillside, and the east wind not perceptible. The sound of the great church bells comes up from the city.

... I wish, my son, that you would now abjure the philosophers. You have had two years of them. You turned to them when I turned to the old church, and I think that I made the best bargain.

To the Same

THE LODGE, 30*th July.*

Storms now prevail, spoiling the raspberries, but washing the dark green 'op to its great good. This morning, after heavy early rain, a warm sun began at 8.30 and the teeming earth sends up an immense and universal perfume.

To the Same

ST. MARY'S CONVENT, MICKLEBAR GATE, YORK, 23*rd August.*

I shall not be able to get to the Minster between four and five. But Le Père Morris says do you come here and you can see me for a quarter of an hour, and then take a walk in the Minster or elsewhere with him. He has a passion for York antiquities, and it will be a refreshment to him to have you. Get a wash and something to eat and then come. I shall count on seeing your darling face. This is a large ordinary-looking house just outside Micklebar Gate. ... We have a good deal of rain here, but the large garden in which we pace silently soon dries. I am glad that I came away, but it was an effort at the moment. ... I enclose also a rather touching letter from Aunt Emily; I *will* go and see her. She has been such a faithful friend to me since 1870.

Yesterday was two years since I made my move.

It is odd, rather, that all that has happened has a sort of fragrance in my memory, not in the least pain. If pain there was, all trace of it has faded. Perhaps in another life we shall so remember even days of anguish here. We shall seem to have lived more truly, even though we suffered keenly.—Ever, my sweet, your loving mother, SIBYL HOLLAND.

Much of my meditation takes the turn of considering my children—here, there, or elsewhere. I thank God that I can trust their lives to His good guidance. There is much to make me anxious could I *do* anything in it, but, as I can't, I try to keep a quiet mind and see the hand of God in all things.

CONCLUSION

In the last days of August 1891, my mother left the convent at York, where the Retreat had been conducted by her friend, Father Morris, S.J., and went for a visit of two or three days to her sister at Cavendish, in Suffolk. Here she seemed to be in excellent health and high spirits. She arrived at Harbledown Lodge on the 2nd of September. On the morning of the 3rd of September, the fifth anniversary of her daughter's death, she was taken at breakfast by a sudden "rigor." The nature of her illness was not well understood, but it was thought to be due to a blood-poisoning from an abscess. Her illness was painful but short. She received the last sacraments from Father Morris, and died on the 23rd of September, in the presence of several members of her family. On the 28th of September she was buried, with the Roman Catholic ceremonial, under the south wall of the chancel of Godmersham, close to the grave of the daughter whom she had so ardently loved.

Over that grave, five years earlier, she had caused to be engraved the words from the Latin psalm, "Domine ne moreris," in our version, "Lord, make no long tarrying," an expression of her own hope not to live too long. When death came she received it as a gracious gift from God. My sister, who was with her throughout the illness, wrote at the time: "She longed to die. All through her illness this was her one cry, 'Oh, that God would take me now, *now!* Oh, that this might be my last bed! If He would let me go now, I should think it such a mercy.' She settled everything with a view to this, and gave me many messages."

LINES BY A FRIEND

M. S. H.

23RD SEPTEMBER 1891.

CARVE no stone above her head,
Rather let her praise be read
In the shining eyes of youth
Taught by her to gaze at Truth;
Let her honour be approved
In the deeds of those she loved,
And each life inspired by her
Be her worthy chronicler.

Never soul more chastely wise
Watched the world through deeper eyes;
Hardly shall the future tell
What the influence of her spell;
How her speech's virgin gold
Took the grace of antique mould;
How her heart like altar fire
Burned with flame of high desire;
How divine Philosophy,
Handmaid of the Lord, stood nigh,
Prompting her the Truths that wrought
In her every look and thought.—
All has fled; no written scroll
Holds the story of her Soul;
In Time's archives is set forth
No escutcheon of her worth—
Naught remains save memory!

Nay; such sweetness cannot die;
Though her name be never set
In Fame's tarnished coronet.

As within a garden green
Shall that dearest name be seen,
Showing as in lilies writ,
And with roses framing it.
We who hung upon her words
Caught the throb of heavenly chords
Touching harmonies of earth
Into a diviner birth;
Felt the Stoic's rigid School
Soften into Christian rule;
Learnt what hidden virtue lies
In the life which fools despise;
Longed to play the nobler part
With the right chivalric heart.
Honeyed lore of poet and sage;
Simples of the golden age,
These, as into sweets distilled,
All her days with fragrance filled,
These, as garlands wreathed and fair,
Guard her solemn sepulchre.

All Love's herald could proclaim
Lies within her twofold name,
Mary, hers, whose home was blest
By the living Lord as guest;
Sibyl, her majestic eyes
Rapt in lofty mysteries,
But, if childhood met her sight,
Melted into loving light.
Precious as her counsel's store,
Yet her comforting was more;
When she stood by misery
With divining sympathy,
When her every grace and power
Found in Love its crowning dower.

Where the hallowed sunshine fills
That lone vale 'mid Kentish hills,

Where her stainless child has rest
'Neath her native earth's kind breast,
Let her sleep, while April rain
Calls the blossoms forth again,
While the nightingales rejoice,
And the wild bee's murmurous voice
Hums the sombre trees among
Like an echo of old song.
While the fading leaves shall fall
To one lonely thrush's call,
While the snow shall drift and pass
Like a shadow on life's glass,
While the world shall onward roll
Nearer its mysterious goal.

Strew with violets dim the sod,
Leave her Epitaph with God.
ETHEL COXON.

February 1892.

March, 1898.

MR. EDWARD ARNOLD'S
New Books & Announcements.

LONDON: 37 BEDFORD STREET.

Telegraphic Address: 'Scholarly, London.'

New and Forthcoming Works.

WITH THE BRITISH MISSION TO MENELIK, 1897.

By COUNT GLEICHEN,
Captain Grenadier Guards, Intelligence Officer to the Mission.

With numerous Illustrations by the Author and a Map. Demy 8vo., 16s.

This book gives the only authentic account of the extremely interesting mission to Menelik in 1897. Every day the relations of this country with Abyssinia are becoming more important as our advance up the Nile progresses; while in Somaliland and at Kassala we shall shortly find ourselves face to face with the 'Empire of Ethiopia.' Much has happened since Sir Gerald Portal's Mission to Abyssinia some years ago, and the present expedition, headed by Mr. Rennell Rodd, passed through an entirely new country and had opportunities never before enjoyed by Englishmen of examining its resources and observing the power of Menelik's military dominion.

Count Gleichen has already made a literary reputation by his work, 'With the Camel Corps up the Nile,' and has written an entertaining and very valuable book.

MANY MEMORIES OF MANY PEOPLE.

By Mrs. M. C. SIMPSON (*née* NASSAU-SENIOR).

One vol., demy 8vo., 16s.

'Mrs. Simpson's work should appeal with success to a wide circle of readers. It is charmingly written, and pleasant to read.'—*Standard.*

'A delightful volume.'—*Daily News.*

'Mrs. Simpson has something interesting to say about nearly every woman of note in the middle portion of the century. The whole book is good reading.'—*Athenæum.*

'This is a delightful book. A long succession of familiar names flit across Mrs. Simpson's pages, and she has something interesting or amusing to tell us about all of them.'—*Guardian.*

'There is not a dull page in it from first to last, and the present generation will have no excuse for ignorance of all that was best and most brilliant in the society of the middle of this century as long as a copy of "Many Memories" remains accessible.'—*Manchester Guardian.*

Three New Works of Fiction.

A REPUTATION FOR A SONG.

By MAUD OXENDEN.

Author of 'Interludes.'

Crown 8vo., 6s.

THE FALSE CHEVALIER.

By W. D. LIGHTHALL.

Crown 8vo., 6s.

THE MERMAID OF INISH-UIG.

By R. W. K. EDWARDS.

Crown 8vo., 3s. 6d.

HARROW SCHOOL.

Edited by E. W. HOWSON and G. TOWNSEND WARNER.

With a Preface by EARL SPENCER, K.G., D.C.L.,
Chairman of the Governors of Harrow School,

And Contributions by Old Harrovians and Harrow Masters.

Illustrated with a large number of original full-page and other Pen-and-ink Drawings by Mr. HERBERT MARSHALL,

With several Photogravure Portraits and reproductions of objects of interest.

In one volume, crown 4to., One Guinea net.

A numbered Large-Paper Edition, limited to 150 copies, Three Guineas net.

This book will contain articles on the origin and history of the School and its buildings, and its connection with the town, embodying much information hitherto unpublished; also on the Headmasters of the School, Harrovian Statesmen, Harrovian Men of Letters, the Benefactions, Reminiscences of School Life in Old Days, Cricket, Football, and other branches of School Sports, School Songs and Music, and the Social Life of the School.

Articles have been contributed by the following:

E. E. BOWEN; H. MONTAGU BUTLER, D.D., Master of Trinity College, Cambridge, and late Headmaster of Harrow School; EDWARD M. BUTLER; C. COLBECK; Professor W. J. COURTHOPE, C.B.; the EARL OF CREWE; Rev. J. A. CRUIKSHANK; Sir HENRY S. CUNNINGHAM, K.C.S.I.; Sir CHARLES DALRYMPLE, Bart., M.P.; Rev. B. H. DRURY; SPENCER W. GORE; E. GRAHAM; W. O. HEWLETT; A. F. HORT; E. W. HOWSON; the Right Rev. BISHOP JENNER; B. P. LASCELLES; Hon. E. CHANDOS LEIGH, Q.C.; Right Hon. W. H. LONG, M.P.; Rev. HASTINGS RASHDALL; C. S. ROUNDELL, Governor of Harrow School; the EARL SPENCER, K.G., D.C.L., Chairman of the Governors; P. M. THORNTON, M.P.; G. TOWNSEND WARNER; and the Rev. J. E. C. WELLDON, Headmaster of Harrow School.

A full Prospectus can be had post-free on application.
The work will be ready for publication in June.

LESSONS IN OLD TESTAMENT HISTORY.

By the VENERABLE ARCHDEACON AGLEN.

With Maps. One vol., crown 8vo., 4s. 6d.

The Archdeacon of St. Andrews is known to literature for his scholarly contributions to the 'Encyclopædia Britannica,' for his translation of the Odes of Horace, and as the editor of 'Selections from the Writings of Dean Stanley.'

CHURCH AND REALM IN STUART TIMES.

A Course of Ten Illustrated Lectures arranged to accompany a Series of 600 Lantern Illustrations.

By the Rev. C. ARTHUR LANE,
Author of 'Illustrated Notes on English Church History.'

One vol., crown 8vo., 3s. 6d. net.

For twelve years Mr. Lane has been engaged in popularizing, by his Church lectures, the history of the National Church of England. This volume is indispensable to clergymen and others who desire to give popular lectures on Church History. The lantern slides to accompany the lectures are supplied by the Church Committee for Church Defence.

LETTERS OF MARY SIBYLLA HOLLAND.

Selected and Edited by her Son, BERNARD HOLLAND.

One vol., crown 8vo., 7s. 6d. net.

This book has the charm of a collection of letters written, with no thought but to please, convey affection, help or console, by a person gifted with sympathy, and of a nature of rare distinction. The writer has also the power of style, the inmost soul of literature.

New Volume of The Sportsman's Library.

THE CHASE, THE TURF, AND THE ROAD.

By NIMROD.

Edited by the Right Hon. Sir HERBERT MAXWELL, Bart., M.P.

With a Photogravure Portrait of the Author by D. MACLISE, R.A., and with Coloured Photogravure and other Plates from the original Illustrations by ALKEN, and several reproductions of old Portraits.

Large 8vo., handsomely bound, 15s. Also a Large-Paper Edition, limited to 200 copies, Two Guineas net.

This Edition is based on the first Edition of Apperley's famous work; Alken's Plates will be reproduced to their original size, and it may confidently be claimed that it forms the finest Edition of the book yet published.

For earlier volumes of 'The Sportsman's Library,' see pp. 13 and 18 of this catalogue.

A MINGLED YARN.

The Autobiography of Edward Spencer Mott

(NATHANIEL GUBBINS),

Author of 'Cakes and Ale,' etc.

1 vol., large crown 8vo., 12s. 6d.

This volume is the candid record of a life full of varied experiences. The author, with a wealth of anecdote and a rare fund of cynical humour, gives some account of his school-days, a vivid narrative of the years he spent as a lieutenant in the Queen's service in India, of existence in a cholera camp and in a Burmese gaol. Under the pseudonym of 'Nathaniel Gubbins' he is widely known as a sporting journalist, and no small portion of the work is devoted to the history and stories of the racecourse.

STUDIES ON MANY SUBJECTS.

By S. H. REYNOLDS.

One vol., demy 8vo., 10s. 6d.

The late Rev. Samuel Harvey Reynolds was a scholar of Exeter College, Oxford, and a Fellow and Tutor of Brasenose College, and Vicar of East Ham from 1871 to 1893. He was the author of 'The Rise of the Modern European System,' and edited Bacon's 'Essays' and Selden's 'Table Talk' for the Clarendon Press. He wrote for the *Times* from 1873 to 1896, and died in February, 1897. These studies deal with a number of economic, political, and critical subjects.

NEW AND COMPLETELY REVISED EDITION.

POULTRY-KEEPING

As an Industry for Farmers and Cottagers.

By EDWARD BROWN, F.L.S.

Fully Illustrated by LUDLOW.

1 vol., demy 4to., cloth, 6s.

The continued popularity and demand for this work has justified a new edition, which has been thoroughly re-cast and revised by the author.

'... We are glad to welcome the appearance of an excellent volume by Mr. Edward Brown. The author has acquired so solid a reputation in connection with this subject that any praise of his work is superfluous.'—*Morning Post.*

'Mr. Brown is one of our best-known and most capable experts, and he has here presented the fruits of his wide knowledge and experience in, perhaps, the most useful form they could have taken.... His book is, indeed, a thoroughly practical and trustworthy guide to poultry in health and disease; and whether a dozen hens be kept or a hundred, it will be their owner's own fault if, with Mr. Brown's excellent manual at hand, they fail to derive profit from their stock.'—*St. James's Gazette.*

Works of Fiction.

RECENTLY PUBLISHED.

THE KING WITH TWO FACES.

By M. E. COLERIDGE,

Author of 'The Seven Sleepers of Ephesus,' etc.

One vol., crown 8vo., 6s.

Fifth Edition.

'We despair of giving to those who have not read this beautiful romance an adequate impression of the delicacy and variety of its portraiture, the freshness, subtlety, and distinction of its dialogue, and the poignant interest excited in the fortunes of the leading *dramatis personæ*. In the whole range of contemporary fiction we know of no more picturesque Royal figure than that of Gustavus as he is limned by Miss Coleridge. Above all, the book has to a quite exceptional degree the quality of glamour. Fresh from its perusal, and still under the spell of its magic, we are fain to re-echo Schumann's historic greeting addressed to Chopin in a review of his earliest published pianoforte works, "Hats off, gentlemen! A genius."'—*Spectator*.

'One of the very rare novels which yield so much pleasure that it almost stifles criticism. Miss Coleridge's quality is that of perfectly original brilliancy in romantic narration. Her style is at once placid and spirited, full of colour without heaviness and luxury, correct, rapid, adequate, with no tedious research of "the word," or preciosity. Her imagination is wonderfully vivid; for scenes and moments, colour, form, atmosphere, are all felt and conveyed in her pictures, which are not too numerous, and are never tedious.'—*Times*.

'One of the cleverest historical novels of late years.'—*Literature*.

'This is one of the most remarkable stories that we have read for many a day. . . . Gustavus is throughout a magnificent figure. . . . It is a bold thing to say, but we hardly remember in fiction the figure of a king more finely drawn. . . . We desire to welcome this fascinating book.'—*Westminster Gazette*.

'The curious, complex, many-sided nature of the Swedish monarch, the charm he exercised on all brave and generous-minded men with whom he came in contact, his rapidity of decision and action, his strange superstitions and his undaunted valour, are set forth with skill and convincingness. M. E. Coleridge has done very well indeed.'—*Daily Chronicle*.

Third Edition.

PAUL MERCER.

A Tale of Repentance among Millions.

By the Hon. and Rev. JAMES ADDERLEY.

Author of 'Stephen Remarx.'

One vol., crown 8vo., 3s. 6d.

'Will be welcomed by all the large number of readers who enjoyed the same author's "Stephen Remarx." Mr. Adderley may, perhaps, be regarded as the nearest representative of Charles Kingsley in modern Christian Socialism.'—*Daily Chronicle*.

'Mr. Adderley writes so well when he pleases, and has such an eye for humour and for character, that literature must almost grudge him even to the newest side of an old church.'—*Athenæum*.

'Exhibits all the artless sincerity, the humour, and the hopeful idealism which gave to "Stephen Remarx" its interest and charm. We hope that its readers may be numbered by thousands.'—*Church Times*.

THE SON OF A PEASANT.

By EDWARD McNULTY,

Author of 'Misther O'Ryan,' etc.

One vol., crown 8vo., 6s.

'A remarkably clever representation of Irish life . . . The dialogue is racy of the soil. . . . A work of ability, and it will give keen enjoyment to those who know and appreciate the Irish character.'—*Pall Mall Gazette.*

'An excellent Irish story. The book is full of knowledge of Irish character, and altogether it is a welcome relief from the ordinary run of novels.'—*Standard.*

'It is long since we have read an Irish story so consistently well written as this. It is thoroughly to the end, and its humour is racy of the soil.'—*Glasgow Herald.*

JOB HILDRED.

Artist and Carpenter.

By Dr. RICHARDS.

Edited by ELLEN F. PINSENT.

Author of 'Jenny's Case,' 'No Place for Repentance,' etc.

One vol., crown 8vo., 3s. 6d.

'A good piece of work. It is original; it impresses the reader as a genuine bit of life. Lady Elizabeth is an admirable sketch, and Sally Hildred is very nearly a creation to be proud of.'—*Guardian.*

'Mrs. Pinsent possesses the power of feeling with and for her characters in high degree, and combines with it the rare faculty of telling her story in simple and charming style. . . . This book will greatly increase her reputation.'—*Birmingham Daily Post.*

NETHERDYKE.

By R. J. CHARLETON,

Author of 'Newcastle Town,' etc.

One vol., crown 8vo., 6s.

'"Netherdyke" is first and foremost an adventure story, and is unquestionably entitled to be reckoned among the best of its class. Mr. Charleton is an excellent and clear narrator.'—*Newcastle Leader.*

'The stirring times of the '45 are admirably chronicled.'—*Dundee Advertiser.*

'The narrative of the events is graphic and effective.'—*Freeman's Journal.*

'Will be appreciated by boys and all lovers of stirring scenes.'—*Eastern Morning News.*

Works of History and Biography Recently Published.

THIRD EDITION.

RECOLLECTIONS OF AUBREY DE VERE.

In one volume, demy 8vo., with Portrait, 16s.

'The most genial, charming, and amusing volume of reminiscences of the year.'—*Truth*.

'It presents the portrait of a noble figure, a man of letters in a sense peculiar to a day now disappearing, a man of responsible leisure, of serious thought, of grave duties, of high mind.'—*Athenæum*.

'The recollections are likely to be widely read, for they will interest our readers.'—*Spectator*.

'There are brisk studies of character, quaint old stories, bits of exquisite descriptions, excellent jests, anecdotes of famous men.'—*Pall Mall Gazette*.

'These "Recollections" will appeal to many sympathies, personal, political, social, literary, and religious. As a Catholic the author enjoyed the intimate friendship of Cardinal Newman and Cardinal Manning, and these pages throw additional and interesting sidelights on the character and genius of each of these distinguished men. Few "Recollections" of late years, if any, furnish more pleasant reading than these.'—*Morning Post*.

'A remarkable book, full of good humour and good sense, and one which no reader will wish to lay down once he has taken it up. Mr. Aubrey de Vere has long had an "audience fit though few," and the appearance of the present volume will be a point of interest both for those who knew and valued his poems, and for those who knew him for an Irishman of the "ould stock," with many kindly reminiscences of his country through more than one generation.'—*St. James's Gazette*.

'They are the recollections of one whose mind has been concerned with great thoughts and subjects, and whose way has lain with great men.'—*Freeman's Journal*.

THE AUTOBIOGRAPHY AND LETTERS
OF THE
RT. HON. JOHN ARTHUR ROEBUCK,
Q.C., M.P.

Edited by ROBERT EADON LEADER.

With two Portraits, demy 8vo., 16s.

'The political struggles in which Roebuck took a prominent part have passed into history. Nevertheless, this book is welcome. It is a substantial and permanent contribution to the literature of Parliamentary biography. Mr Leader has done his work well, and Roebuck the man as well as Roebuck the Parliamentarian is made to stand clearly before the mind's eye.'—*Globe*.

'Mr. Leader is to be congratulated on the ability with which he has carried through what must have been a most laborious task. He has given not only the record of a remarkable man, but a valuable picture of the working of our Parliamentary system.'—*Morning Post*.

'Mr. Leader has done a good work; he has produced for the public a lifelike portrait of a remarkable public man.'—*Sheffield Telegraph*.

A MEMOIR OF ANNE J. CLOUGH,

Principal of Newnham College, Cambridge.

By her Niece, BLANCHE CLOUGH.

In one volume, 8vo., 12s. 6d.

'Her niece's work as editor has been done with admirable skill. Those who knew and loved Miss Clough will feel that not a word too much has been said and that nothing has been left out which could help to make a rare and lovable personality more fully realised by those who would fain have known her better.'—*Guardian*.

'The memoir is thoroughly worthy of its subject, and must earn the gratitude of every reader. A complicated story has been clearly and simply told; a complicated character has been drawn with rare tact and sympathy.'—*Speaker*.

'Miss B. Clough has unfolded with singular discretion, clearness, and sympathy the early history of an important institution, and the personality of a great pioneer.'—*Spectator*.

ROME: THE MIDDLE OF THE WORLD.

By ALICE GARDNER,

Lecturer in History at Newnham College;
Author of '*Friends of the Olden Time*,' etc.

With Illustrations and Map. Crown 8vo., 3s. 6d.

'Miss Gardner's book on the Emperor Julian reconciled many readers to a singularly interesting personality of which they had previously heard little beyond the opprobrium of "apostasy." In her present volume she addresses a younger audience, but in treating of a much wider subject she displays the same grasp and scholarship. We fancy Miss Gardner knows what youthful patience and attention are, and her method of appealing to the imagination by a series of strongly-lined pictures will probably do more to make Roman history a living thing to children than serried dates and a philosophical argument of causes and effects.'—*Saturday Review*.

FAITH WHICH WORKETH BY LOVE.

A Sermon Preached after the Funeral of the Princess Mary, Duchess of Teck.

By the Very Rev. S. REYNOLDS HOLE, Dean of Rochester,
Author of '*The Memories of Dean Hole*.'

Bound in vellum.   1s. net.

Works in General Literature and Art.

RECENTLY PUBLISHED.

Dedicated by Special Permission to Her Majesty the Queen.

OLD ENGLISH GLASSES.

An Account of Glass Drinking-Vessels in England from Early Times to the end of the Eighteenth Century.

With Introductory Notices of Continental Glasses during the same period, Original Documents, etc.

By ALBERT HARTSHORNE,
Fellow of the Society of Antiquaries.

Illustrated by nearly 70 full-page Tinted or Coloured Plates in the best style of Lithography, and several hundred outline Illustrations in the text. Super royal 4to., price Three Guineas **net**.

'It would be difficult to overestimate the value of this book to the collector. It would be but scanty praise to say that this book is a noble quarto. It is that and much more. With its beautiful type, ample margins and luxurious paper, its hundreds of illustrations, many of them whole-page lithographs of exceptional merit, it is an exceedingly fine example of typography, while its half-vellum binding is in admirable keeping with the care and taste which has been lavished upon the interior.'—*Standard*.

'An important contribution to the library of the serious antiquary and collector.'—*Times*.

'Mr. Hartshorne has been fortunate in finding a subject about which literally nothing was known, even by would-be connoisseurs, and he has risen to the height of his opportunity in a wonderful way. A fortnight ago the collector of old English Glasses was working in darkness... to-day such a collector has but to become the possessor of this sumptuous quarto and the whole sequence of glass-making, not only in England but on the Continent, from primitive times to the end of the last century, is before him. It is a monograph which must remain the one authority on English glasses.'—*Daily Chronicle*.

'No more sumptuous monograph on any artistic subject **has been published** this **year** than Mr. Hartshorne's volume.'—*Westminster Gazette*.

THE CHIPPENDALE PERIOD IN ENGLISH FURNITURE.

By K. WARREN CLOUSTON.

With 200 Illustrations by the Author.

Demy 4to., handsomely bound.   One Guinea, net.

'This handsome volume is enriched with illustrations which will be of great value to collectors, and of interest to any person of taste. It fills a distinct gap in the annals of art, and that in a manner not too technical for the Philistine in search of enlightenment.'—*Daily Telegraph*.

'A very attractive volume.'—*Pall Mall Gazette*.

'In Mr. Clouston's handsome quarto, with its 200 illustrations charmingly drawn by the author and admirably reproduced, we have an attractively written history of a remarkable artistic movement and the man who directed. Mr. Clouston has done his work thoroughly well, and has produced a book which will be of real value not only to the serious student of the history of furniture, but to every reader who wishes **to** be well informed upon a topic at once so pleasant and so popular.'—*Standard*.

SECOND EDITION.

STYLE.

By WALTER RALEIGH,

Professor of English Literature at University College, Liverpool;
Author of 'Robert Louis Stevenson,' etc.

One vol., crown 8vo., 5s.

'Professor Raleigh has produced a finished masterpiece, where the men before him, masters as they were, gave us brilliant sketches or clever studies. His ingenuity of thought, restraint of expression, austerity of judgment, his prudent counsel and wise suggestion are worthy of all praise. A model treatise on a most difficult and important theme.'—*Pall Mall Gazette.*

'In our judgment Mr. Raleigh's volume on "Style" is an amazingly good and pre-eminently interesting and suggestive book. His whole treatment of his subject is vigorous, manly, and most sensible.'—*Speaker.*

'As brimful of discerning criticism and fruitful suggestion as it is throughout lively and inspiriting.'—*St. James's Gazette.*

'Mr. Raleigh's volume is the fruit of much reading and more thinking. It is informed by the true literary spirit; it is full of wisdom, inclining now and then to paradox; and it is gay with quaintnesses and unexpected epigrams.'—*Times.*

'A fascinating little volume.'—*Spectator.*

BALLADS OF THE FLEET.

By RENNELL RODD, C.B., C.M.G.

One vol., crown 8vo., cloth, 6s.

'Mr. Rodd's ballads as a whole reach a high level of achievement. They have much of Macaulay's "go," and something better than Macaulay's rhetoric.'—*Pall Mall Gazette.*

'The verse is full of colour and animation and fine feeling; simple withal, and vigorous without noise or brag.'—*Daily Chronicle.*

'Many-sided in its charm, no less than it its appeal.'—*Standard.*

MORE BEASTS (FOR WORSE CHILDREN).

By H. B. and B. T. B.,

Authors of 'The Bad Child's Book of Beasts.'

One vol., 4to., 3s. 6d.

'The authors of this book have discovered a new continent in the world of nonsense. Their second book, which sings and illustrates this new world, is to the full as original and delightful as the first.'—*Spectator.*

'It has created a furore.'—*Daily Mail.*

'Even better and wittier than the first volume.'—*Westminster Budget.*

The Sportsman's Library.

Edited by the Rt. Hon. Sir HERBERT MAXWELL, Bart., M.P.

TWO RECENT VOLUMES.

REMINISCENCES OF A HUNTSMAN.

By the HON. GRANTLEY F. BERKELEY.

With a Coloured Frontispiece and the original Illustrations by JOHN LEECH, and several Coloured Plates and other Illustrations by G. H. JALLAND.

Large 8vo., handsomely bound, 15s. Also a Large-Paper Edition, limited to 200 copies, Two Guineas net.

'The latest addition to the sumptuous "Sportsman's Library" is here reproduced with all possible aid from the printer and binder, with illustrations from the pencils of Leech and G. H. Jalland.'—*Globe*.

'The Hon. Grantley F. Berkeley had one great quality of the *raconteur*. His self-revelations and displays of vanity are delightful.'—*Times*.

THE ART OF DEER-STALKING.

By WILLIAM SCROPE.

With Frontispiece by EDWIN LANDSEER, and 9 Photogravure Plates of the original Illustrations.

Large 8vo., handsomely bound, 15s. Also a Large-Paper Edition, limited to 200 copies, Two Guineas net.

'With the fine illustrations by the Landseers and Scrope himself, this forms a most worthy number of a splendid series.'—*Pall Mall Gazette*.

'Among the works published in connection with field sports in Scotland, none probably have been more sought after than those of William Scrope, and although published more than fifty years ago, they are still as fresh as ever, full of pleasant anecdote, and valuable for the many practical hints which they convey to inexperienced sportsmen.'—*Field*.

'Judged by the standard of lasting popularity, and by certain subtle qualities that make its pages interesting to those who have read them often, William Scrope's entertaining narrative of deer-stalking in the forest of Atholl must take high rank among works on sport.'—*Daily News*.

Volumes of Sport, Travel and Adventure.

RECENTLY PUBLISHED.

BENIN, THE CITY OF BLOOD.
An Account of the Benin Expedition.

By R. H. BACON, Commander R.N.

Illustrated by W. H. OVEREND.

In one volume, demy 8vo., 7s. 6d.

'Commander Bacon was intelligence officer to the expedition, and his personal record of the advance on Ologbo, of the fighting in the bush and at the crossroads and Agagi, of the capture of Benin, and of the horrors of human sacrifice, and the practice of Ju-Ju, is as fascinating as it evidently is complete and accurate.'—*Daily Mail.*

'Should be read not only by those who care for adventure, but also by those who care for history. It is difficult in a short space to give any idea of the striking way Commander Bacon brings the horrors and trials of the campaign vividly before the reader, or to give even a vague notion of the loathsome practice of Ju-Ju, or the terrible picture of slaughter and sacrifice Benin presented when it was at last reached.'—*Saturday Review.*

WILD NORWAY:
With Chapters on the Swedish Highlands, Jutland, and Spitzbergen.

By ABEL CHAPMAN, Author of 'Wild Spain,' etc.

With seventeen full-page Illustrations and numerous smaller ones by the Author and CHARLES WHYMPER.

Demy 8vo., 16s.

'There is not a chapter in this book which would not be missed.'—*Spectator.*

'A very good, very accurate, and deeply interesting book of wild life and natural history.'—*Illustrated Sporting and Dramatic News.*

'Will be read with keen interest by the angler, the hunter of wild game, and the student of bird life.'—*Scotsman.*

'It will be found not only an invaluable but a delightful companion by the sportsman, the angler, and the ornithologist.'—*Times.*

FIRE AND SWORD IN THE SUDAN.

By SLATIN PASHA.

Translated and Edited by COLONEL WINGATE, C.B., Chief of the Intelligence Department Egyptian Army.

A new, revised, and cheaper edition of this famous work.

Illustrated. Price 6s.

In this edition the book has been thoroughly revised by the authors, omitting certain matters of temporary interest, and making it as far as possible a standard work of permanent value for young and old. The striking illustrations by Mr. Talbot Kelly have been retained.

Also the complete work, demy 8vo., One Guinea.

THROUGH UNKNOWN AFRICAN COUNTRIES.

The First Expedition from Somaliland to Lake Rudolf and Lamu.

A Narrative of Scientific Exploration and Sporting Adventures.

By A. DONALDSON SMITH, M.D., F.R.G.S.

With nearly thirty full-page Plates and numerous smaller Illustrations by A. D. McCORMICK, CHARLES WHYMPER, etc., and detailed Maps of the countries traversed.

Super royal 8vo., One Guinea net.

' Will be of the greatest interest to sportsman, traveller, and man of science.'—*Pall Mall Gazette.*
' Since the publication of Stanley's "Across the Dark Continent," there has been no work of African travel equal, in scientific importance and thrilling interest, to Dr. Donaldson Smith's book. As a book of exciting sport, apart from its geographical and ethnological usefulness, it deserves to stand alongside the best experiences of the toughest Anglo-Indian shikaris.'—*Daily Telegraph.*
' While to the large class of people interested in African exploration this book is indispensable, sportsmen will find in its pages a wealth of exciting incidents rarely equalled in similar works.'—*St. James's Gazette.*

SOLDIERING AND SURVEYING IN BRITISH EAST AFRICA, 1891-1894.

An Account of the Survey for the Uganda Railway, and the various Campaigns in the British Protectorate during the last few years.

By Major J. R. MACDONALD, R.E.

Illustrated from Sketches and Photographs by the Author and numerous Plans and a Map.

Demy 8vo., 16s.

' No country in the world has had greater need of an impartial historian than Uganda, and, strange to say, though the bitter feelings engendered by the struggles of the past ten years have not had time to cool, one has been found among the actors in these stormy scenes—Major Macdonald. . . . No one who reads this exciting book of adventure can regret that we are spending £3,000,000 on the railway. Major Macdonald writes with considerable literary and historical skill, and his sketches and maps are all excellent.'—*Pall Mall Gazette.*
' The illustrations from photographs and sketches are better than any we have seen of this part of the Dark Continent, and the maps are distinctly good.'—*Daily Chronicle.*
' A well written and useful addition to our knowledge of Uganda.'—*Literature.*

MEMORIES OF THE MONTHS.

Leaves from a Field Naturalist's Note-book.

By the Right Hon. Sir HERBERT MAXWELL, Bart., M.P.

Crown 8vo., with four Photogravure Illustrations, 6s.

' It is a very long time since we have read so pleasant a book as this.'—*Daily Chronicle.*
' Most agreeably and freshly written.'—*Field.*
' The easy style, the graphic descriptions of bird-life, and of the ways of beasts and fishes, the clever sketches of sport, the happy introductions of plant-lore and of fragments of myth and legend, will ensure a warm welcome for this delightful volume.'—*Daily News.*
' Charming in language, and at the same time so varied in character that they never become tedious.'—*Athenæum.*

Volumes of Travel, Sport, and Adventure.

Bacon—THE CITY OF BLOOD. (*See page* 14.)

Balfour—TWELVE HUNDRED MILES IN A WAGGON. A Narrative of a Journey in Cape Colony, the Transvaal, and the Chartered Company's Territories. By ALICE BLANCHE BALFOUR With nearly forty original Illustrations from Sketches by the Author, and a Map. Demy 8vo. cloth, 16s.

Beynon—WITH KELLY TO CHITRAL. By Lieutenant W. G. L. BEYNON, D.S.O., 3rd Goorkha Rifles, Staff Officer to Colonel Kelly with the Relief Force. With Maps, Plans, and Illustrations. Demy 8vo., 7s. 6d.

Bottome — A SUNSHINE TRIP: Glimpses of the Orient. Extracts from Letters written by MARGARET BOTTOME. With Portrait, elegantly bound, 4s. 6d.

Bull—THE CRUISE OF THE 'ANTARCTIC.' To the South Polar Regions. By H. J. BULL, a member of the Expedition. With frontispiece by W. L. WYLLIE, A.R.A., and numerous full-page illustrations by W. G. BURN-MURDOCH. Demy 8vo., 15s.

Chapman—WILD NORWAY. (*See page* 14.)

Colvile—THE LAND OF THE NILE SPRINGS. By Colonel Sir HENRY COLVILE, K.C.M.G., C.B., recently British Commissioner in Uganda. With Photogravure Frontispiece, 16 full-page Illustrations and 2 Maps. Demy 8vo., 16s.

Custance—RIDING RECOLLECTIONS AND TURF STORIES. By HENRY CUSTANCE, three times winner of the Derby. One vol., crown 8vo., cloth, 2s. 6d.

Freshfield — THE EXPLORATION OF THE CAUCASUS. By DOUGLAS W. FRESHFIELD, lately President of the Alpine Club and Honorary Secretary of the Royal Geographical Society. With Contributions by H. W. HOLDER, J. G. COCKIN, H. WOOLLEY, M. DE DÉCHY, and Prof. BONNEY, D.SC., F.R.S. Illustrated by 3 Panoramas, 74 full-page Photogravures, about 140 Illustrations in the text, chiefly from Photographs by VITTORIO SELLA, and 4 Original Maps, including the first authentic map of the Caucasus specially prepared from unpublished sources by Mr. FRESHFIELD. In two volumes, large 4to., 600 pp., Three Guineas net.

Gordon—PERSIA REVISITED. With Remarks on H.I.M. Mozuffer-ed-Din Shah, and the Present Situation in Persia (1896). By General Sir T. E. GORDON, K.C.I.E., C.B., C.S.I. Formerly Military Attaché and Oriental Secretary to the British Legation at Teheran, Author of 'The Roof of the World,' etc. Demy 8vo., with full-page illustrations, 10s. 6d.

Hall—FISH TAILS AND SOME TRUE ONES. By BRADNOCK HALL, Author of 'Rough Mischance.' With an original Etching by the Author and twelve full-page Illustrations by T. H. MCLACHLAN. Crown 8vo., 6s.

Hole—A LITTLE TOUR IN AMERICA. By the Very Rev. S. REYNOLDS HOLE, Dean of Rochester, Author of 'The Memories of Dean Hole' 'A Book about Roses,' etc. With numerous Illustrations. Demy 8vo., 16s.

Hole—A LITTLE TOUR IN IRELAND. By 'OXONIAN' (the Very Rev. S. REYNOLDS HOLE). With nearly forty Illustrations by JOHN LEECH. Large crown 8vo., 6s.

Knight-Bruce—MEMORIES OF MASHONALAND. By the late Right Rev. Bishop KNIGHT-BRUCE, formerly Bishop of Mashonaland. 8vo., 10s. 6d.

Macdonald—SOLDIERING AND SURVEYING IN BRITISH EAST AFRICA. (*See page* 15.)

McNab—ON VELDT AND FARM—in Cape Colony, Bechuanaland, Natal, and the Transvaal. By FRANCES MCNAB. With Map. Crown 8vo., 300 pages, 3s. 6d.

Maxwell—THE SPORTSMAN'S LIBRARY. (*See pages* 5, 13, *and* 18.)

Maxwell—MEMORIES OF THE MONTHS. (*See page* 15.)

Pike—THROUGH THE SUB-ARCTIC FOREST. A Record of a Canoe Journey for 4,000 miles, from Fort Wrangel to the Pelly Lakes, and down the Yukon to the Behring Sea. By WARBURTON PIKE, Author of 'The Barren Grounds of Canada.' With illustrations by CHARLES WHYMPER, from Photographs taken by the Author, and a Map. Demy 8vo., 16s.

Pollok—FIFTY YEARS' REMINISCENCES OF INDIA. By Lieut.-Colonel POLLOK, author of 'Sport in Burmah.' Illustrated by A. C. CORBOULD. Demy 8vo., 16s.

Portal—THE BRITISH MISSION TO UGANDA. By the late Sir GERALD PORTAL, K.C.M.G. Edited by RENNELL RODD, C.M.G. With an Introduction by the Right Honourable LORD CROMER, G.C.M.G. Illustrated from photos taken during the Expedition by Colonel RHODES. Demy 8vo., 21s.

Portal—MY MISSION TO ABYSSINIA. By the late Sir GERALD H. PORTAL, C.B. With Map and Illustrations. Demy 8vo., 15s.

Slatin—FIRE AND SWORD IN THE SUDAN. (*See page* 14.)

Smith—THROUGH UNKNOWN AFRICAN COUNTRIES. (*See page* 15.)

Stone—IN AND BEYOND THE HIMALAYAS: A Record of Sport and Travel. By S. J. STONE, late Deputy Inspector-General of the Punjab Police. With 16 full-page Illustrations by CHARLES WHYMPER. Demy 8vo., 16s.

AMERICAN SPORT AND TRAVEL.

These books, selected from the Catalogue of MESSRS. RAND MCNALLY & CO., *the well-known publishers of Chicago, have been placed in* MR. EDWARD ARNOLD'S *hands under the impression that many British Travellers and Sportsmen may find them useful before starting on expeditions in the United States.*

Aldrich—ARCTIC ALASKA AND SIBERIA. By HERBERT L. ALDRICH. Crown 8vo., cloth, 4s. 6d.

AMERICAN GAME FISHES. By various Writers. Cloth, 10s. 6d.

Higgins—NEW GUIDE TO THE PACIFIC COAST. By C. A. HIGGINS. Crown 8vo., cloth, 4s. 6d.

Leffingwell—THE ART OF WING-SHOOTING. By W. B. LEFFINGWELL. Crown 8vo., cloth, 4s. 6d.

Shields—CAMPING AND CAMP OUTFITS. By G. O. SHIELDS ('Coquina'). Crown 8vo., cloth, 5s.

Shields—THE AMERICAN BOOK OF THE DOG. By various Writers. Edited by G. O. SHIELDS ('Coquina'). Cloth, 15s.

Thomas—SWEDEN AND THE SWEDES. By WILLIAM WIDGERY THOMAS, Jun., United States Minister to Sweden and Norway. Cloth, 16s.

The Sportsman's Library.

Edited by the RIGHT HON. SIR HERBERT MAXWELL, BART., M.P.

A Re-issue, in handsome volumes, of certain rare and entertaining books on sport, carefully selected by the Editor, and illustrated by the best sporting artists of the day, and with reproductions of old plates.

Library Edition, 15s. a Volume.

Large Paper Edition (limited to 200 copies), 2 guineas a volume.

VOLUME I.
THE LIFE OF A FOX, AND THE DIARY OF A HUNTSMAN.

By THOMAS SMITH, Master of the Hambledon and Pytchley Hounds.

With Illustrations by the Author, and Coloured Plates by G. H. JALLAND.

VOLUME II.
A SPORTING TOUR THROUGH THE NORTHERN PARTS OF ENGLAND AND GREAT PART OF THE HIGHLANDS OF SCOTLAND.

By COLONEL T. THORNTON, of Thornville Royal, in Yorkshire.

With the Original Illustrations by GARRARD, and other Illustrations and Coloured Plates by G. E. LODGE.

VOLUME III.
THE SPORTSMAN IN IRELAND.

By a COSMOPOLITE.

With Coloured Plates and Black and White Drawings by P. CHENEVIX TRENCH, and reproductions of the Original Illustrations drawn by R. ALLEN and engraved by W. WESTALL, A.R.A.

VOLUME IV.
REMINISCENCES OF A HUNTSMAN.

By the HON. GRANTLEY F. BERKELEY.

With a Coloured Frontispiece and the original Illustrations by JOHN LEECH, and several Coloured Plates and other Illustrations by G. H. JALLAND.

VOLUME V.
THE ART OF DEERSTALKING.

By WILLIAM SCROPE.

With Frontispiece by EDWIN LANDSEER, and 9 Photogravure Plates of the original Illustrations.

VOLUME VI.
THE CHASE, THE TURF, AND THE ROAD.

By NIMROD.

With Coloured and other Photogravure Plates by ALKEN, photogravure portrait of the Author by D. MACLISE, R.A., and several reproductions of old portraits.

Works of Fiction.

'Adalet'—HADJIRA: A Turkish Love Story. By 'ADALET.' 1 vol., crown 8vo., cloth, 6s.

Adderley—STEPHEN REMARX. The Story of a Venture in Ethics. By the Hon. and Rev. JAMES ADDERLEY, formerly Head of the Oxford House and Christ Church Mission, Bethnal Green. Twenty-Second Thousand. Small 8vo., elegantly bound, 3s. 6d. Also, in paper cover, 1s.

Adderley—PAUL MERCER. (*See page* 7.)

Blatchford—TOMMY ATKINS. A Tale of the Ranks. By ROBERT BLATCHFORD, Author of 'A Son of the Forge,' 'Merrie England,' etc. New Edition. Crown 8vo., cloth, 3s. 6d.

Charleton—NETHERDYKE. (*See page* 8.)

Cherbuliez—THE TUTOR'S SECRET. (Le Secret du Précepteur.) Translated from the French of VICTOR CHERBULIEZ. One vol., crown 8vo., cloth, 6s.

Cholmondeley—A DEVOTEE: An Episode in the Life of a Butterfly. By MARY CHOLMONDELEY, Author of 'Diana Tempest,' 'The Danvers Jewels,' etc. Crown 8vo., 3s. 6d.

Clifford—LOVE-LETTERS OF A WORLDLY WOMAN. By Mrs. W. K. CLIFFORD, Author of 'Aunt Anne,' 'Mrs. Keith's Crime,' etc. One vol., crown 8vo., cloth, 2s. 6d.

Coleridge—THE KING WITH TWO FACES (*See page* 7.)

Collingwood—THE BONDWOMAN. A Story of the Northmen in Lakeland. By W. G. COLLINGWOOD, Author of 'Thorstein of the Mere,' 'The Life and Work of John Ruskin,' etc. Cloth, 16mo., 3s. 6d.

Crane—GEORGE'S MOTHER. By STEPHEN CRANE. Author of 'The Red Badge of Courage.' Cloth, 2s.

Dunmore—ORMISDAL. A Novel. By the EARL OF DUNMORE, F.R.G.S., Author of 'The Pamirs.' One vol., crown 8vo., cloth, 6s.

Ford—ON THE THRESHOLD. By ISABELLA O. FORD, Author of 'Miss Blake of Monkshalton.' One vol., crown 8vo., 3s. 6d.

Gaunt—DAVE'S SWEETHEART. By MARY GAUNT. One vol., 8vo., cloth, 3s. 6d.

Hall—FISH TAILS AND SOME TRUE ONES. Crown 8vo., 6s.

Hutchinson—THAT FIDDLER FELLOW: A Tale of St. Andrews. By HORACE G. HUTCHINSON, Author of 'My Wife's Politics,' 'Golf,' 'Creatures of Circumstance,' etc. Crown 8vo., cloth, 2s. 6d.

Knutsford—THE MYSTERY OF THE RUE SOLY. Translated by Lady KNUTSFORD from the French of H. DE BALZAC. Crown 8vo., cloth, 3s. 6d.

McNulty—MISTHER O'RYAN. An Incident in the History of a Nation. By EDWARD MCNULTY. Small 8vo., elegantly bound, 3s. 6d.

McNulty—SON OF A PEASANT. (*See page* 8.)

Montrésor—WORTH WHILE. By F. F. MONTRÉSOR, Author of 'Into the Highways and Hedges.' Crown 8vo., cloth, 2s. 6d.

Oxenden—INTERLUDES. By MAUD OXENDEN. Crown 8vo., 6s.

Pinsent—JOB HILDRED. (*See page* 8).

Prescott—A MASK AND A MARTYR. By E. LIVINGSTON PRESCOTT, Author of 'Scarlet and Steel.' Cloth, 6s.

Spinner—A RELUCTANT EVANGELIST, and other Stories. By ALICE SPINNER, Author of 'Lucilla,' 'A Study in Colour,' etc. Crown 8vo., 6s.

Williams—THE BAYONET THAT CAME HOME. By N. WYNNE WILLIAMS. Crown 8vo., 3s. 6d.

Tales of Adventure for Boys.

Clowes—THE DOUBLE EMPEROR. By W. LAIRD CLOWES, Author of 'The Great Peril,' etc. Illustrated. Crown 8vo., 3s. 6d.

Fawcett—SWALLOWED BY AN EARTHQUAKE. By E. D. FAWCETT. Illustrated. Crown 8vo., 3s. 6d.

Fawcett—HARTMANN THE ANARCHIST; or, The Doom of the Great City. By E. DOUGLAS FAWCETT. With sixteen full-page and numerous smaller Illustrations by F. T. JANE. Crown 8vo., cloth, 3s. 6d.

Fawcett—THE SECRET OF THE DESERT. By E. D. FAWCETT. With numerous full-page Illustrations. Crown 8vo., cloth, 3s. 6d.

Hervey—THE REEF OF GOLD. By MAURICE H. HERVEY. With numerous full-page Illustrations, handsomely bound. Gilt edges, 5s.

Hervey—ERIC THE ARCHER. By MAURICE H. HERVEY. With numerous full-page Illustrations. Handsomely bound, crown 8vo., 5s.

Munroe—THE FUR SEAL'S TOOTH. By KIRK MUNROE. Fully illustrated. Crown 8vo., cloth, 5s.

Munroe—SNOW-SHOES AND SLEDGES. By KIRK MUNROE. Fully illustrated. Crown 8vo., cloth, 5s.

Munroe—RICK DALE. By KIRK MUNROE. Fully illustrated. Crown 8vo., cloth, 5s.

Nash—BAREROCK; or, The Island of Pearls. By HENRY NASH. With numerous Illustrations by LANCELOT SPEED. Large crown 8vo., handsomely bound, gilt edges, 5s.

Works on Science and Philosophy.

Bryan—THE MARK IN EUROPE AND AMERICA. A Review of the Discussion on Early Land Tenure. By ENOCH A. BRYAN, A.M., President of Vincennes University, Indiana. Crown 8vo., cloth, 4s. 6d.

Burgess—POLITICAL SCIENCE AND COMPARATIVE CONSTITUTIONAL LAW. By JOHN W. BURGESS, Ph.D., LL.D., Dean of the University Faculty of Political Science in Columbia College, U.S.A. In two volumes, demy 8vo., cloth, 25s.

Fawcett—THE RIDDLE OF THE UNIVERSE. Being an Attempt to determine the First Principles of Metaphysics considered as an Inquiry into the Conditions and Import of Consciousness. By EDWARD DOUGLAS FAWCETT. One vol., demy 8vo., 14s.

Hopkins—THE RELIGIONS OF INDIA. By E. W. HOPKINS, Ph.D. (Leipzig), Professor of Sanskrit and Comparative Philology in Bryn Mawr College. One volume, demy 8vo., 8s. 6d. net.

Ladd—LOTZE'S PHILOSOPHICAL OUTLINES. Dictated Portions of the Latest Lectures (at Göttingen and Berlin) of Hermann Lotze. Translated and edited by GEORGE T. LADD, Professor of Philosophy in Yale College. About 180 pages in each volume. Crown 8vo., cloth, 4s. each. Vol. I. Metaphysics. Vol. II. Philosophy of Religion. Vol. III. Practical Philosophy. Vol. IV. Psychology. Vol. V. Æsthetics. Vol. VI. Logic.

THE JOURNAL OF MORPHOLOGY. Edited by C. O. WHITMAN, Professor of Biology in Clark University, U.S.A. Three numbers in a volume of 100 to 150 large 4to. pages, with numerous plates. Single numbers, 17s. 6d.; subscription to the volume of three numbers, 45s. Volumes I. to XII. can now be obtained, and the first number of Volume XIII. is ready.

Morgan—ANIMAL LIFE AND INTELLIGENCE. By Professor C. LLOYD MORGAN, F.G.S., Principal of University College, Bristol. With 40 Illustrations and a Photo-etched Frontispiece. Second Edition. Demy 8vo., cloth, 16s.

Morgan—HABIT AND INSTINCT. A Study in Heredity. By C. LLOYD MORGAN, F.G.S. Demy 8vo., 16s.

Morgan—THE SPRINGS OF CONDUCT. By Professor C. LLOYD MORGAN, F.G.S. Cheaper Edition. Large crown 8vo., 3s. 6d.

Morgan—PSYCHOLOGY FOR TEACHERS. By Professor C. LLOYD MORGAN, F.G.S. With a Preface by J. G. FITCH, M.A., LL.D., late one of H.M. Chief Inspectors of Training Colleges. One vol., crown 8vo., cloth, 3s. 6d. net.

Paget—WASTED RECORDS OF DISEASE. By CHARLES E. PAGET, Lecturer on Public Health in Owens College, Medical Officer of Health for Salford, etc. Crown 8vo., 2s. 6d.

Pearson—THE CHANCES OF DEATH, AND OTHER STUDIES IN EVOLUTION. By KARL PEARSON, F.R.S., Author of 'The Ethic of Free Thought,' etc. In two vols., demy 8vo., with Illustrations, 25s. net.

CONTENTS OF VOL. I.—The Chances of Death—The Scientific Aspect of Monte Carlo Roulette—Reproductive Selection—Socialism and Natural Selection—Politics and Science—Reaction—Women and Labour—Variation in Man and Woman.

CONTENTS OF VOL. II.—Woman as Witch—Ashiepattle; or, Hans seeks his Luck—Kindred Group Marriage—The German Passion Play—Index.

Perry—CALCULUS FOR ENGINEERS. By Professor JOHN PERRY, F.R.S. Crown 8vo., 7s. 6d.

THE PHILOSOPHICAL REVIEW. Edited by J. G. SCHURMAN, Professor of Philosophy in Cornell University, U.S.A. Six Numbers a year. Single Numbers, 3s. 6d.; Annual Subscription, 14s. post free. The first number was issued in January, 1892.

Shaw—A TEXT-BOOK OF NURSING FOR HOME AND HOSPITAL USE. By C. WEEKS SHAW. Revised and largely re-written by W. RADFORD House Surgeon at the Poplar Hospital, under the supervision of Sir DYCE DUCKWORTH, M.D., F.R.C.P. Fully Illustrated, crown 8vo., 3s. 6d.

Young—A GENERAL ASTRONOMY. By CHARLES A. YOUNG, Professor of Astronomy in the College of New Jersey, Associate of the Royal Astronomical Society, Author of *The Sun*, etc. In one vol., 550 pages, with 250 Illustrations, and supplemented with the necessary tables. Royal 8vo., half morocco, 12s. 6d.

Works in General Literature.

Aglen—OLD TESTAMENT HISTORY. (*See page* 4.)

Bell—DIANA'S LOOKING GLASS, and other Poems. By the Rev. CANON BELL, D.D., Rector of Cheltenham, and Hon. Canon of Carlisle. Crown 8vo., cloth, 5s. net. **POEMS OLD AND NEW.** Cloth, 7s. 6d. **THE NAME ABOVE EVERY NAME, and other Sermons.** Cloth, 5s. **THE GOSPEL AND POWER OF GOD.** Crown 8vo., cloth, 3s. 6d.

Bell—KLEINES HAUSTHEATER. Fifteen Little Plays in German for Children. By Mrs. HUGH BELL. Crown 8vo., cloth, 2s.

Most of these little plays have been adapted from the author's 'Petit Théâtre,' the remainder from a little book of English plays by the same writer entitled 'Nursery Comedies.'

Butler—SELECT ESSAYS OF SAINTE BEUVE. Chiefly bearing on English Literature. Translated by A. J. BUTLER, Translator of 'The Memoirs of Baron Marbot.' One vol., 8vo., cloth, 5s. net.

Clouston—EARLY ENGLISH FURNITURE. (*See page* 5.)

Collingwood—THORSTEIN OF THE MERE: a Saga of the Northmen in Lakeland. By W. G. COLLINGWOOD, Author of 'Life of John Ruskin,' etc. With Illustrations. Price 10s. 6d.

Collins—A TREASURY OF MINOR BRITISH POETRY. Selected and Arranged, with Notes, by J. CHURTON COLLINS, M.A. Crown 8vo., 7s. 6d.

Cook—THE DEFENSE OF POESY, otherwise known as An APOLOGY FOR POETRY. By Sir PHILIP SIDNEY. Edited by A. S. COOK, Professor of English Literature in Yale University. Crown 8vo., cloth, 4s. 6d.

Cook—A DEFENCE OF POETRY. By PERCY BYSSHE SHELLEY. Edited, with notes and introduction, by Professor A. S. COOK. Crown 8vo., cloth, 2s. 6d.

Davidson—A HANDBOOK TO DANTE. By Giovanni A. Scartazzini. Translated from the Italian, with notes and additions, by Thomas Davidson, M.A. Crown 8vo., cloth, 6s.

Ellacombe—THE PLANT-LORE AND GARDEN-CRAFT OF SHAKESPEARE. By Henry N. Ellacombe, M.A., Vicar of Bitton. Illustrated by Major E. B. Ricketts. Large crown 8vo., 10s. 6d.

Fleming—THE ART OF READING AND SPEAKING. By the Rev. Canon Fleming, Vicar of St. Michael's, Chester Square. Third edition. Cloth, 3s. 6d.

Garnett—SELECTIONS IN ENGLISH PROSE FROM ELIZABETH TO VICTORIA. Chosen and arranged by James M. Garnett, M.A., LL.D. 700 pages, large crown 8vo., cloth, 7s. 6d.

Goschen—THE CULTIVATION AND USE OF IMAGINATION. By the Right Hon. George Joachim Goschen. Crown 8vo., cloth, 2s. 6d.

GREAT PUBLIC SCHOOLS. Eton — Harrow — Winchester — Rugby — Westminster — Marlborough — Cheltenham — Haileybury — Clifton — Charterhouse. With nearly 100 Illustrations by the best artists. Cheaper edition. One vol., large Imperial 16mo., handsomely bound, 3s. 6d.

Gummere—OLD ENGLISH BALLADS. Selected and Edited by Francis B. Gummere, Professor of English in Haverford College, U.S.A. Crown 8vo., cloth, 5s. 6d.

Harrison—STUDIES IN EARLY VICTORIAN LITERATURE. By Frederic Harrison, M.A., Author of 'The Choice of Books,' etc. New and Cheaper Edition, large crown 8vo., cloth, 3s. 6d.

Hartshorne—OLD ENGLISH GLASSES. (*See page* 11.)

Herschell—THE BEGGARS OF PARIS. Translated from the French of M. Louis Paulian by Lady Herschell. Crown 8vo., 1s.

Hole — ADDRESSES TO WORKING MEN FROM PULPIT AND PLATFORM. By the Very Rev. S. Reynolds Hole, Dean of Rochester. One vol., crown 8vo., 6s.

Hudson—THE LIFE, ART, AND CHARACTERS OF SHAKESPEARE. By Henry N. Hudson, LL.D., Editor of *The Harvard Shakespeare*, etc. 969 pages, in two vols., large crown 8vo., cloth, 21s.

Hudson — THE HARVARD EDITION OF SHAKESPEARE'S COMPLETE WORKS. A fine Library Edition. By Henry N. Hudson, LL.D., Author of 'The Life, Art, and Characters of Shakespeare.' In twenty volumes, large crown 8vo., cloth, £6. Also in ten volumes, £5.

Hunt—Leigh Hunt's 'WHAT IS POETRY?' An Answer to the Question, 'What is Poetry?' including Remarks on Versification. By Leigh Hunt. Edited, with notes, by Professor A. S. Cook. Crown 8vo., cloth, 2s. 6d.

Kuhns—THE TREATMENT OF NATURE IN DANTE'S 'DIVINA COMMEDIA.' By L. OSCAR KUHNS, Professor in Wesleyan University, Middleton, U.S.A. Crown 8vo., cloth, 5s.

Lang—LAMB'S ADVENTURES OF ULYSSES. With an Introduction by ANDREW LANG. Square 8vo., cloth, 1s. 6d. Also the Prize Edition, gilt edges, 2s.

Maud—WAGNER'S HEROES. Parsifal—Tannhauser—Lohengrin—Hans Sachs. By CONSTANCE MAUD. Illustrated by H. GRANVILLE FELL. Second Edition, crown 8vo., 5s.

Maud—WAGNER'S HEROINES. Brunhilda—Senta—Isolda. By CONSTANCE MAUD. Illustrated by J. W. MAUD. Crown 8vo., 5s.

Morrison—LIFE'S PRESCRIPTION, In Seven Doses. By D. MACLAREN MORRISON. Crown 8vo., parchment, 1s. 6d.

Raleigh—STYLE. (*See page* 12.)

Rodd—FEDA, and other Poems, chiefly Lyrical. By RENNELL RODD, C.M.G. With etched Frontispiece. Crown 8vo., cloth, 6s.

Rodd—THE UNKNOWN MADONNA, and other Poems. By RENNELL RODD, C.M.G. With Frontispiece by RICHMOND. Crown 8vo., cloth, 5s.

Rodd—THE VIOLET CROWN, AND SONGS OF ENGLAND. By RENNELL RODD, C.M.G. With Photogravure Frontispiece. Crown 8vo., cloth, 5s.

Rodd—THE CUSTOMS AND LORE OF MODERN GREECE. By RENNELL RODD, C.M.G. With 7 full-page Illustrations. 8vo., cloth, 8s. 6d.

Rodd—BALLADS OF THE FLEET. (*See page* 12.)

Schelling—A BOOK OF ELIZABETHAN LYRICS. Selected and Edited by F. E. SCHELLING, Professor of English Literature in the University of Pennsylvania. Crown 8vo., cloth, 5s. 6d.

Schelling—BEN JONSON'S TIMBER. Edited by Professor F. E. SCHELLING. Crown 8vo., cloth, 4s.

Sichel—THE STORY OF TWO SALONS. Madame de Beaumont and the Suards. By EDITH SICHEL, Author of 'Worthington Junior.' With Illustrations. Large crown 8vo., cloth, 10s. 6d.

Thayer—THE BEST ELIZABETHAN PLAYS. Edited, with an Introduction, by WILLIAM R. THAYER. 612 pages, large crown 8vo., cloth, 7s. 6d.

WINCHESTER COLLEGE. Illustrated by HERBERT MARSHALL. With Contributions in Prose and Verse by OLD WYKEHAMISTS. Demy 4to., cloth, 25s. net. A few copies of the first edition, limited to 1,000 copies, are still to be had.

Works of History and Biography.

Benson and Tatham—MEN OF MIGHT. Studies of Great Characters. By A. C. BENSON, M.A., and H. F. W. TATHAM, M.A., Assistant Masters at Eton College. Second Edition. Crown 8vo., cloth, 3s. 6d.

Boyle—THE RECOLLECTIONS OF THE DEAN OF SALISBURY. By the Very Rev. G. D. BOYLE, Dean of Salisbury. With Photogravure Portrait. 1 vol., demy 8vo., cloth, 16s.

Cawston and Keane—THE EARLY CHARTERED COMPANIES. A.D. 1296-1858. By GEORGE CAWSTON, barrister-at-law, and A. H. KEANE, F.R.G.S. Large crown 8vo., with Frontispiece, 10s. 6d.

Clough—MEMOIRS OF ANNE CLOUGH. (*See page* 10.)

De Vere—RECOLLECTIONS OF AUBREY DE VERE. (*See page* 9.)

Fowler—ECHOES OF OLD COUNTY LIFE. By J. K. FOWLER, of Aylesbury. Second Edition, with numerous Illustrations, 8vo., 10s. 6d. Also a Large-paper edition, of 200 copies only, 21s. net.

Gardner—ROME : THE MIDDLE OF THE WORLD. (*See page* 10.)

Gardner—FRIENDS OF THE OLDEN TIME. (*See page* 28.)

Hare—MARIA EDGEWORTH : her Life and Letters. Edited by AUGUSTUS J. C. HARE, Author of 'The Story of Two Noble Lives,' etc. Two vols., crown 8vo., with Portraits, 16s. net.

Hole—THE MEMORIES OF DEAN HOLE. By the Very Rev. S. REYNOLDS HOLE, Dean of Rochester. With the original Illustrations from sketches by LEECH and THACKERAY. Twelfth thousand, crown 8vo., 6s.

Hole—MORE MEMORIES : Being Thoughts about England Spoken in America. By the Very Rev. S. REYNOLDS HOLE, Dean of Rochester. With Frontispiece. Demy 8vo., 16s.

Kay—OMARAH'S HISTORY OF YAMAN. The Arabic Text, edited, with a translation, by HENRY CASSELS KAY, Member of the Royal Asiatic Society. Demy 8vo., cloth, 17s. 6d. net.

Lecky—THE POLITICAL VALUE OF HISTORY. By W. E. H. LECKY, D.C.L., LL.D. An Address delivered at the Midland Institute, reprinted with additions. Crown 8vo., cloth, 2s. 6d.

Le Fanu—SEVENTY YEARS OF IRISH LIFE. By the late W. R. LE FANU. New and Popular Edition. Crown 8vo., 6s.

Macdonald—THE MEMOIRS OF THE LATE SIR JOHN A. MACDONALD, G.C.B., First Prime Minister of Canada. Edited by JOSEPH POPE, his Private Secretary. With Portraits. Two vols., demy 8vo., 32s.

Milner—ENGLAND IN EGYPT. By Sir ALFRED MILNER, K.C.B., Governor of Cape Colony and High Commissioner to South Africa. Popular Edition, with Map, and full details of the British position and responsibilities, 7s. 6d.

Milner—ARNOLD TOYNBEE. A Reminiscence. By Sir ALFRED MILNER, K.C.B., Author of 'England in Egypt.' Crown 8vo., paper, 1s.

Oman—A HISTORY OF ENGLAND. By CHARLES OMAN, Fellow of All Souls' College, and Lecturer in History at New College, Oxford; Author of 'Warwick the Kingmaker,' 'A History of Greece,' etc. Crown 8vo., cloth, 5s. Also in two parts, 3s. each. Part I., to A.D. 1603; Part II., from 1603 to present time.

Pilkington—IN AN ETON PLAYING FIELD. The Adventures of some old Public School Boys in East London. By E. M. S. PILKINGTON. Fcap. 8vo., handsomely bound, 2s. 6d.

Pulitzer—THE ROMANCE OF PRINCE EUGENE. An Idyll under Napoleon the First. By ALBERT PULITZER. With numerous Photogravure Illustrations. Two vols., demy 8vo., 21s.

Raleigh—ROBERT LOUIS STEVENSON. By WALTER RALEIGH, Professor of English Literature at Liverpool University College. Second edition. Crown 8vo., cloth 2s. 6d.

Ransome—THE BATTLES OF FREDERICK THE GREAT. Extracted from Carlyle's 'History of Frederick the Great,' and edited by CYRIL RANSOME, M.A., Professor of History at the Yorkshire College, Leeds. With numerous Illustrations by ADOLPH MENZEL. Square 8vo., 3s. 6d.

Rochefort—THE ADVENTURES OF MY LIFE. By HENRI ROCHEFORT. Second Edition. Two vols., large crown 8vo., 25s.

Roebuck—AUTOBIOGRAPHY AND LETTERS. (*See page 9.*)

Santley—STUDENT AND SINGER. The Reminiscences of CHARLES SANTLEY. New Edition. Crown 8vo., cloth, 6s.

Sherard—ALPHONSE DAUDET: a Biography and Critical Study. By R. H. SHERARD, Editor of 'The Memoirs of Baron Meneval,' etc. With Illustrations. Demy 8vo., 15s.

Tollemache—BENJAMIN JOWETT, Master of Balliol. A Personal Memoir. By the Hon. LIONEL TOLLEMACHE, Author of 'Safe Studies,' etc. Third Edition, with portrait. Crown 8vo., cloth, 3s. 6d.

Twining—RECOLLECTIONS OF LIFE AND WORK. Being the Autobiography of LOUISA TWINING. One vol., 8vo., cloth, 15s.

Practical Science Manuals.

GENERAL EDITOR: PROFESSOR RAPHAEL MELDOLA, F.R.S.

STEAM BOILERS. By GEORGE HALLIDAY, late Demonstrator at the Finsbury Technical College. With numerous Diagrams and Illustrations. Crown 8vo., 400 pages, 5s. [*Ready.*

AGRICULTURAL CHEMISTRY. By T. S. DYMOND, of the County Technical Laboratory, Chelmsford. [*In preparation.*

ELECTRIC TRACTION. By ERNEST WILSON, Wh. Sc., M.I.E.E., Lecturer and Demonstrator in the Siemen's Laboratory, King's College, London. [*In preparation.*

Works upon Country Life and Pastimes.

Brown—PLEASURABLE POULTRY-KEEPING. By E. BROWN, F.L.S. Fully illustrated. One vol., crown 8vo., cloth, 2s. 6d.

Brown—POULTRY-KEEPING AS AN INDUSTRY FOR FARMERS AND COTTAGERS. (*See page* 6.)

Brown—INDUSTRIAL POULTRY-KEEPING. By EDWARD BROWN. Illustrated. Paper boards, 1s. A small handbook chiefly intended for cottagers and allotment-holders.

Brown—POULTRY FATTENING. By E. BROWN, F.L.S. Fully illustrated. New Edition. Crown 8vo., 1s. 6d.

Clouston.—EARLY ENGLISH FURNITURE. (*See page* 11.)

Cunningham—THE DRAUGHTS POCKET MANUAL. By J. G. CUNNINGHAM. An Introduction to the Game in all its branches. Small 8vo., with numerous diagrams, 2s. 6d.

Ellacombe—IN A GLOUCESTERSHIRE GARDEN. By the Rev. H. N. ELLACOMBE, Vicar of Bitton, and Honorary Canon of Bristol. Author of 'Plant Lore and Garden Craft of Shakespeare.' With new illustrations by Major E. B. RICKETTS. Second Edition. Crown 8vo., cloth, 6s.

Gossip—THE CHESS POCKET MANUAL. By G. H. D. GOSSIP. A Pocket Guide, with numerous Specimen Games and Illustrations. Small 8vo., 2s. 6d.

Hartshorne—OLD ENGLISH GLASSES. (*See page* 11.)

Hole—A BOOK ABOUT THE GARDEN AND THE GARDENER. By the Very Rev. S. REYNOLDS HOLE, Dean of Rochester. Second edition. Crown 8vo., 6s.

Hole—A BOOK ABOUT ROSES. By the Very Rev. S. REYNOLDS HOLE, Dean of Rochester. Fifteenth Edition. Illustrated by H. G. MOON and G. ELGOOD. Presentation Edition with coloured plates, 10s. 6d. ; Popular Edition, 3s. 6d.

Holt—FANCY DRESSES DESCRIBED. By ARDERN HOLT. An Alphabetical Dictionary of Fancy Costumes. With full accounts of the Dresses. About 60 Illustrations by LILLIAN YOUNG. Many of them coloured. One vol., demy 8vo., 7s. 6d. net.

Kenney-Herbert—FIFTY BREAKFASTS : containing a great variety of New and Simple Recipes for Breakfast Dishes. By Colonel KENNEY-HERBERT ('Wyvern'). Small 8vo., 2s. 6d. FIFTY DINNERS. Small 8vo., cloth, 2s. 6d. FIFTY LUNCHES. Small 8vo., cloth, 2s. 6d.

Kenney-Herbert—COMMON-SENSE COOKERY : based on Modern English and Continental Principles, Worked out in Detail. By Colonel A. KENNEY-HERBERT ('Wyvern'). Large crown 8vo., over 500 pp., 7s. 6d.

Shorland—CYCLING FOR HEALTH AND PLEASURE. By L. H. PORTER, Author of 'Wheels and Wheeling,' etc. Revised and edited by F. W. SHORLAND, Amateur Champion 1892-93-94. With numerous Illustrations, small 8vo., 2s. 6d.

White—PLEASURABLE BEE-KEEPING. By C. N. WHITE, Lecturer to the County Councils of Huntingdon, Cambridgeshire, etc. Fully Illustrated. One vol., crown 8vo., cloth, 2s. 6d.

WILD FLOWERS IN ART AND NATURE. By J. C. L. SPARKES, Principal of the National Art Training School, South Kensington, and F. W. BURBIDGE, Curator of the University Botanical Gardens, Dublin. With 21 Full-page Coloured Plates by H. G. MOON. Royal 4to., handsomely bound, gilt edges, 21s.

Books for the Young.

FIVE SHILLINGS EACH.

SNOW-SHOES AND SLEDGES. By KIRK MUNROE. Fully illustrated. Crown 8vo., cloth, 5s.
RICK DALE. By KIRK MUNROE. Fully illustrated. Crown 8vo., cloth, 5s.
ERIC THE ARCHER. By MAURICE H. HERVEY. With numerous full-page Illustrations. Handsomely bound, crown 8vo., 5s.
THE FUR SEAL'S TOOTH. By KIRK MUNROE. Fully illustrated. Crown 8vo., cloth, 5s.
HOW DICK AND MOLLY WENT ROUND THE WORLD. By M. H. CORNWALL LEGH. With numerous Illustrations. Foolscap 4to., cloth, 5s.
HOW DICK AND MOLLY SAW ENGLAND. By M. H. CORNWALL LEGH. With numerous Illustrations. Foolscap 4to., 5s.
DR. GILBERT'S DAUGHTERS. By MARGARET HARRIET MATHEWS. Illustrated by CHRIS. HAMMOND. Crown 8vo., cloth, 5s.
THE REEF OF GOLD. By MAURICE H. HERVEY. With numerous full-page Illustrations, handsomely bound. Gilt edges, 5s.
BAREROCK; or, The Island of Pearls. By HENRY NASH. With numerous Illustrations by LANCELOT SPEED. Large crown 8vo., handsomely bound, gilt edges, 5s.

THREE SHILLINGS AND SIXPENCE EACH.

TALES FROM HANS ANDERSEN. With nearly 40 Original Illustrations by E. A. LEMANN. Small 4to., handsomely bound in cloth, 3s. 6d.
THE SNOW QUEEN, and other Tales. By HANS CHRISTIAN ANDERSEN. Beautifully illustrated by Miss E. A. LEMANN. Small 4to., handsomely bound, 3s. 6d.
HUNTERS THREE. By THOMAS W. KNOX, Author of 'The Boy Travellers,' etc. With numerous Illustrations. Crown 8vo., cloth, 3s. 6d.
THE SECRET OF THE DESERT. By E. D. FAWCETT. With numerous full-page Illustrations. Crown 8vo., cloth, 3s. 6d.
JOEL: A BOY OF GALILEE. By ANNIE FELLOWS JOHNSTON. With ten full-page Illustrations. Crown 8vo., cloth, 3s. 6d.
THE MUSHROOM CAVE. By EVELYN RAYMOND. With Illustrations. Crown 8vo., cloth, 3s. 6d.
THE DOUBLE EMPEROR. By W. LAIRD CLOWES, Author of 'The Great Peril,' etc. Illustrated. Crown 8vo., 3s. 6d.
SWALLOWED BY AN EARTHQUAKE. By E. D. FAWCETT. Illustrated. Crown 8vo., 3s. 6d.
HARTMANN THE ANARCHIST; or, The Doom of the Great City. By E. DOUGLAS FAWCETT. With sixteen full-page and numerous smaller Illustrations by F. T. JANE. Crown 8vo., cloth, 3s. 6d.
ANIMAL SKETCHES: a Popular Book of Natural History. By Professor C. LLOYD MORGAN, F.G.S. Crown 8vo., cloth, 3s. 6d.

TWO SHILLINGS EACH.

THE CHILDREN'S FAVOURITE SERIES. A Charming Series of Juvenile Books, each plentifully Illustrated, and written in simple language to please young readers. Price 2s. each; or, gilt edges, 2s. 6d.

- My Book of Wonders.
- My Book of Travel Stories.
- My Book of Adventures.
- My Book of the Sea.
- My Book of Fables.
- Deeds of Gold.
- My Book of Heroism.
- My Book of Perils.
- My Book of Fairy Tales.
- My Book of History Tales.
- My Story Book of Animals.
- Rhymes for You and Me.
- My Book of Inventions.

ONE SHILLING AND SIXPENCE EACH.

The Children's Hour Series.

All with Full-page Illustrations.

THE PALACE ON THE MOOR. By E. DAVENPORT ADAMS. 1s. 6d.
TOBY'S PROMISE. By A. M. HOPKINSON. 1s. 6d.
MASTER MAGNUS. By Mrs. E. M. FIELD. 1s. 6d.
MY DOG PLATO. By M. H. CORNWALL LEGH. 1s. 6d.

FRIENDS OF THE OLDEN TIME. By ALICE GARDNER, Lecturer in History at Newnham College, Cambridge. Second Edition. Illustrated. Square 8vo., 2s. 6d.

THE INTERNATIONAL EDUCATION SERIES.

THE INTELLECTUAL AND MORAL DEVELOPMENT OF THE CHILD. By GABRIEL COMPAYRÉ. 6s.

TEACHING THE LANGUAGE-ARTS. Speech, Reading, Composition. By B. A. HINSDALE, Ph.D., LL.D., University of Michigan. 4s. 6d.

THE PSYCHOLOGY OF THE NUMBER, AND ITS APPLICATION TO METHODS OF TEACHING ARITHMETIC. By JAMES A. MCLELLAN, A.M., and JOHN DEWEY, Ph.D. 6s.

THE SONGS AND MUSIC OF FROEBEL'S MOTHER PLAY. By SUSAN E. BLOW. 6s.

THE MOTTOES AND COMMENTARIES OF FROEBEL'S MOTHER PLAY. By SUSAN E. BLOW and H. R. ELIOT. 6s.

HOW TO STUDY AND TEACH HISTORY. By B. A. HINSDALE, Ph.D., LL.D. 6s.

FROEBEL'S PEDAGOGICS OF THE KINDERGARTEN; or, His Ideas concerning the Play and Playthings of the Child. Translated by J. JARVIS. Crown 8vo., cloth, 6s.

THE EDUCATION OF THE GREEK PEOPLE, AND ITS INFLUENCE ON CIVILIZATION. By THOMAS DAVIDSON. Crown 8vo., cloth, 6s.

SYSTEMATIC SCIENCE TEACHING. By EDWARD G. HOWE. Crown 8vo., cloth, 6s.

EVOLUTION OF THE PUBLIC SCHOOL SYSTEM IN MASSACHUSETTS. By GEORGE H. MARTIN. Crown 8vo., cloth, 6s.

THE INFANT MIND; or, Mental Development in the Child. Translated from the German of W. PREYER, Professor of Physiology in the University of Jena. Crown 8vo., cloth, 4s. 6d.

ENGLISH EDUCATION IN THE ELEMENTARY AND SECONDARY SCHOOLS. By ISAAC SHARPLESS, LL.D., President of Haverford College, U.S.A. Crown 8vo., cloth, 4s. 6d.

EMILE; or, A Treatise on Education. By JEAN JACQUES ROUSSEAU. Translated and Edited by W. H. PAYNE, Ph.D., LL.D., President of the Peabody Normal College, U.S.A. Crown 8vo., cloth, 6s.

EDUCATION FROM A NATIONAL STANDPOINT. Translated from the French of ALFRED FOUILLÉE by W. J. GREENSTREET, M.A., Head Master of the Marling School, Stroud. Crown 8vo., cloth, 7s. 6d.

THE MORAL INSTRUCTION OF CHILDREN. By FELIX ADLER, President of the Ethical Society of New York. Crown 8vo., cloth, 6s.

THE PHILOSOPHY OF EDUCATION. By JOHANN KARL ROSENKRANZ, Doctor of Theology and Professor of Philosophy at Königsberg. (Translated.) Crown 8vo., cloth, 6s.

A HISTORY OF EDUCATION. By Professor F. V. N. PAINTER. 6s.

THE VENTILATION AND WARMING OF SCHOOL BUILDINGS. With Plans and Diagrams. By GILBERT B. MORRISON. Crown 8vo., 4s. 6d.

FROEBEL'S 'EDUCATION OF MAN.' Translated by W. N. HAILMAN. Crown 8vo., 6s.

ELEMENTARY PSYCHOLOGY AND EDUCATION. By Dr. J. BALDWIN. Illustrated, crown 8vo., 6s.

THE SENSES AND THE WILL. Forming Part I. of 'The Mind of the Child.' By W. PREYER, Professor of Physiology in the University of Jena. (Translated.) Crown 8vo., 6s.

THE DEVELOPMENT OF THE INTELLECT. Forming Part II. of 'The Mind of the Child.' By Professor W. PREYER. (Translated.) Crown 8vo., 6s.

HOW TO STUDY GEOGRAPHY. By FRANCIS W. PARKER. 6s.

A HISTORY OF EDUCATION IN THE UNITED STATES. By RICHARD A. BOONE, Professor of Pedagogy in Indiana University. Crown 8vo., 6s.

EUROPEAN SCHOOLS; or, What I Saw in the Schools of Germany, France, Austria, and Switzerland. By L. R. KLEMM, Ph.D. With numerous Illustrations. Crown 8vo., 8s. 6d.

PRACTICAL HINTS FOR TEACHERS. By GEORGE HOWLAND, Superintendent of the Chicago Schools. Crown 8vo., 4s. 6d.

SCHOOL SUPERVISION. By J. L. PICKARD. 4s. 6d.

HIGHER EDUCATION OF WOMEN IN EUROPE. By HELENE LANGE. 4s. 6d.

HERBART'S TEXT-BOOK IN PSYCHOLOGY. By M. K. SMITH. 4s. 6d.

PSYCHOLOGY APPLIED TO THE ART OF TEACHING. By Dr. J. BALDWIN. 6s.

THE SCHOOL SYSTEM OF ONTARIO. By the Hon. GEORGE W. ROSS, LL.D. 4s. 6d.

FROEBEL'S EDUCATIONAL LAWS FOR ALL TEACHERS. By JAMES L. HUGHES. 6s.

SCHOOL MANAGEMENT AND SCHOOL METHODS. By Dr. J. BALDWIN. 6s.

THE NATIONAL REVIEW.

Edited by L. J. MAXSE.

Price Half-a-crown Monthly.

The 'National Review' is the leading Unionist and Conservative Review in Great Britain. Since it passed into the control and editorship of Mr. Leo Maxse, most of the leaders of the Unionist Party have contributed to its pages, including the Marquis of Salisbury, Mr. Arthur Balfour, Mr. J. Chamberlain, and Lord George Hamilton. The episodes of the month, which give a masterly review of the important events of the preceding month, form a valuable feature of the Review, which now occupies a unique position among monthly periodicals.

PUBLICATIONS OF THE INDIA OFFICE AND OF THE GOVERNMENT OF INDIA.

Mr. EDWARD ARNOLD, having been appointed Publisher to the Secretary of State for India in Council, has now on sale the above publications at 37 Bedford Street, Strand, and is prepared to supply full information concerning them on application.

INDIAN GOVERNMENT MAPS.

Any of the Maps in this magnificent series can now be obtained at the shortest notice from Mr. EDWARD ARNOLD, Publisher to the India Office.

The following Catalogues of Mr. Edward Arnold's Publications will be sent post free on application:

CATALOGUE OF WORKS OF GENERAL LITERATURE.

GENERAL CATALOGUE OF EDUCATIONAL WORKS, including the principal publications of Messrs. Ginn and Company, Educational Publishers, of Boston and New York, and of Messrs. E. L. Kellogg and Company, of New York.

CATALOGUE OF WORKS FOR USE IN ELEMENTARY SCHOOLS. With Specimen Pages.

ILLUSTRATED LIST OF BOOKS FOR PRESENTS AND PRIZES.

Index to Authors.

	PAGE
ADAMS.—The Palace on the Moor	28
ADDERLEY.—Stephen Remarx	19
,, Paul Mercer	7
AGLEN.—Old Testament History	4
ALDRICH.—Arctic Alaska	17
AMERICAN GAME FISHES	17
BACON.—City of Blood	14
BALFOUR.—Twelve Hundred Miles in a Waggon	16
BELL, MRS.—Kleines Haustheater	23
BELL (REV. CANON).—The Gospel the Power of God	22
,, Sermons	22
,, Diana's Looking Glass	22
,, Poems Old and New	22
BENSON.—Men of Might	25
BERKELEY.—Reminiscences of a Huntsman	13
BEYNON.—With Kelly to Chitral	16
BLATCHFORD.—Tommy Atkins	19
BOTTOME.—A Sunshine Trip	13
BOYLE.—Recollections of the Dean of Salisbury	25
BROWN.—Works on Poultry Keeping	27
BRYAN.—Mark in Europe	21
BULL.—The Cruise of the 'Antarctic'	16
BURBIDGE.—Wild Flowers in Art	27
BURGESS.—Political Science	21
BUTLER.—Select Essays of Sainte Beuve	22
CAWSTON.—The Early Chartered Companies	25
CHAPMAN.—Wild Norway	14
CHARLETON.—Netherdyke	8
CHERBULIEZ.—The Tutor's Secret	19
CHILDREN'S FAVOURITE SERIES	28
CHILDREN'S HOUR SERIES	28
CHOLMONDELEY.—A Devotee	19
CLIFFORD.—Love-Letters	16
CLOUGH.—Memoir of Anne J. Clough	10
CLOUSTON.—Early English Furniture	11
CLOWES.—Double Emperor	28
COLERIDGE.—King with Two Faces	7
COLLINGWOOD.—Thorstein	19
,, The Bondwoman	19
COLLINS.—A Treasury of Minor British Poetry	22
COLVILE.—Land of the Nile Springs	16
COOK.—Sidney's Defense of Poesy	22
,, Shelley's Defence of Poetry	22
COSMOPOLITE.—Sportsman in Ireland	10
CRANE.—George's Mother	19
CUNNINGHAM.—Draughts Manual	27
CUSTANCE.—Riding Recollections	16
DAVIDSON.—Handbook to Dante	23
DE VERE.—Recollections	9
DUNMORE.—Ormisdal	19

	PAGE
EDWARDS.—Mermaid of Inish-Uig	2
ELLACOMBE. — In a Gloucestershire Garden	2
ELLACOMBE.—The Plant Lore of Shakespeare	23
FAWCETT.—Hartmann the Anarchist	28
,, Riddle of the Universe	21
,, Secret of the Desert	28
,, Swallowed by an Earthquake	28
FIELD.—Master Magnus	28
FLEMING.—Art of Reading and Speaking	23
FORD.—On the Threshold	19
FOWLER.—Echoes of Old County Life	25
FRESHFIELD.—Exploration of the Caucasus	16
GARDNER.—Friends of Olden Time	28
,, Rome: Middle of World	10
GARNETT.—Selections in English Prose	23
GAUNT.—Dave's Sweetheart	19
GLEICHEN.—With the British Mission to Menelik	1
GORDON.—Persia Revisited	16
GOSCHEN.—Cultivation and Use of the Imagination	23
GOSSIP.—Chess Pocket Manual	27
GREAT PUBLIC SCHOOLS	23
GUMMERE.—Old English Ballads	23
HADJIRA	19
HALL.—Fish Tails	16
HANS ANDERSEN.—Snow Queen	28
,, Tales from	28
HARE.—Life and Letters of Maria Edgeworth	25
HARRISON.—Early Victorian Literature	23
HARROW SCHOOL	3
HARTSHORNE.—Old English Glasses	11
HERSCHELL.—Parisian Beggars	23
HERVEY.—Eric the Archer	28
,, Reef of Gold	28
HIGGINS. — New Guide to the Pacific Coast	17
HOLE.—Addresses to Working Men	23
,, Book about Roses	27
,, Book about the Garden	27
,, Little Tour in America	16
,, Little Tour in Ireland	16
,, Memories	25
,, More Memories	25
HOLLAND.—Letters of	4
HOLT.—Fancy Dresses Described	27
HOPKINSON.—Toby's Promise	28
HOPKINS.—Religions of India	21
HUDSON.—Life, Art, and Characters of Shakespeare	23
,, Harvard Shakespeare	23
HUNT—What is Poetry?	23

	PAGE
HUTCHINSON.—That Fiddler Fellow	19
INTERNATIONAL EDUCATION SERIES	29
JOHNSTON.—Joel; a Boy of Galilee	28
KAY.—Omarah's Yaman	25
KENNEY-HERBERT.—Fifty Breakfasts	27
,, ,, Fifty Dinners	27
,, ,, Fifty Lunches	27
,, ,, Common-sense Cookery	27
KNIGHT-BRUCE.—Memories of Mashonaland	16
KNOX.—Hunters Three	28
KNUTSFORD.—Mystery of the Rue Soly	20
KUHNS.—The Treatment of Nature in Dante	24
LANE.—Church and Realm	4
LANG.—Lamb's Adventures of Ulysses	24
LEADER.—Autobiography of Roebuck	2
LECKY.—Political Value of History	25
LE FANU.—Seventy Years of Irish Life	25
LEFFINGWELL.—Art of Wing-Shooting	17
LEGH.—How Dick and Molly went round the World	28
LEGH.—How Dick and Molly saw England	28
LEGH.—My Dog Plato	28
LIGHTHALL.—The False Chevalier	2
LOTZE.—Philosophical Outlines	20
MACDONALD.— Memoirs of Sir John Macdonald	25
MACDONALD.—Soldiering and Surveying in British East Africa	15
MAUD.—Wagner's Heroes	24
,, Wagner's Heroines	24
MAXWELL.—The Sportsman's Library	18
,, Memories of the Months	15
MCNAB.—On Veldt and Farm	17
MCNULTY.—Misther O'Ryan	20
,, Son of a Peasant	8
MILNER.—England in Egypt	25
,, Arnold Toynbee	26
MONTRÉSOR.—Worth While	20
More Beasts for Worse Children	12
MORGAN.—Animal Life	21
,, Habit and Instinct	21
,, Psychology for Teachers	21
,, Springs of Conduct	21
MORPHOLOGY, JOURNAL OF	21
MORRISON.—Life's Prescription	24
MUNROE.—Fur Seal's Tooth	28
,, Rick Dale	28
,, Snow-shoes and Sledges	28
NASH.—Barerock	28
NATIONAL REVIEW	30
NIMROD.—Chase, Turf, and Road	5
OMAN.—History of England	26
OXENDEN.—Interludes	20

	PAGE
OXENDEN.—A Reputation for a Song	2
PAGET.—Wasted Records of Disease	21
PEARSON.—The Chances of Death	21
PERRY.—Calculus for Engineers	21
PHILOSOPHICAL REVIEW	22
PIKE.—Through the Sub-Arctic Forest	17
PILKINGTON.—An Eton Playing-Field	26
PINSENT—Job Hildred	8
POLLOK.—Fifty Years' Reminiscences of India	17
POPE.—Memoirs of Sir John Macdonald	25
PORTAL.—British Mission to Uganda	14
,, My Mission to Abyssinia	14
PRACTICAL SCIENCE MANUALS	26
PRESCOTT.—A Mask and a Martyr	20
PULITZER.—Romance of Prince Eugene	26
RALEIGH.—Robert Louis Stevenson	26
,, Style	12
RANSOME.—Battles of Frederick the Great	26
RAYMOND.—Mushroom Cave	28
REYNOLDS.—Studies on Many Subjects	6
ROCHEFORT.—The Adventures of My Life	26
RODD.—Ballads of the Fleet	12
RODD.—Works by Rennell Rodd	24
ROEBUCK.—Autobiography	9
SANTLEY.—Student and Singer	26
SCHELLING.—Elizabethan Lyrics	24
,, Ben Jonson's Timber	24
SCROPE.—Art of Deer-Stalking	13
SHAW.—A Text Book of Nursing	22
SHERARD.—Alphonse Daudet	26
SHIELDS.—Camping and Camp Outfits	17
SHIELDS.—American Book of the Dog	17
SHORLAND.— Cycling for Health and Pleasure	27
SICHEL.—The Story of Two Salons	24
SIMPSON.—Many Memories of Many People	2
SLATIN.—Fire and Sword in the Sudan	14
SMITH.—The Life of a Fox	10
,, Through Unknown African Countries	15
SPENCER.—A Mingled Yarn	5
SPINNER.—A Reluctant Evangelist	20
STONE.—In and Beyond the Himalayas	17
TATHAM.—Men of Might	25
THAYER.—Best Elizabethan Plays	24
THOMAS.—Sweden and the Swedes	17
THORNTON.—A Sporting Tour	10
TOLLEMACHE.—Benjamin Jowett	26
TWINING.— Recollections of Life and Work	26
WHITE.—Pleasurable Bee-Keeping	27
WILD FLOWERS IN ART AND NATURE	27
WILLIAMS.— The Bayonet that came Home	20
WINCHESTER COLLEGE	24
YOUNG.—General Astronomy	22

www.ingramcontent.com/pod-product-compliance
Lightning Source LLC
Chambersburg PA
CBHW030302240426

43673CB00040B/1032